The Descendants of Richard Thomas Taylor

Taylor

With information on his ancestors
to the 800s in England

by

David G. Conklin

Please direct all correspondence and book orders to:

David G. Conklin
965 Ranch Lane
Kalispell, MT 59901
Tel: 406-210-4989
conklind@hotmail.com

Library of Congress Control Number: 2022952284

ISBN 978-1-7362441-3-5

Printed for the author by
Moore Graphics
11200 W. Wisconsin Ave. #6
Youngtown, AZ 85363

Cover photos:

Front: center-*Taylor family Coat of Arms;*
from left -*Richard Lemuel Taylor; Richard Thomas Taylor;*
Roxie Ann Gibbs; Richard Lamuel Taylor

Back: top-*David G. Conklin*;
from left - *Rev. Dr. Rowland Taylor; John "The Immigrant" Taylor;*
Elizabeth Lawes Nunne; Martha Montague Thompson

Acknowledgments

I would first like to thank my wife Mary Guerra, her late mother Nettie Taylor, sister Tecla Guerra, Aunt Marjorie Taylor, and her Taylor cousins for giving me permission to interview them, capture their memories on tape, and to use their family memories and photos. These recollections provided almost all of the information on Richard Thomas and Roxie Ann Taylor that did not come from official government records available in the public domain. I also want to further acknowledge the work of my wife Mary, who as always, is my editor-in-chief and biggest supporter.

I also wish to thank my good friend and former college roommate Arnold Browning, who co-authored the very interesting family history "*The Descendants of Emory R. Wilder: 1889-1967*" (Browning, Arnold J. & Justin W. Wilder, 2009) and provided the format and impetus for this family history. Also many thanks to my West Valley Genealogical Society volunteer proof reader Susan C. Beckmann who's knowledge of the subject and detailed feedback was invaluable. Also thanks to Jody Johnson and Catherine Caine for their valuable corrections and comments.

Thanks to all of you who have provided me with your family information, stories, documents and photos. All illustrations not credited were provided by the author or from public domain sources. In a way, you, members of the Taylor family, are the authors of this book. I am just the recorder of the information that was provided. You encouraged me by your interest in learning more about the origins of the Taylor family. Any errors or omissions, however, are mine alone. Please send me your corrections and any additional information, and I will include them in a future edition of this book.

It is my hope that this first edition will encourage someone in this branch of the Taylor family to update this book in the future. Perhaps one of the cousins or their children will want to update their branch of the family. I would be happy to provide files and advice to any family member who would like to write a book and extend the Taylor family history.

December 2022

About the Author

A Montana resident for more than forty years, David G. "Dave" Conklin is a retired park ranger who lives in the Flathead Valley. Although he has B.S. and M.S. degrees in Forestry and Wildlife Management, and an M.B.A., one of his first professional assignments was writing the *Montana Historic Preservation Plan* (Conklin D. , 1975) and nominating historic sites to the National Register of Historic Places. As a park ranger, he worked to preserve historic parks associated with people who made the country what it is today. While in Helena, Montana Dave built a log cabin where he lived with his family near the old mining town of Unionville. After retiring he published his first book, *Montana History Weekends* (Conklin D. , 2002).

Dave began gathering information about his family and his wife Mary's family in 1978 while still working in Helena, Montana, to include local and family oral histories on audio and videotape as well as photos, documents and notes. After retiring he trained as a Broadcast Journalist for the Army National Guard and served two years in Iraq during Operation Iraqi Freedom where he was awarded the Bronze Star during combat operations. In 2015 Dave retired again, began taking genealogy classes, and started work on his memoirs and family histories. His most recent genealogy book, *The Descendants of Jose Antonio Guerra*, was published in 2020 (Conklin D. G., 2020) and is available at major genealogical libraries in the U.S., or from the author himself. He is a member of the West Valley Genealogical Society, Youngtown, Arizona and splits his time between Kalispell, Montana and Sun City, Arizona.

The Author
David G. "Dave" Conklin, Apr 2017

CONTENTS

Introduction

My purpose in compiling this information is to promote an appreciation of the Taylor family history and appreciation of both those born into the family, and those like me, who married into the family. I have centered this book on my spouse Mary Guerra's mother Nettie Taylor's parents, Richard Thomas Taylor and Roxie Ann Gibbs. Although I knew very little about them until I began this project, I am thankful that I knew Mary's mother and father Nettie Taylor and Guadalupe Guerra who were still alive to meet our children, their grandchildren.

When we look at our parents and grandparents we often catch glimpses of ourselves, and it's not just from shared DNA. The people who raise us shape us, almost invisibly, through the values they convey, their convictions, and especially through their actions. I hope that this book will cause you to think about the legacy that you leave your children. Our grandparents passed on to us a strong work ethic, moral values, self-discipline, concern for neighbors, the importance of hospitality, and the importance of love and family.

I have included brief information about each person's education, occupation, military and public service when that information was available. I would hope that Richard and Roxie would be pleased to know that many in the family seek to honor their parents, their communities, their country, and each other.

The findings presented here are based solely on my research, primarily over the past five years. The discovery of additional sources or interpretations may affect the conclusions.

The Format

The National Genealogical Society Quarterly (NGSQ) generation numbering system format is used in this book in order of descent from the oldest paternal ancestor, Harger Taylefer (b. 1287) to twenty-second generation Bryson Kurt Taylor (b. 2002). I only show the direct lineage for each of the ancestors of Harger Taylefer. I list all of the children for each ancestor, but only the ancestors of Harger Taylefer are listed in the next generation. Details and stories from ancestors' lives are mentioned when available. I included all the descendants of Harger Taylefer that I found. As this book goes back twenty-two generations to include female ancestor lines, it has been a challenge as there are more than 177 descendants of only Harger Taylefer and the number continues to increase.

Names: In this book I have repeated the variations of the Taylor and Gibbs surnames (e.g., Taylefer, Taylifer, Taylor, Gibbes, Gibbs) based on the most common usage for that individual or generation. However, poor spelling and not hearing the name spoken correctly by immigration, census, and other government officials can make the name of a person or location almost incomprehensible. It is not hard to see why some non-English family members adopted English pronunciation and spelling of their names soon after they began attending schools in the USA (i.e. Robert John Gibbes' son Thomas changed his surname to Gibbs).

Also, the given names of Richard, Thomas, John, William, etc. as well as the Taylor surname itself are very common English and Irish names (like John Smith and Thomas Jones), making it very difficult to trace the correct family as almost every generation produced a Richard, Thomas, John, or William in multiple families. I was careful to choose the best evidence based on name, location, birth, marriage, and death dates but much of this data has not yet been found for some ancestors, and for others what was listed in one reference may be incorrect or disputed by another.

Chapter 1 is about the Taylor ancestors. Practically all the information about Richard Thomas Taylor's ancestors was obtained from published sources describing England, Ireland, and its ethnic history due to the lack of sources from family ancestors themselves. Where published sources exist for the more noteworthy Taylors, I have tried to summarize the relevant content.

Chapter 2 is about the lives of Richard Thomas Taylor and Roxie Ann Gibbs who are the focus of this book and the parents of Nettie LaVonne Taylor, my mother-in-law.

The remaining chapters follow the descendants of Richard Taylor and Roxie Gibbs with a separate chapter for each of Richard and Roxie's children who lived to be adults, beginning with the oldest, Elsie (Chapter 3) to the youngest, Marjorie (Chapter 9).

Each descendant is assigned a NGSQ number. Also, for both ancestors and descendants, a small number appears after their first name, or after their middle name if they have a middle name. This number indicates what generation of descendant this person is compared to the person listed at the beginning of the chapter. For example, in Chapter 8 the "4" after Isabelle Iona Conklin signifies that she is the 4th generation descending from Nettie Taylor who is listed at the beginning of Chapter 8 as person number 1. This is true except for Chapter 2 where the "18" after Richard Thomas Taylor signifies that he is the 18th generation descending from Harger Taylefer who is listed in Chapter 1 as person number 1.

Each of Richard's ancestors' names appears in parentheses after his name. First, his 15th great grandfather Harger Taylefer is followed by a superscript "1" indicating that Harger Taylefer is the first generation that I have any information on. If we someday find Harger's father, he would become the 1st generation, and so on.

For descendants that married a person that already had children, I have included these children and their families in the book. Although they are not descendants by blood line, they are part of the Taylor family through marriage. Similarly, adopted children are included when their information was provided.

This book was developed with the "Family Tree Maker" computer application (MacKiev, 2019). Each chapter that presents a descendant of Richard Thomas Taylor is developed from a separate "Descendant" genealogy report file and "Smart Story" file built with Family Tree Maker. Each file has a number for each descendant of the primary person starting with "2." When there is a plus sign in front of the number, it indicates that the descendant also had children who will be listed again under the next generation farther along in the book.

This methodology is used to keep all of the descendants of each of Richard's children in one chapter. If we had just used one file for all the descendants, the family members would appear mixed throughout this section of the book, because the report file lists all descendants by generation. You can also use the index to find the name and page with information for that individual. Richard's ancestors are also listed by name in the index.

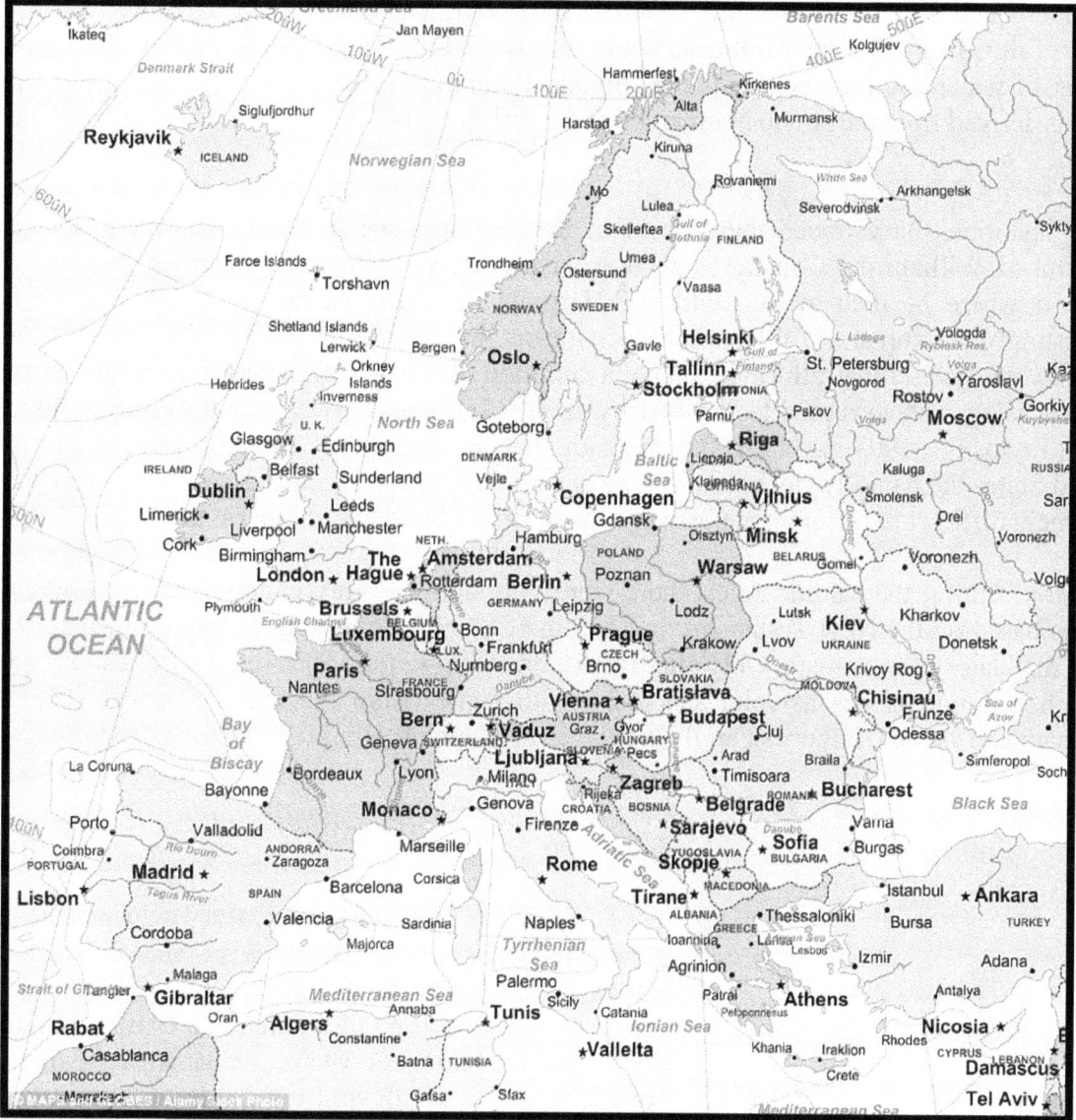

A map of Europe showing the relationship of countries with Taylor ancestors.
From freeworldmaps.net.

Taylor Family Movement

In Western Europe during the early Middle Ages people were referred to by a single given name unless they were part of the aristocracy or needed to be distinguished by place of birth.

(i.e. William of Nottingham), distinguishing features, or occupation. So before about 1450 there were few fixed hereditary surnames, making tracing a family's past extremely difficult.

The surname Taylor was one of many given to those because of their occupation, in this case a tailor or maker of clothes. Taylor is a common early English, Scottish, Irish, and American surname, spelled variously over the centuries as Tayler, Taylour, Talord, Tayllour, Tayleur, Taliur, Talur, Tailor, Tailer, Taillor, Tailleur, Taillour, Tailur, Talar, Tailur, Tailour, Talor, and Taylor, of which the last spelling is now the most common (Taylor I. T., 1945, p. 287). The name is derived from the Anglo Norman French word "taliator," from "taliere" (to cut) (Hanks, 2003).

Some historians have traced the descent of the Taylor name to Baron Taillefer, Norman Minstrel of William the Conqueror, who accompanied William in the Norman invasion of England where he died at the Battle of Hastings in 1066 (Taylor I. T., 1945, p. 287). Interestingly, the surname Taillefer in French means "hewer of iron" (Wikipedia, 2020). There is a prevalent belief that all Taylors have a common origin in Baron Taillefer, whose name over the years was corrupted to Taylefer by about 1250, then to Taylor and its variations by 1350 (Taylor E. , 1903, p. 11). Today the name has become a very common surname. In the United States the name Taylor is the 10th most prevalent surname, making genealogy research extremely difficult to differentiate between the different branches of the Taylor family.

Similarly, during the Middle Ages, there were only about twenty common names given to infants based on the New Testament. In 1545 the Catholic Church made the use of a saint's name mandatory for baptism. Only after the Reformation in the 1600s did the Protestants add to such common names as John and Mary with names from the Old Testament such as Abraham and Jacob (Halbert's Family Heritage, 1998, pp. 4, 10).

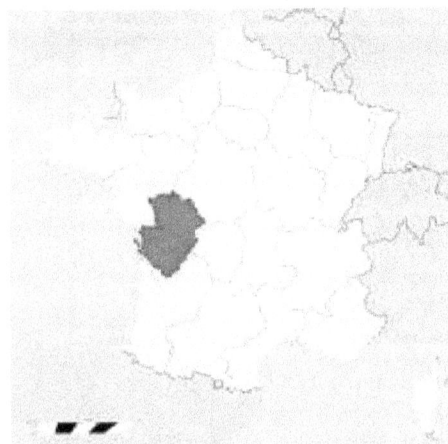

Left: Map of France highlighting the province of Angouleme.

If we follow the prevalent belief, the Taylor ancestors were early Counts of Angouleme, a province in Western France as far back as 866 AD. The House of Angouleme later became the House of Taillefer, and Baron Taillefer was the Norman minstrel who accompanied William the Conqueror and was killed at the Battle of Hastings on his conquest of England in 1066. For this sacrifice, the House of Taillefer was awarded large estates in the county of Kent, England and named Earls of Pennington. It is reported that in the 1200's a descendant, Harger Taylefer , held vast estates in the county of Kent and that by the 1300's Sir John Taylifer of Homestall in Shadoxhurst, County of Kent was a knight under King Edward III (Logan, 1926, p. 2).

The histories of the Taylor family that we can trace are the movements of Harger Taylefer 's descendants. The history begins in Kent in the 1300's when Edward III was king of England.

From there, the Taylor family branched out over England, Scotland, and Ireland. In 1509 John Thomas Taylor was one of the Royal Chaplains at Henry VII's funeral; and later Royal Ambassador to Burgundy and France. In 1527 he had been appointed one of the commissioners to try the validity of King Henry VIII's marriage to Catalina of Aragon.

Map of British Isles showing the county of Kent in the far southeast.

During the 1500's, King Henry VIII broke with the Church of Rome and established the Church of England (Anglican Church). Some objected to parts of the newly formed religion and wanted to simplify or "purify" it. They became known as "Puritans" and faced severe laws against dissention. Born in 1510, John Taylor's son the Rev. Dr. Rowland Taylor was influential in the religious reformation of England. Then during the reign of Queen Mary I she enforced draconian measures to return to the Catholic Church, becoming known as "Bloody Mary." At the time of Rev. Taylor's death he was rector of a small church in Hadley, England.

The English Parliament banned the William Tyndale English Bible in 1543 (Foxe, 2001, p. 121) During this time, many people who opposed Catholic Church teachings were put to death. Taylor opposed several Catholic teachings, including celibacy of a priest and the way the church practiced Holy Communion. On March 26, 1554 he was arrested for heresy because he was spreading the word of God in public and was burned at the stake on February 9, 1555 (Foxe, 2001, p. 179). In order to escape persecution, by 1620 the first Pilgrims had arrived in America and ten years later the first Puritans came to establish a separate church. Emigration from England to the American colonies began and soon after, the Taylors became part of the history of America.

The seventeenth century saw the foundation of the Thirteen American Colonies. Small estates were created, and religious toleration was proclaimed for all except Catholics. By the end of the century an influx of English and Scottish-Irish settlers had arrived, followed by Jews, Protestants, Moravians from Germany, and Huguenots from France. By 1650 more than twenty-five apparently unrelated Taylors had settled in New England and more than seventy-five further down the Atlantic Coast (Taylor I. T., 1945, p. 288). One of those was Colonel James Henry "The Elder" Taylor who arrived in Williamsburg, Virginia with his family in 1635 on the ship "True Love" from Carlisle, England. He later took part in the Revolutionary War. He was a plantation owner and as the population near the eastern seacoast grew, as farmland became scarce, and as the threat of Indian attacks reduced, he took advantage of a society supported in the North by the forced labor of indentured servants and in the South by a mass of slaves multiplied by yearly shiploads from Africa (Churchill, 1991, p. 258). One of his grandsons was John Penn, one of the signers of the Declaration of Independence, and his descendants include Presidents James Madison and Zachary Taylor.

During the eighteenth century the Taylors continued to expand in America and participated in the Revolutionary War. The southern branch of the family moved through Virginia, Pennsylvania, North Carolina, and South Carolina. According to U.S. Census records, by 1820 Dempsey Taylor, son of William Abraham Taylor of Waxhaw, South Carolina, had moved from Duplin County North Carolina to Telfair, Georgia. Their descendants established themselves in the cotton, tobacco, and turpentine industries in south central Georgia. By 1857, when Wilcox County was created from Irwin, Dooly and Pulaski counties, this branch of the Taylor family had settled on both sides of the Ocmulgee River, which is the east boundary of Wilcox County, and was a major north-south transportation corridor until the railroads were established.

According to one source, Wilcox County in south central Georgia was an especially good place for raising cattle and sheep; for farming cotton, tobacco, peanuts, watermelons and cantaloupe; for producing lumber and turpentine from the extensive southern pine forests; and for businesses that support these agricultural industries. It is no surprise that for the past two centuries many Taylors living in Georgia have listed their occupation on the federal census as "farmer" (McDonald, 1987, p. 111).

Right: Map of Wilcox County. Courtesy mapsoftheworld.com.

For the Taylors in Ireland, the middle of the 1840s marked the onset of catastrophe for the Irish potato crop. A partial failure of the vital staple crop in 1845 was followed by a complete failure the following year, which was in turn followed by an especially cruel winter. In 1848, the crop failed once again. Starvation and disease became common as many farmers were driven penniless from their homes. The Irish Potato Famine resulted in one of the most dramatic waves of migration in history, bringing many more Taylors to America.

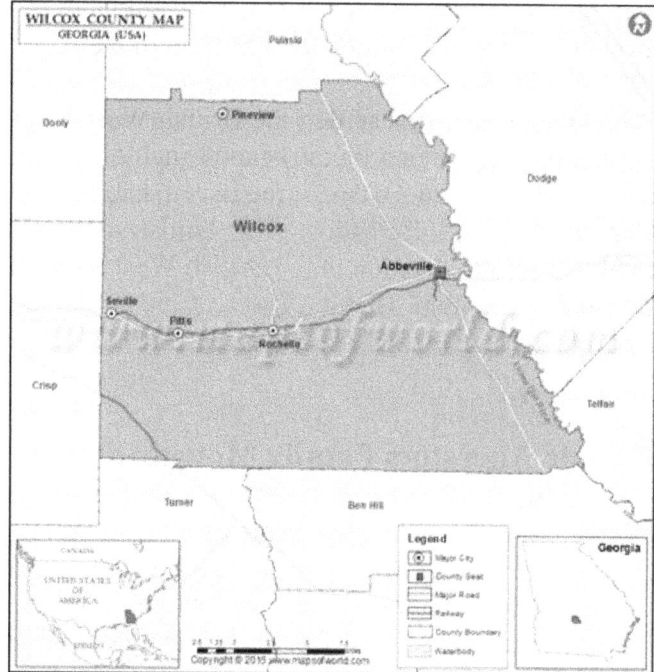

In the 1860s several Taylors fought and died for the Confederate States of America during the Civil War. In the early 1900s Richard Thomas. Taylor moved his family from Georgia to Florida, Oklahoma, and then Idaho in search of farmland on which to raise his family. Since then, the Taylors have expanded throughout the U.S. and participated in both world wars.

The Taylor name also spread to other parts of the world besides America including Europe, Australia, New Zealand and the Caribbean. The Taylors from Normandy had settled in northern France and were intermarrying with the natives. From there, they swept through England and Scotland and eventually came to Ireland in 1169.

Approximately 50,000 convicts, including many Taylors, were sent by Britain to North America from the 1600s up until the end of the American War of Independence. Around this time, machinery was also becoming more popular in Britain; therefore, laborers and farm workers were being put out of work and driven towards the cities. This, in turn, led to increased crime rates and eventually overcrowded prisons. Therefore William Pitt, the British Prime Minister at the time, decided that Australia would be the answer to his problems.

Thus the Taylor name expanded into Australia. Over a span of 81 years (1787-1868), an estimated 160,000 convicts were sent from Britain to Australia. Many of the convicts worked as laborers. Smith, Jones, William, Brown, and Johnson were the five most common surnames among the convicts, but there were many Taylors as well; and interestingly there were 603 men recorded with the name John Smith.

Taylor emigration to New Zealand followed in the footsteps of the European explorers, such as Captain Cook's voyage of 1769-70. First came sealers, whalers, missionaries and traders. By 1838, the British New Zealand Company had begun buying land from the Māori tribes and selling it to settlers. After the Treaty of Waitangi in 1840, many British families set out on the arduous six-month journey from Britain to New Zealand to start a new life.

When the British first settled the British West Indies around 1604, they made many attempts to establish settlements on the islands, including Saint Lucia and Grenada, and the Taylor name continued to spread. By 1627, the British had managed to establish settlements on St. Kitts (St. Christopher) and Barbados. The British continued to expand the settlements including establishing a Federation in the British West Indies by 1674. These islands included Barbados, Bermuda, Cayman Island, Turks, Caicos, Jamaica and Belize (then known as British Honduras) (House of Names, 2021, p. 170).

Female Ancestors Family Movement

Although the Taylor family name came from the British Isles, the familial DNA comes from female ancestors as well as male. As the Taylors married, their spouses passed on their ancestry to Taylor descendants as well. For example DNA results (see Appendix 2. DNA Ethnicity Reports) for four cousins from this branch of the Taylor family living today show anywhere from 28% to 51% England and NW European ethnicity. These results show that Mary Guerra has only 28% England and NW European ethnicity and is the only one of the four cousins to also have Spanish, Native American, Jewish, and African ethnicity. There are no surprises here even though her mother Nettie was a Taylor, as we know that her father Guadalupe Guerra was of Spanish descent and his ancestry includes the above ethnic groups. Therefore Mary Guerra's children will pass on these additional ethnicities that her Taylor mother and other Taylors do not have (Conklin D. G., 2020, p. 9).

Similarly, these DNA results for Dennis R. Taylor show 18% Scottish and 4% Germanic ethnicity while his sister Arlene Taylor has more than twice as much Scottish (40%) and no Germanic ethnicity. Again there are no surprises here as their father Art Taylor's wife Hazel McClure is a descendant of Scottish ancestors and passed on more of this ethnicity to her daughter than to her son Dennis (see Appendix 2. DNA Ethnicity Reports, p. 161).

Therefore as we can see, when the Taylors married, their spouses passed on their ancestry to Taylor descendants as well. For example, John Thomas Taylor, oldest of triplets, and the great grandson of Sir John Taylor, Lord of Rothbury (1403-1466) of Shadoxhurst, England, married Lady Susan Rowland, granddaughter of both John Rowland, Master of the Tower of London (1440-1466) and heir of Sir John Hanson of Woodhouse (1442-1520). These ancestors in turn include John's father John William Taylor I (1450-1525) who married Margaret Sarah De Fairsted (1457-1530), daughter of Humphrey De Fairsted (1431-1457) and Anne Boyle (1435-1499).

Art and Hazel (McClure) Taylor and their children
at the Taylor Family Reunion at Palisades Lake, Idaho.
From left to right: Art Taylor, Hazel (McClure) Taylor, Dennis, Arlene.
Author photo Aug 1975.

Also when Capt. Thomas John Taylor II (1573-1618) married Lady Margaret Swinderby (1578-1672) from Denmark, she brought along her ancestry which subsequently travelled to America with them. The couple became the direct ancestors of five US presidents (Abraham Lincoln, James Madison, Zachary Taylor, William Henry Harrison, and Benjamin Harrison) and one actress (Elizabeth Taylor).

Famous Taylor Ancestors

According to the website *Born of Greatness.weebly.com* (Taylor Ancestors, 2020) the Taylor family tree can be traced back 1,242 years to the year 770 in Auvergne, Aquitaine France and includes the Emperor of Rome, Charlemagne (Charles the Great). The Taylors were members of French and English royalty. Other Taylor ancestors hale from Prussia and Copenhagen, Denmark. The tree includes Methodist Episcopal ministers, farmers, colonels, and generals, with the most notable being Zachary Taylor who became the 12th President of the United States. Taylor ancestors also include Rev. Dr. Rowland Taylor and William Tyndale who were Christian martyrs charged with heresy and burned at the stake.

A selection of noteworthy Taylors throughout the world are discussed below chronologically by birthdate. Unless otherwise noted, the following information is from (House of Names, 2021).

Baron Taillefer (1028-1066), Norman Minstrel of William the Conqueror, led the charge at the Battle of Hastings and died there in 1066. For his great services, his family was given large landed possessions in the county of Kent, which descended to his posterity during the Reigns of Henry III, Richard II, Henry IV and Henry V. His descendants became the Earls of Pennington, who bear the same arms as those brought to the colony of Virginia by John William Taylor, "The Immigrant" (Lytton, 1895, p. 53).

Rev. Dr. Rowland Taylor (1510-1555), was influential in the religious reformation of England during the reign of Queen Mary I. At the time of his death he was rector of a small church in Hadley, England. Taylor opposed several Catholic teachings, including celibacy of a priest and the way the church practiced Holy Communion. On March 26, 1554 he was arrested for heresy because he was spreading the word of God in public. He was burned at the stake in 1555 (Foxe, 2001, p. 179).

Zachary Taylor (1784-1850), was a general and national hero in the United States Army from the time of the Mexican-American War and the War of 1812, earning the nickname "Old Rough-and-Ready" for his indifference to hardship. Sent to Texas in anticipation of war with Mexico, he defeated the Mexican army at the battles of Palo Alto and Resaca de la Palma (1846). Taylor ignored orders to remain in Monterrey and marched south to defeat a large Mexican force at the Battle of Buena Vista (1847). He became a national hero and was nominated as the Whig candidate for president (1848). His brief term was marked by a controversy over slavery in the new territories that produced the Compromise of 1850 and by a scandal involving members of his cabinet. He died, probably of cholera, after only 16 months in office and was succeeded by Millard Fillmore (Churchill, 1991).

Sarah Knox Taylor (1814-1835). Wife of Jefferson Davis, Confederate States of America (CSA) President, Sarah Knox "Knoxie" Taylor Davis was the daughter of the 12th U.S. President Zachary Taylor and part of the notable Lee Family. She met Jefferson Davis when living with her father and family at Fort Crawford, Wisconsin during the Black Hawk War in 1832. They married in 1835 and she died of malaria only three months later.

Frederick Winslow Taylor (1856-1915) was an American mechanical engineer widely known for his methods to improve industrial efficiency. His book, "The Principles of Scientific Management," described his pioneering work in applying engineering principles to the work done on the factory floor. Taylor was instrumental in the creation and development of the branch of engineering that is now known as industrial engineering. He made his fortune patenting steel-process improvements. As a result, scientific management is sometimes referred to as "Taylorism."

George W. Taylor (1901-1972) was an American professor of industrial relations at the Wharton School at the University of Pennsylvania and recipient of the Presidential Medal of Freedom.

Maxwell Davenport Taylor (1901-1987) was a senior United States Army officer and diplomat of the mid-20th century. He served with distinction in World War II, most notably as commander of the 101st Airborne Division, nicknamed "The Screaming Eagles." After the war, he served as the fifth chairman of the Joint Chiefs of Staff, having been appointed by President John F. Kennedy. He is the father of biographer and historian John Maxwell Taylor and of military historian and author Thomas Happer Taylor. A controversial figure, Taylor along with Robert McNamara, was considered to be the one that played a major role during the early days of the Vietnam War to send more combat troops to Vietnam.

Elizabeth Taylor (1932-2011) was a British-American actress. She began her career as a child actress in the early 1940s and was one of the most popular stars of classical Hollywood cinema in the 1950s. She then became the highest paid movie star in the 1960s, remaining a well-known public figure for the rest of her life. In 1999, the American Film Institute named her the seventh-greatest female screen legend of Classic Hollywood cinema.

James Vernon Taylor (1948-), American six-time Grammy Award winning singer-songwriter and guitarist, was inducted into the Rock and Roll Hall of Fame in 2000 and received the Presidential Medal of Freedom in 2015.

Chapter 1. Ancestors of Richard Thomas Taylor

This chapter presents the ancestors of Richard Thomas Taylor beginning with Wulgrin D'Angouleme, the Count of Angouleme, who lived in the mid-800s. For more information about the context of the Taylor ancestors' life and times in England see *"Churchill's History of the English Speaking Peoples"* (Churchill, 1991); and in America see *"History of John Taylor of Hadley."* (Taylor E. , 1903).

It is believed that many English Taylors are NOT descendants of folks who practiced the art of sewing clothes, but rather were descendants of a Norman who came to England. According to a French genealogist, the original ancestor of the Taylors whose name originated in this fashion was Wulgrin, ancestor of the Baron William Ivo Taillefer. Wulgrin was given the title of Count of Perigord and Angouleme in Normandy by his kinsman Charles the Bold of France. According to Burke's History of the Landed Gentry of England, the Norman Baron Taillefer accompanied William the Conqueror in his invasion of England in 1066, and fell at the Battle of Hastings. The name has been variously spelled, from Taillefer, Taliaferro, Taylefer, Taylard, and finally modernized into Taylor (Rixford, 1993, pp. 8, 137).

Since I cannot yet show a direct lineage from Baron Taillefer for several generations to his suspected descendant Harger Taylefer, I have chosen to deal with these ancestors separately under the House of Taillefer. Then under the House of Taylor I deal with the known descendants of Harger Taylefer. If in the future a direct lineage is found between these ancestors, then these two houses could be merged into one family lineage.

House of Taillefer - Generation 1

1. **WULGRIN**[I] **D'ANGOULEME.** He died in 866 AD. He married **ROGERLINDE D'TOULOUSE.**

Wulgrin, the Count of Perigord and Angouleme, is the earliest ancestor that I have been able to trace so far. Angouleme is a city in southwestern France and capital of the Department of Charente. The countship dates from the ninth century.

Wulgrin D'Angouleme and Rogerlinde D'Toulouse had the following child:
+2. i. ALDWIN[2] D'ANGOULEME. He died in 915 AD.

Generation 2

2. ALDWIN[2] D'ANGOULEME (Wulgrin[1]). He held the title of Count of Angouleme. He died in 915 AD.

Aldwin D'Angouleme had the following child:
+3. i. WILLIAM[3] TAILLEFER I. He died about 956 AD.

Generation 3

3. WILLIAM[3] TAILLEFER I (Aldwin[2] D'Angouleme, Wulgrin[1] D'Angouleme). He died about 956 AD.

William Taillefer I had the following child:
+4. i. ARMAND[4] TAILLEFER. He died about 1006. He married HILDEGARDE.

Generation 4

4. ARMAND[4] TAILLEFER (William[3] I, Aldwin[2] D'Angouleme, Wulgrin[1] D'Angouleme). He died about 1006. He married **HILDEGARDE**.

Armand Taillefer and Hildegarde had the following child:
+5. i. WILLIAM[5] TAILLEFER II was born about 930 AD in Angouleme, France. He died prior to 1028 in Angouleme, France. He married GIRBERGE D'ANJOU.

Generation 5

5. WILLIAM[5] TAILLEFER II (Armand[4], William[3] I, Aldwin[2] D'Angouleme, Wulgrin[1] D'Angouleme) was born about 930 AD in Angouleme, France. He also held the title of Count of Angouleme. He died prior to 1028 in Angouleme, France. He married **GIRBERGE D'ANJOU**.

William Taillefer II and Girberge D'Anjou had the following child:
+6. i. GEOFREY[6] TAILLEFER was born about 955 AD. He died prior to 1040. He married PETRONILLE D'ARCHIAC.

Generation 6

6. GEOFREY[6] TAILLEFER (William[5] II, Armand[4], William[3] I, Aldwin[2] D'Angouleme, Wulgrin[1] D'Angouleme) was born about 955 AD. He died prior to 1040. He married **PETRONILLE D'ARCHIAC**.

Geofrey Taillefer and Petronille D'Archiac had the following children:

7. i.   BARON WILLIAM IVO[7] TAILLEFER was born about 1028 in Normandy, France. He died on 14 Oct 1066 in Hastings, Sussex, England (Battle of Hastings).

8. ii.   FOULQUES TAILLEFER was born about 1030 in Normandy, France. He died after 1089 in Normandy, France. He married CONDO.

Generation 7

7. BARON WILLIAM IVO[7] TAILLEFER was born about 1028 in Normandy, France. He died on 14 Oct 1066 in Hastings, Sussex, England (Battle of Hastings). Taillefer's given name was Ivo according to one source (Churchill, 1991, p. 40); or William according to another (Rixford, 1993, p. 137) so I have chosen to use both to best identify him as the same person. William Ivo Taillefer was also known by the title of Baron, and General of the Norman Army, as well as Chassard, and Le Chauser. His cause of death was being speared by Leofwine, brother of King Harold of England at the Battle of Hastings. He was described as having deep auburn hair, light hazel eyes, and "gigantic height" (Lytton, 1895, p. 53).

Taillefer was also the Norman Minstrel of William the Conqueror and led the charge at the Battle of Hastings becoming the first Norman killed there in 1066. Lytton describes the scene:

In the midst of the Duke's cohort was the sacred gonfanon (flag), and in front of it and of the whole line, rode a strange warrior of gigantic height. And as he rode, the warrior sang. . . . This warrior, in front of the Duke and the horsemen, seemed beside himself with the joy of battle. As he rode, and as he chanted, he threw up his sword in the air like a gleeman, catching it nimbly as it fell . . . and, dashing forward to the very front of a detachment of Saxon riders, shouted "A Taillefer! A Taillefer!" And by voice and gesture challenged forth someone to single combat (Lytton, 1895, p. 53).

Left: An artist's rendition of the charge of Baron William Ivo Taillefer at the Battle of Hastings. Courtesy wordpress.com.

After killing two Saxon riders in succession with his sword, Taillefer was himself killed by King Harold's brother Leofwine's spear. Thus began the Battle of Hastings.

After the Battle William I, Duke of Normandy was proclaimed "William the Conqueror, King of England," the first King of England of the Norman line. By 1071, King William was able to proclaim that all of England was his domain. He granted half of his lands to the Norman Barons in return for their aid. For Taillefer's gallant death, his family was given large landed possessions in the county of Kent, which descended to his posterity during the Reigns of Henry III, Richard II, Henry IV and Henry V. His descendants became the Earls of Pennington, who bear the same arms as those brought to the colony of Virginia by James "The Immigrant" Taylor.

Taylor family Coat of Arms
Motto: "Always forward, however little."

House of Taylor - Generation 1

1. HARGER[1] **TAYLEFER** was born in 1287 in Ospringe, Kent, England. He died in 1335 in Ospringe, Kent, England. He married **MARIE MONTGOMERY**, daughter of Walter de Montgomery and Alice de Chaddesdon. She was born in 1291 in Ospringe, Kent, England.

Harger (or Hanger) Taylefer is reportedly the great grandson of Baron Taillefer and one of the first Earls of Pennington, however we do not have any documentation to identify his immediate ancestors. Until we do, he is identified here as the first generation of the Taylor lineage.

Harger Taylefer and Marie Montgomery had the following child:
+**2.** i. SIR JOHN[2] TAYLIFER was born in 1327 in Shadoxhurst, Kent, England (Homestall [homestead]). He died in 1377 in Shadoxhurst, Kent, England. He married MARGARET WELMOTE. She was born on 12 Jun 1328 in Kent, England (Welmote). She died in 1380 in Shadoxhurst, Kent, England (Homestall).

2. Sir John[2] Taylifer (Harger[1] Taylefer) was born in 1327 in Shadoxhurst, Kent, England (Homestall). He died in 1377 in Shadoxhurst, Kent, England (Homestall). He married **Margaret Welmote**. She was born on 12 Jun 1328 in Kent, England (Welmote). She died in 1380 in Shadoxhurst, Kent, England (Homestall).

Sir John was also known as John of the Homestall, and Sir John Taylor. He was a Knight under King Edward III (1312-1377). John Marius Wilson's Imperial Gazetteer of England and Wales described Shadoxhurst in the 1870s:

> SHADOXHURST, a parish, with a village, in West Ashford district, Kent; 4 miles SW by S of Ashford railroad station. Post-town, Ashford. . . The property is subdivided. The living [quarters] is a rectory in the diocese of Canterbury. Value, £109. Patron, the Lord Chancellor. The church is tolerable; and there are a Wesleyan chapel and a parochial school.

Right: Saints Peter and Paul Parish Church in Shadoxhurst, Kent, England.

Sir John Taylifer and Margaret Welmote had the following children:

3.   i.   John[3] Taylor was born about 1375 in Shadoxhurst, Kent, England.

+4.   ii.   William Taylor I was born in 1377 in Shadoxhurst, Kent, England. He died in 1422 in Shadoxhurst, Kent, England. He married Jane Marshall about 1397. She was born in 1377 in Shadoxhurst, Kent, England. She died in 1437 in Shadoxhurst, Kent, England.

Generation 3

4. William³ Taylor I (Sir John² Taylifer, Harger¹ Taylefer) was born in 1377 in Shadoxhurst, Kent, England. He died in 1422 in Shadoxhurst, Kent, England. He married **Jane Marshall** about 1397. She was born in 1377 in Shadoxhurst, Kent, England. She died in 1437 in Shadoxhurst, Kent, England.

This generation was the first to begin using Taylor as a surname led by William's older brother John Taylor. So far I have found very little information about William or John, except that they were born in Shadoxhurst, Kent, England, as was their father Sir John Taylifer (b. 1327).

William Taylor I and Jane Marshall had the following child:

+5.   i.   Sir John⁴ Taylor was born in 1403 in Shadoxhurst, Kent, England. He died in 1466 in Eastwell Manor, Shadoxhurst, Kent, England. He married Lady Margaret Hamley, daughter of Arthur Cornwall Hamley, in 1428 in Kent, England (Saints Peter and Paul Parish Church). She was born in 1409 in Halwin, Cornwall, England. She died on 20 Apr 1493 in Knowle, Warwickshire, England.

Generation 4

5. Sir John⁴ Taylor (William³ I, Sir John² Taylifer, Harger¹ Taylefer) was born in 1403 in Shadoxhurst, Kent, England. He died in 1466 in Eastwell Manor, Shadoxhurst, Kent, England. He married **Lady Margaret Hamley**, daughter of Arthur Cornwall Hamley, in 1428 in Kent, England (Saints Peter and Paul Parish Church). She was born in 1409 in Halwin, Cornwall, England. She died on 20 Apr 1493 in Knowle, Warwickshire, England.

Sir John Taylor was also known as Fitz Alexander de Taylor of Knowle, and Sir John of Schodochurst. He held the title of Lord of Rothbury.

Sir John Taylor and Lady Margaret Hamley had the following child:

+6.   i.   William⁵ Taylor II was born in 1429 in Shadoxhurst, Kent, England. He died on 20 Aug 1493 in Shadoxhurst, Kent, England (as per probate of will). He married Joane Gilbard in 1450 in Shadoxhurst, Kent, England. She was born in 1432 in Shadoxhurst, Kent, England. She died on 21 Aug 1493 in Shadoxhurst, Kent, England.

6. WILLIAM⁵ TAYLOR II (Sir John⁴, William³ I, Sir John² Taylifer, Harger¹ Taylefer) was born in 1429 in Shadoxhurst, Kent, England. He died on 20 Aug 1493 in Shadoxhurst, Kent, England. He married **Joane Gilbard** in 1450 in Shadoxhurst, Kent, England. She was born in 1432 in Shadoxhurst, Kent, England. She died on 21 Aug 1493 in Shadoxhurst, Kent, England.

William Taylor II signed his will on 20 Aug 1493 in Shadoxhurst, Kent, England. He was known by the title of Master of the Rolls of The Court of Chancery. He was employed as a game warden of Needwood Forest in Barton-under-Needwood, Staffordshire, England. William's wife, Joane Gilbard was reportedly the first woman on record to give birth to triplets which all survived.

William Taylor II and Joane Gilbard had the following children:

+7. i. JOHN WILLIAM⁶ TAYLOR I was born in 1450 in Shadoxhurst, Kent, England (1st of 3 triplets). He died in 1525 in Shadoxhurst, Kent, England. He married Margaret Sarah De Fairsted, daughter of Humphrey De Fairsted and Anne Boyle, in 1477 in Shadoxhurst, Kent, England (Saints Peter and Paul Parish Church). She was born in 1457 in Shadoxhurst, Kent, England (Fairsted Manor). She died in 1530 in Shadoxhurst, Kent, England (Barton-under-Needwood).

ii. ROWLAND TAYLOR was born in 1450 in Shadoxhurst, Kent, England (2d of 3 triplets).

iii NATHANIEL TAYLOR I was born in 1450 in Shadoxhurst, Kent, England (3d of 3 triplets).

iv. ELIZABETH TAYLOR.

Generation 6

7. JOHN WILLIAM⁶ TAYLOR I (William⁵ II, Sir John⁴, William³ I, Sir John² Taylifer, Harger¹ Taylefer) was born in 1450 in Shadoxhurst, Kent, England. He died in 1525 in Shadoxhurst, Kent, England. He married **Margaret Sarah De Fairsted**, daughter of Humphrey De Fairsted and Anne Boyle, in 1477 in Shadoxhurst, Kent, England (Saints Peter and Paul Parish Church). She was born in 1457 in Shadoxhurst, Kent, England (Fairsted Manor). She died in 1530 in Shadoxhurst, Kent, England (Barton-under-Needwood).

John William Taylor I purchased More Court in Ivie Church in about 1500. His wife, Margaret Sarah De Fairsted, was the sole heir of Humphrey De Fairsted and acquired his estates and arms.

John William Taylor I and Margaret Sarah De Fairsted had the following children:

+8.　i.　JOHN THOMAS[7] TAYLOR was born in 1478 in Rothbury, Northumberland, England. He died in 1534 in Rothbury, Northumberland, England. He married Lady Susan Rowland, daughter of Sir John Rowland Jr and Lady Agnes Hansen, in 1509 in Rothbury, Northumberland, England. She was born in 1482 in Rothbury, Northumberland, England. She died in 1513 in Rothbury, Northumberland, England.

9.　ii.　WILLIAM TAYLOR III was born about 1484 in Shadoxhurst, Kent, England. He died about 1541.

10.　iii.　JOANE TAYLOR was born in 1504 in England. She died on Feb 1582/83 in Shadoxhurst, Kent, England. She married Robert Lucy in 1522 in England. He was born in 1502 in England. He died in 1585 in Woodchurch, Kent, England.

Generation 7

8. JOHN THOMAS[7] TAYLOR (John William[6] I, William[5] II, Sir John[4], William[3] I, Sir John[2] Taylifer, Harger[1] Taylefer) was born in 1478 in Rothbury, Northumberland, England. He died in 1534 in Rothbury, Northumberland, England. He married **Lady Susan Rowland**, daughter of Sir John Rowland Jr and Lady Agnes Hansen, in 1509 in Rothbury, Northumberland, England. She was born in 1482 in Rothbury, Northumberland, England. She died in 1513 in Rothbury, Northumberland, England.

John Taylor had a successful career as a priest and civil servant, culminating in a post as Master of the Rolls from 1527 to 1534. John Taylor and Susan Rowland were the parents of Rowland Taylor, prominent Protestant martyr (d. 1555). He died in 1534 when his son Rowland received his L.L.D. from Cambridge at the age of 24.

John Thomas Taylor and Lady Susan Rowland had the following child:

+11.　i.　REV. DR. ROWLAND[8] TAYLOR was born on 06 Oct 1510 in Rothbury, Northumberland, England. He died on 09 Feb 1554/55 in Hadleigh, Suffolk, England (age 44). He married Lady Margaret Elizabeth Tyndale in 1534 in Rothbury, Northumberland, England. She was born on 06 Oct 1510 in Rothbury, Northumberland, England. She died on 09 Feb 1555 in Hadleigh, Suffolk, England.

11. REV. DR. ROWLAND[8] TAYLOR (John Thomas[7], John William[6] I, William[5] II, Sir John[4], William[3] I, Sir John[2] Taylifer, Harger[1] Taylefer) was born on 06 Oct 1510 in Rothbury, Northumberland, England. He died on 09 Feb 1554/55 in Hadleigh, Suffolk, England. He married **Lady Margaret Elizabeth Tyndale** in 1534 in Rothbury, Northumberland, England. She was born on 06 Oct 1510 in Rothbury, Northumberland, England. She died on 09 Feb 1555 in Hadleigh, Suffolk, England.

The Reverend Doctor Rowland Taylor was influential in the religious reformation of England during the reign of Queen Mary I. In 1530 and 1534 he received degrees from the University of Cambridge. At the time of his death he was rector of a small church in Hadleigh, England. The English Parliament banned the William Tyndale English Bible in 1543. During this time, many people who opposed the Catholic Church teachings were put to death. Taylor opposed several Catholic teachings, including celibacy of a priest and the way the church practiced Holy Communion. On March 26, 1554 he was arrested for heresy and committed to Clink Prison. Thus the saying "He was put in the Clink." The following year he was taken to Aldham Common near the town of Hadleigh and died a religious martyr after being burned at the stake on February 9, 1555 (Foxe, 2001, p. 179).

Above, left: Sketch of St Mary's Church and Deanery Tower in Hadleigh.
Above, right: 1999 photo by Rog Frost of St Mary's Church and Deanery Tower in Hadleigh.
Courtesy Creative Commons.org.

Lady Margaret Tyndale, wife of Rev. Dr. Rowland Taylor, was the niece of William Tyndale who was tried and denounced for his New English Bible translation. Tyndale was burned at the stake at Hadleigh, England in 1536 (Foxe, 2001, p. 121).

Rev. Dr. Rowland Taylor and Lady Margaret Elizabeth Tyndale had the following child:

+12. i. THOMAS JOHN[9] TAYLOR I was born on 15 Sep 1548 in Cambridge, Cambridgeshire, England. He died on 01 Oct 1588 in London, Middlesex, England (St. Stephen Coleman Street). He married Elizabeth Eddings Burwell in 1572 in Hadleigh, Suffolk, England. She was born in 1552 in Hadley, Shropshire, England. She died in 1580.

Generation 9

12. THOMAS JOHN[9] TAYLOR I (Rev. Dr. Rowland[8], John Thomas[7], John William[6] I, William[5] II, Sir John[4], William[3] I, Sir John[2] Taylifer, Harger[1] Taylefer) was born on 15 Sep 1548 in Cambridge, Cambridgeshire, England. He died on 01 Oct 1588 in London, Middlesex, England (St. Stephen Coleman Street). He married **Elizabeth Eddings Burwell** in 1572 in Hadleigh, Suffolk, England. She was born in 1552 in Hadley, Shropshire, England. She died in 1580.

Thomas John Taylor I lived in Hadleigh, an ancient market town in Suffolk, East Anglia, England. It derived its prosperity from its wool and cloth industries. It has a 15th century timber-framed Guildhall and many fine examples of timber and brick buildings, some with highly detailed 17th century plasterwork or "pargeting." Most of these buildings can be found on High Street, Benton Street, and the immediate area. St. Mary Church is located on Church Street, and the red brick Tudor gateway to the now demolished medieval deanery, next to the church, is where the Oxford Movement began in 1833. This changed the face of Anglican churches forever. Like the nearby town of East Bergholt, Hadleigh was also known during the 16th century for its Protestant radicalism (findagrave.com/memorial #23000159).

Thomas John Taylor I and Elizabeth Eddings Burwell had the following children:

+13. i. CAPT THOMAS JOHN[10] TAYLOR II was born on 15 Mar 1573/74 in Hadleigh, Suffolk, England He died in 1618 in Hadleigh, Suffolk, England. He married Lady Margaret Elizabeth Swinderby, daughter of Andrew Swinderby and Margreta Mitchell Anderson, on 09 Oct 1599 in Hadleigh, Suffolk, England. She was born on 08 Jul 1578 in København, Kobenhavn, Denmark. She died on 02 Jul 1672 in Hadleigh, Suffolk, England.

14. ii. NATHANIEL TAYLOR was born in 1578 in Cambridge, Suffolk, England. He died in 1668 in Ireland.

15. iii. EDMUND TAYLOR was born in 1580 in Cambridge, Suffolk, England. He died in 1670 in Ireland.

Generation 10

13. CAPT. THOMAS JOHN[10] TAYLOR II (Thomas John[9] I, Rev. Dr. Rowland[8], John Thomas[7], John William[6] I, William[5] II, Sir John[4], William[3] I, Sir John[2] Taylifer, Harger[1] Taylefer) was born on 15 Mar 1573/74 in Hadleigh, Suffolk, England as the first child of Thomas John Taylor I and Elizabeth Eddings Burwell. He had two siblings, namely: Nathaniel, and Edmund. He died in 1618 in Hadleigh, Suffolk, England. When he was 25, he married Lady **Margaret Elizabeth Swinderby**, daughter of Andrew Swinderby and Margreta Mitchell Anderson, on 09 Oct 1599 in Hadleigh, Suffolk, England. Capt Thomas John Taylor II lived in St. Mark's Parish in 1721. He was known by the title of Captain. He lived in London. He was buried in Hadleigh, Suffolk, England (St. Mary's Churchyard; Find A Grave #18652140).

There is considerable confusion over whether James Taylor, father of Col. James Taylor II, was the son of Capt. Thomas Taylor II or his grandson, son of John (I conclude that James is the Captain's grandson). At any rate, there is evidence that Capt. Thomas J. Taylor, II and Margaret Swinderby were the direct ancestors of 5 US presidents (Abraham Lincoln, James Madison, Zachary Taylor, William Henry Harrison, and Benjamin Harrison) as well as actress Elizabeth Taylor. Captain Taylor's wife, Lady Margaret Elizabeth Swinderby became the first of Danish ancestry in this branch of the Taylor family.

According to Our Taylor Ancestors (Taylor Ancestors, 2020), Capt. Thomas John Taylor II emigrated from England before 1626 (despite his reported death in 1618), when he was one of the original land owners and earliest settlers of Elizabeth City, Warwick County, Virginia. By 1643 he had 600 acres in Warwick County. His plantation was named after Windmill Point, a high bluff dividing the Warwick River and Potash Creek at their confluence and facing Mulberry Island. He was probably a Bristol sea captain long engaged in the Virginia trade who retired from the sea.

Lady Margaret Elizabeth Swinderby was born on 08 Jul 1578 in Kobenhavn, Kobenhavn, Denmark as the first child of Andrew Swinderby and Margreta Mitchell Anderson. She died on 02 Jul 1672 in Hadleigh, Suffolk, England. When she was 21, she married Capt. Thomas John Taylor II son of Thomas John Taylor I and Elizabeth Eddings Burwell, on 09 Oct 1599 in Hadleigh, Suffolk, England. Lady Swinderby was buried in Hadley, Middlesex. England (St. Mary's Churchyard; Find A Grave #18652168)

Capt Thomas John Taylor II and Lady Margaret Elizabeth Swinderby had the following child:
+16. i. JOHN WILLIAM "THE IMMIGRANT"[11] TAYLOR was born on 10 Aug 1607 in Carlisle, Cumberland, England (Pennington Castle). He died on 16 Jan 1651/52 in Lancaster County, Virginia, USA. He married Elizabeth Lawes Nunne on 07 May 1627 in London, England (St Gregory by St Paul). She was born on 10 Aug 1608 in Hadley, Middlesex. England. She died on 28 Feb 1658/59 in Lancaster County, Virginia, USA.

Generation 11

16. JOHN WILLIAM "THE IMMIGRANT"[11] TAYLOR (Capt Thomas John[10] II, Thomas John[9] I, Rev. Dr. Rowland[8], John Thomas[7], John William[6] I, William[5] II, Sir John[4], William[3] I, Sir John[2] Taylifer, Harger[1] Taylefer) was born on 10 Aug 1607 in Carlisle, Cumberland, England (Pennington Castle). He died on 16 Jan 1652/53 in Lancaster County, Virginia, USA. He married **Elizabeth Lawes Nunne** on 07 May 1627 in London, England (St Gregory by St Paul). She was born on 10 Aug 1608 in Hadley, Middlesex. England. She died on 28 Feb 1658/59 in Lancaster County, Virginia, USA.

The Earl of Pennington, Col. John William Taylor became "The Immigrant" when he left England for the colony of Williamsburg, Virginia in about 1648. One source says by August 1, 1652 he was living on land bordering Fleets Bay on the North shore of the Rappahannock River in Lancaster County, Virginia. On that date Teague Floyne, who was later to help inventory John Taylor's estate, patented land adjoining John Taylor on Fleets Bay. Four months later, on November 29, 1652, John Taylor and Tobias Horton were formally granted patents for adjoining tracts on Fleets Bay. John Taylor was given a patent for 400 acres for transporting eight immigrants, probably by paying for their passage. John Taylor died sometime shortly before January 10, 1653. He was buried in Northumberland County, Virginia, USA (Wicomico Parish Church Cemetery; Find A Grave #219294247).

Elizabeth Lawes Nunne was born on 10 Aug 1608 in Hadleigh, Suffolk, England. She died on 28 Feb 1658/59 in Lancaster County, Virginia, USA. When she was 18, she married John William "The Immigrant" Taylor, son of Capt. Thomas John Taylor II and Lady Margaret Elizabeth Swinderby on 07 May 1627 in London, England (St Gregory by St Paul). When she was 45, she married Tobias Horton in 1654 in Lancaster County, Virginia, USA. Elizabeth Lawes Nunne arrived in Maryland, USA in 1640. She was also known as Elizabeth Jones, Flowers, Nunn, Nin, Nunne, Nynne, Nynn, Taylor, and Horton. She was buried in Northumberland, Virginia, USA (Wicomico Parish Church Cemetery: Find A Grave #219354565).

Sources say John married Elizabeth in England in 1627. After his death she was appointed administrator of his estate by the Lancaster County, Virginia court (Lancaster Co., VA WB-1, p. 24; Lancaster County, Virginia Deeds and Wills, 1652-1657). In 1654 after John's death Elizabeth Taylor became Elizabeth Taylor Horton when she married Tobias Horton, a wealthy planter, surveyor and businessman with whom she founded a dynasty. Sources say Horton arrived in America as early as 1638.

Horton bought 1,400 acres near the Indian town of Wicomoco, located on the southside of Corotoman, from Francis Morrison, which was originally owned by John Taylor I. On October

10, 1654 Tobias and Elizabeth hired Hugh Brent and Teague Floyne to make an inventory of the late John Taylor's estate. It included three old Bibles, 70 other books, and £9,590 worth of tobacco. On July 1, 1659 Tobias Horton paid John Taylor's debt of £6,173. At the Lancaster County court on May 15, 1663 Elizabeth requested that cattle which belonged to John Taylor be given to his orphans (Abstracts, Lancaster County, Virginia, wills, 1653-1800).

John William "The Immigrant" Taylor and Elizabeth Lawes Nunne had the following child:
+17.   i.   JAMES HENRY "THE ELDER"[12] TAYLOR I was born on 12 Feb 1634/35 in Carlisle, Cumberland, England (Earl, Hare). He died on 30 Apr 1698 in Bowling Green, Caroline County, Virginia, USA. He married (1) Mary Frances Walker, daughter of Thomas Walker and Elizabeth Gregory, in 1666 in New Kent County, Virginia, USA. She was born in 1640 in Leamington Hastings, Warwickshire, England. She died on 22 Sep 1680 in Bowling Green, Caroline County, Virginia, USA. He married (2) Mary Bishop Gregory on 10 Aug 1682 in New Kent, Virginia, USA. She was born on 16 Feb 1664/65 in Sittenbourne, Rappahannock, Virginia, USA. She died on 02 Apr 1747 in Bowling Green, Caroline, Virginia, USA.

Generation 12

17. JAMES HENRY "THE ELDER"[12] TAYLOR I (John William "The Immigrant"[11], Capt. Thomas John[10] II, Thomas John[9] I, Rev. Dr. Rowland[8], John Thomas[7], John William[6] I, William[5] II, Sir John[4], William[3] I, Sir John[2] Taylifer, Harger[1] Taylefer) was born on 12 Feb 1634/35 in Carlisle, Cumberland, England (Pennington Castle) as the first child of John William "The Immigrant" Taylor and Elizabeth Lawes Nunne. He died on 30 Apr 1698 in Bowling Green, Caroline County, Virginia, USA. When he was 30, he married (1) **Mary Frances Walker**, daughter of William Thomas Walker and Elizabeth Gregory, on 17 Jan 1665/66 in New Kent County, Virginia, USA. When he was 47, he married (2) **Mary Bishop Gregory** on 10 Aug 1682 in New Kent County, Virginia, USA.

James Henry "The Elder" Taylor I arrived in Williamsburg, James City County, Virginia, USA in Dec 1635. He lived in Caroline County, Virginia, USA in 1650 (Monte Bello). He lived in Virginia, USA in 1651. He was also known as "James The Elder." He was known by the title of Colonel, Doctor. He was buried in Hopewell, Caroline County, Virginia, USA (Hare Forest Plantation Cemetery, 10th Ave and Davis St., Sec D Site 4709-A; Find A Grave #18538665).

Left: Pennington Castle, Carlisle, England. Birthplace of John Taylor "The Immigrant" and James Taylor "The Elder." Courtesy Ancestry.com.

Colonel James Taylor, a Revolutionary War veteran, was born at his ancestral home, Pennington Castle, about 20 miles from Carlisle, England. He arrived in Virginia with his family in 1635 on the ship "True Love." He was an ancestor of President Zachary Taylor, Zachary's cousin James Madison and John Penn, signer of the Declaration of Independence. James Taylor became a large landowner and prominent citizen in the Williamsburg Colony. He was a lawyer and a public official and served as a member of the House of Burgesses. He was Sheriff of New Kent County in 1690 and Vestryman of Saint George's Parish. James built his home along the Mattaponi River and named it "Hare Forest." His home was in King and Queen County, Virginia which was later divided and became part of Orange County, where his children were born. His home is now located in Caroline County, Virginia.

An old ring handed down in the family is said to have once been his property. Engraved upon the ring is the crest of the Taylor Clan of Pennington Castle. James Taylor was a lineal descendant of the Earls of Pennington. The crest is a naked arm cupped at the shoulder embowed holding an arrow with the motto "Consequitur Quodeunque Petit" variously translated as "Always forward, however little," or "Strikes what he aims at," or "gains what he seeks" (Walker, 1964, p. p. 163).

Crest of the Taylor Clan of Pennington Castle:
A naked arm cupped at the shoulder embowed holding an arrow
with the motto "Consequitur Quodeunque Petit".

Mary Frances Walker was the first wife of James Taylor I and by some accounts had three children with him until her death in 1680. She was buried in Caroline County, Virginia USA (Find A Grave #18538707).

Mary Bishop Gregory married James Taylor I on 10 Aug 1682 according to the Erasmus Taylor family Bible. She raised her two young step-children, James Jr and Sarah, and had four surviving children of her own with James Taylor. She may have had as many as four other children with James who did not survive youth. When James died in 1698, Mary was left with four children between the ages of 2-14. Mary's step-children from James's first wife had left or were soon to leave home. James Jr was 24 and would marry the following year, and Sarah was already married. Mary was buried in Hopewell, Caroline County, Virginia, USA (Hare Forest Plantation Cemetery, Find A Grave #18531133).

James Henry "The Elder" Taylor I and Mary Frances Walker had the following children:

+18.   i.   WILLIAM NATHANIEL[13] TAYLOR was born in 1671 in Antrim, Argmagh, Ulster, Ireland. He died in 1730 in Locustville, Accomack, Virginia, USA. He married Ruth Janet Paul, daughter of John Clother Paul and Dorothy Walker, in 1700 in Antrim, Antrim, Northern Ireland. She was born on 09 Feb 1682/83 in Inveresk, Midlothian, Scotland. She died in 1732 in Staunton, Augusta, Virginia, USA.

+19.   ii.   JAMES WALKER TAYLOR II was born on 14 Mar 1672/73 in Accomack, Accomack, Virginia, USA. He died on 26 Jun 1729 in Orange Co., Virginia, USA. He married Martha Montague Thompson, daughter of William Thompson and Ellen Montague, on 23 Feb 1698/99 in King and Queen, Virginia, USA. She was born on 06 Feb 1678/79 in Carlisle, Cumbria, England. She died on 19 Nov 1762 in Greenfield, Orange, VA.

20.   iii.   SARAH TAYLOR was born on 30 Jun 1676 in New Kent County, Virginia, USA. She died in 1745 in Locustville, Accomack, Virginia, USA.

James Henry "The Elder" Taylor I and Mary Bishop Gregory had the following children:

21.   i.   ANN[13] TAYLOR was born on 12 Jan 1684 in Hare Forest Plantation, Caroline County, Virginia, USA. She died in 1729 in St George Parish, Spotsylvania County, Virginia, USA.

22.   ii.   MARY BISHOP TAYLOR was born on 29 Jun 1688 in Caroline, Virginia, USA. She died on 10 Jun 1770 in Bowling Green, Caroline, Virginia, USA. She married Henry Pendleton, son of Philip Pendleton and Isabella Hurt, in 1701 in Caroline Co, Virginia, USA. He was born in 1683 in King and Queen County, Virginia, USA. He died in May 1721 in Caroline Co, Virginia, USA.

23.   iii   EDMUND TAYLOR was born on 05 Jul 1690 in New Kent, Virginia, USA (Hare Forest). He died in 1755 in Spotsylvania, Spotsylvania, Virginia, USA.

+24.   iv.   COL.JOHN POWELL TAYLOR was born on 18 Nov 1696 in Orange, Virginia, USA. He died on 22 Mar 1780 in Townsville, Granville, North Carolina, USA. He married Catherine Pendleton, daughter of Philip Pendleton and Isabella Hurt, on 14 Feb 1715/16 in VA. She was born on 08 Dec 1699 in King and Queen County, Virginia, USA. She died on 26 Jul 1774 in Granville County, N. Carolina, USA.

18. WILLIAM NATHANIEL[13] **TAYLOR** (James Henry "The Elder"[12] I, John William "The Immigrant"[11], Capt Thomas John[10] II, Thomas John[9] I, Rev. Dr. Rowland[8], John Thomas[7], John William[6] I, William[5] II, Sir John[4], William[3] I, Sir John[2] Taylifer, Harger[1] Taylefer) was born in 1671 in Antrim, Argmagh, Ulster, Ireland. He died in 1730 in Locustville, Accomack, Virginia, USA. He married **Ruth Janet Paul**, daughter of John Clother Paul and Dorothy Walker, in 1700 in Antrim, Antrim, Northern Ireland. She was born on 09 Feb 1682/83 in Inveresk, Midlothian, Scotland. She died in 1732 in Staunton, Augusta, Virginia, USA.

William Nathaniel Taylor and Ruth Janet Paul had the following children:

+25. i. WILLIAM ABRAHAM LAWRENCE[14] TAYLOR was born on 13 Apr 1690 in Ballitore, Kildare, Ireland. He died on 03 Mar 1775 in Waxhaw, Lancaster, South Carolina, USA. He married Mary Dinah Atherton, daughter of General Henry Atherton and Jennetta "Jane" Thelwall, in 1719 in East Caln, Chester, Pennsylvania, USA. She was born on 06 Aug 1691 in Lancashire, England (Farnworth near Prescot). She died on 05 Sep 1758 in Lancaster, South Carolina, USA.

26. ii. JAMES WALKER TAYLOR III was born in 1703. He died in 1784 in Cecil, Maryland, USA. He married ALICE THORNTON.

27. iii. MATHEW TAYLOR was born in 1707 in Armagh, Ulster, Ireland. He died on 03 Jan 1784 in Cecil, Maryland, USA.

19. JAMES WALKER[13] **TAYLOR II** (James Henry "The Elder"[12] I, John William "The Immigrant"[11], Capt Thomas John[10] II, Thomas John[9] I, Rev. Dr. Rowland[8], John Thomas[7], John William[6] I, William[5] II, Sir John[4], William[3] I, Sir John[2] Taylifer, Harger[1] Taylefer) was born on 14 Mar 1672/73 in Accomac, Accomack, Virginia, USA. He died on 26 Jun 1729 in Orange Co., Virginia, USA. He married **Martha Montague Thompson**, daughter of Col. William Thompson of the Royal Army and Ellen Montague, on 23 Feb 1698/99 in King and Queen, Virginia, USA. She was born on 06 Feb 1678/79 in Carlisle, Cumbria, England. She died on 19 Nov 1762 in Greenfield, Orange, VA.

James Walker Taylor II was born in New Kent County, Virginia, which later became King & Queen County. He died in Orange in King & Queen County, which later became Orange County. James Taylor II was a Colonel in the Colonial Militia and probably did active duty during the French and Indian War. He accompanied Lieutenant Governor Spotswood on his expedition over the Blue Ridge, was a member of the House of Burgesses and Surveyor General of Virginia Colony. James was granted 13,000 acres of land in what became Orange County and there he built his Bloomsbury Plantation about 1722. His one-and-a-half story frame house of Williamsburg construction about four miles southeast of Orange, VA was still standing as of 1964. He divided his vast holdings among his children. George received Midland (now Yatton), James III got Bloomsbury, Erasmus got Greenfield and Zachary got Meadow Farm. Two of his great grandsons, James Madison and Zachary Taylor, became US Presidents

(Trabue, 1925, p. 16).

Martha MontagueThompson was described as a famous beauty, vivacious, brilliant, with charming manners, proud and queenly, and noted for firmness and dignity. A story by descendant Elizabeth H. Taylor illustrated her courage in time of danger:

> In those early days in the settlement of Virginia, danger from marauding Indians was always imminent. It was necessary that the frontier woman as well as her husband should be constantly ready for defense. The rifle was his constant companion at home or in the field. Every cabin was a semi-fortress that could be barred instantly by the wife and children at the sound of the dreadful war whoop. It was amid such conditions as this that our fair ancestress reared her family. One day, when her husband and elder sons were some distance from the house preparing a field for planting, three savages crept into the kitchen where Martha was supervising the preparations for dinner. Their intent was evidently hostile, but they were not prepared for her method of defense. As they pushed their way into the kitchen and made for the house adjoining, she seized a ladle, dipped it into a pot of hot mush and dashed the boiling liquid on their bare bodies. Howling with rage and pain, they fled into the house and hid under a bed, where she bravely held them at bay, threatening them with further doses of the hot mush, until her husband returned and captured them (Walker, 1964, p. 167).

It is believed that James II and Martha were buried at Bloomsbury in the Taylor-Quarles Cemetery on the property, since this was their original homestead. However the James Taylor I Association believes Martha died at and was buried on the Greenfield Plantation, the home of her son Erasmus, but she does not have a grave marker there.

James Walker Taylor II and Martha Montague Thompson had the following children:

+28.   i.   FRANCES[14] TAYLOR was born on 30 Aug 1700 in Orange County, Virginia, USA. She died on 26 Nov 1761 in Orange County, Virginia, USA. She married Ambrose Madison on 24 Aug 1721. He was born on 17 Jan 1695/96 in Orange County, Virginia, USA. He died on 27 Aug 1732 in Orange County, Virginia, USA (Montpelier Plantation).

29.   ii.   JAMES TAYLOR III was born on 30 Mar 1703 in Essex County, Virginia, USA. He died on 01 Mar 1784 in Rapidan, Culpeper County, Virginia, USA.

+30.   iii.   ZACHARY TAYLOR SR was born on 17 Apr 1707 in Rapidan, Culpeper County, Virginia, USA. He died on 01 Mar 1768 in Rapidan, Culpeper County, Virginia, USA. He married Elizabeth Lee on 23 Feb 1737/38. She was born before 1709 in Virginia, USA. She died on 03 Mar 1743/44.

31.   iv.   GEORGE (COLONEL) TAYLOR was born on 11 Feb 1710/11 in King and Queen County, Virginia, USA. He died on 04 Nov 1792 in Orange County, Virginia, USA.

32.   v.   ERASMUS TAYLOR was born on 05 Sep 1715 in Rapidan, Culpeper County, Virginia, USA. He died on 19 Dec 1794 in Orange County, Virginia, USA (Greenfield).

24. COL. JOHN POWELL[13] TAYLOR (James Henry "The Elder"[12] I, John William "The

Immigrant"[11], Capt Thomas John[10] II, Thomas John[9] I, Rev. Dr. Rowland[8], John Thomas[7], John William[6] I, William[5] II, Sir John[4], William[3] I, Sir John[2] Taylifer, Harger[1] Taylefer) was born on 18 Nov 1696 in Orange, Virginia, USA. He died on 22 Mar 1780 in Townsville, Granville, North Carolina, USA. He married **Catherine Pendleton**, daughter of Philip Pendleton and Isabella Hurt, on 14 Feb 1715/16 in VA. She was born on 08 Dec 1699 in King and Queen County, Virginia, USA. She died on 26 Jul 1774 in Granville County, North Carolina, USA.

In about 1754 John Powell Taylor and his wife Catherine Pendleton settled at Macpelah in North Carolina (two miles south of Townsville in Vance County). This is the old plantation of the Taylor's. It is still in the Taylor family (as of May 2000) though not as large a property holding now as it was then.

Catherine Pendleton married John Powell Taylor, brother of Mary Taylor, wife of her brother, Henry. Her son John Taylor of Carolina was well known. Even more notable is the fact that she became the ancestor of five presidents: James Madison, Zachary Taylor, William Henry Harrison, Benjamin Harrison and John Tyler.

Col. John Powell Taylor and Catherine Pendleton had the following children:

33.   i.   MARY ELIZABETH[14] TAYLOR SR was born on 30 May 1718 in Rapidan, Culpeper County, Virginia, USA. She died on 13 Sep 1757 in Caroline County, Virginia, USA.
34.   ii.   CATHERINE TAYLOR was born on 30 Dec 1719. She died on 04 Nov 1759.
35.   iii.   EDMUND TAYLOR was born on 12 Jun 1723 in Orange County, Virginia, USA. He died in May 1808 in Granville County, North Carolina, USA.
36.   iv.   JOHN TAYLOR JR was born on 07 Sep 1727 in Mecklenburg County, Virginia, USA. He died on 26 Oct 1787 in Granville County, North Carolina, USA.
37.   v.   JAMES TAYLOR was born on 07 Sep 1729 in Orange County, Virginia, USA. He died on 26 Sep 1750 in Townsville, Vance County, North Carolina, USA.
38.   vi.   PHILIP TAYLOR was born on 17 Feb 1731/32 in Orange County, Virginia, USA. He died on 07 Sep 1765 in Townsville, Vance County, North Carolina, USA.
39.   vii.   ELIZABETH LEWIS TAYLOR was born on 09 Jul 1735 in Caroline County, Virginia, USA. She died in 1816 in Granville County, North Carolina, USA.
40.   viii.   LT. COL. WILLIAM TAYLOR was born on 19 Dec 1737 in Rapidan, Culpeper County, Virginia, USA. He died on 05 Nov 1803 in Townsville, Vance County, North Carolina, USA.
41.   ix.   COL. JOSEPH TAYLOR was born on 19 Feb 1741/42 in Virginia, USA. He died on 31 May 1815 in Virginia, USA.

Author Note: Since different branches of the Taylor family from England, Ireland and Scotland settled in several American colonies during the 1600s, since the Taylor name is very common, and since few Taylor family records of that era still exist, I am only speculating until further proof is available that a direct lineage from William Nathaniel Taylor (18) in Generation 13 above and his ancestors exists to William Abraham Lawrence Taylor (25) below. However from Generation 14 and forward many more records exist, and the direct lineage of Taylor family ancestors can be proven, despite that some details may be missing or incorrect.

Generation 14

25. WILLIAM ABRAHAM LAWRENCE[13] **TAYLOR** (James Henry "The Elder"[12] I, John William "The Immigrant"[11], Capt Thomas John[10] II, Thomas John[9] I, Rev. Dr. Rowland[8], John Thomas[7], John William[6] I, William[5] II, Sir John[4], William[3] I, Sir John[2] Taylifer, Harger[1] Taylefer) was born on 13 Apr 1690 in Ballitore, Kildare, Ireland as the first child of William Nathaniel Taylor and Ruth Janet Anne Paul. He had two siblings, namely: James Walker III, and Mathew. He died on 03 Mar 1775 in Waxhaw, Lancaster, South Carolina, USA. When he was 28, he married **Mary Dinah Atherton**, daughter of General Henry Atherton and Jennetta "Jane" Thelwall, in 1719 in East Caln, Chester, Pennsylvania, USA.

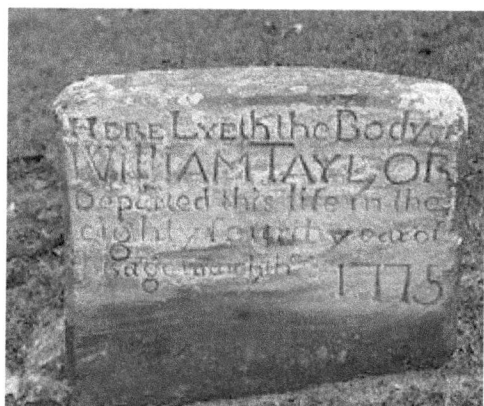

Left: William Taylor's gravestone at Old Waxhaw Presbyterian Church Cemetery. Courtesy findagrave.com (#10224789).

William Abraham Lawrence Taylor was baptized on 25 Jan 1689/90 in Cassington, Oxfordshire, England. He arrived in Caln, Chester, Pennsylvania, USA in 1714. He lived in Caln, Chester, Pennsylvania, USA on 17 Aug 1741. He lived in Philadelphia, Pennsylvania, USA about 1750. He lived in Craven, North Carolina, USA in 1753. He lived in Waxhaw, Lancaster, South Carolina, USA in 1768. He may also have been known as "Cain." He was buried in Riverside, Greenville, South Carolina, USA (Old Waxhaw Presbyterian Church Cemetery; Find A Grave #10224789).

Right: Old Waxhaw Presbyterian Church near Riverside, South Carolina. Courtesy Ancestry.com.

Mary Dinah Atherton was born on 06 Aug 1691 in Liverpool, Lancashire, England (Farnworth near Prescot) as the third child of General Henry Atherton and Jennetta "Jane" Thelwall. She had four siblings, namely: Grace, Henry Jr, William, and Thomas. She died on 05 Sep 1758 in Lancaster, South Carolina, USA. When she was 27, she married William Abraham Lawrence Taylor, son of William Nathaniel Taylor and Ruth Janet Anne Paul, in 1719 in East Caln, Chester, Pennsylvania, USA. Mary Dinah Atherton arrived in Pennsylvania, USA in 1714 (arrived with her brother William and John Holland). She was affiliated with the Quaker religion. She was buried at 2814 Old Hickory Road, Riverside; Lancaster County, South Carolina, USA (Old Waxhaw Presbyterian Church Cemetery; Find A Grave #10224788).

William Abraham Lawrence Taylor and Mary Dinah Atherton had the following children:

42. i. JONATHAN[15] TAYLOR was born in 1720 in South Carolina, USA. He died in 1798.

43. ii. WILLIAM ARTHUR TAYLOR was born in 1722 in South Carolina, USA. He died on 08 Jan 1798 in Waxhaw, Lancaster, South Carolina, USA. He married NELLIE MCMAHAN. She was born in 1725 in South Carolina USA.

44. iii. JOHN TAYLOR was born on 29 Sep 1724 in Waxhaw Settlement, South Carolina. He died in 1798 in Johnston County, North Carolina, USA.

45. iv. ISAAC TAYLOR was born in 1731 in Chester,Craven County, South Carolina, USA. He died in 1786 in Randolph, North Carolina, USA.

46. v. JACOB Q TAYLOR was born in 1731 in Waxhaw, Lancaster, South Carolina, USA. He died on 18 Sep 1784 in Waxhaw, Lancaster, South Carolina, USA.

47. vi. ABRAHAM LAWRENCE TAYLOR was born in 1733 in South Carolina, USA. He died in 1787 in Edgefield, South Carolina, USA.

+48. vii. DEMPSEY TAYLOR was born in 1744 in Edgecombe, Edgecombe, North Carolina, USA. He died on 17 Jan 1837 in Irwin County, Georgia, USA. He married Sarah Sally Swinson, daughter of Theophilus Swinson and Elizabeth Allen, on 01 Oct 1783 in Bladen, North Carolina, USA. She was born in 1756 in Sampson, North Carolina, USA. She died in Aug 1859 in Wilcox, Georgia, USA (lived with son John Dennis Taylor at time of death at age 103).

28. FRANCES[14] TAYLOR (James Walker[13] II, James Henry "The Elder"[12] I, John William "The Immigrant"[11], Capt Thomas John[10] II, Thomas John[9] I, Rev. Dr. Rowland[8], John Thomas[7], John William[6] I, William[5] II, Sir John[4], William[3] I, Sir John[2] Taylifer, Harger[1] Taylefer) was born on 30 Aug 1700 in Orange County, Virginia, USA. She died on 26 Nov 1761 in Orange County, Virginia, USA. She married **Ambrose Madison** on 24 Aug 1721. He was born on 17 Jan 1695/96 in Orange County, Virginia, USA. He died on 27 Aug 1732 in Orange County, Virginia, USA (Montpelier Plantation).

Ambrose Madison and Frances Taylor had the following child:

+49. i. JAMES[15] MADISON SR was born on 27 Mar 1723 in Orange County, Virginia, USA. He died on 27 Feb 1801 in Orange County, Virginia, USA (Montpelier Plantation). He married Eleanor Rose Conway on 13 Sep 1749. She was born on 09 Jan 1730/31 in King George, Virginia, USA (Port Conway). She died on 11 Feb 1829 in Orange County, Virginia, USA (Montpelier Plantation).

30. ZACHARY[14] TAYLOR SR (James Walker[13] II, James Henry "The Elder"[12] I, John William "The Immigrant"[11], Capt Thomas John[10] II, Thomas John[9] I, Rev. Dr. Rowland[8], John Thomas[7], John William[6] I, William[5] II, Sir John[4], William[3] I, Sir John[2] Taylifer, Harger[1] Taylefer) was born on 17 Apr 1707 in Rapidan, Culpeper County, Virginia, USA. He died on 01 Mar 1768 in Rapidan, Culpeper County, Virginia, USA. He married **Elizabeth Lee** on 23 Feb 1737/38. She was born before 1709 in Virginia, USA. She died on 03 Mar 1743/44.

Zachary Taylor Sr. and Elizabeth Lee had the following child:

+50. i. Lt. COL. RICHARD LEE[15] TAYLOR was born on 03 Mar 1743/44 in Orange County, Virginia, USA. He died on 19 Jan 1829 in Woodford, Kentucky, USA. He married Sara Dabney Strother on 20 Aug 1779 in Orange County, Virginia, USA. She was born on 14 Dec 1760 in Orange County, Virginia, USA. She died on 13 Dec 1822 in Woodford, Kentucky, USA.

Generation 15

48. DEMPSEY[15] **TAYLOR** (William Abraham Lawrence[14], William Nathaniel[13], James Henry "The Elder"[12] I, John William "The Immigrant"[11], Capt Thomas John[10] II, Thomas John[9] I, Rev. Dr. Rowland[8], John Thomas[7], John William[6] I, William[5] II, Sir John[4], William[3] I, Sir John[2] Taylifer, Harger[1] Taylefer) was born 15 Oct 1759 in Duplin County, North Carolina, USA. He died on 17 Jan 1837 in Irwin County, Georgia, USA. He married **Sarah Sally Swinson**, daughter of Theophilus Swinson and Elizabeth Allen, on 01 Oct 1783 in Dublin, Bladen County, North Carolina, USA. She was born on 09 Mar 1763 in Sampson, North Carolina, USA. She died in Aug 1859 in Wilcox, Georgia, USA (lived with son John Dennis Taylor at time of death at age 96).

Dempsey was the son of William Taylor and Mary Atherton of Bladen County, North Carolina. During the American Revolution he served with Brig. Gen. Francis Marion's militia in the Carolinas. One story about this militia goes like this:

> In early 1781, Revolutionary War militia leader Francis Marion and his men were camping on Snow's Island, South Carolina, when a British officer arrived to discuss a prisoner exchange. As one militiaman recalled years later, a breakfast of sweet potatoes was roasting in the fire, and after the negotiations Marion, known as the "Swamp Fox," invited the British soldier to share breakfast. According to a legend that grew out of the much-repeated anecdote, the British officer was so inspired by the Americans' resourcefulness and dedication to the cause—despite their lack of adequate provisions, supplies or proper uniforms—that he promptly switched sides and supported American independence (Crawford, 2007).

After his military service Dempsey Taylor and Sarah Sally Swinson were married in Bladen County, North Carolina where their son John Dennis was born. The family went to Georgia sometime before 1800 and Dempsey registered for the 1805 Land Lottery but drew no land. A few years later, Dempsey moved his family down to Telfair County where they appear in the 1820 Census. Dempsey and Sally then moved to Irwin County, Georgia where they lived the rest of their lives. The Revolutionary War Pension application of Dempsey's widow Sally was submitted in 1858 only a year prior to her death at age 96 in 1859. In it she stated that her husband Dempsey Taylor died January 17, 1837 in Irwin County, Georgia.

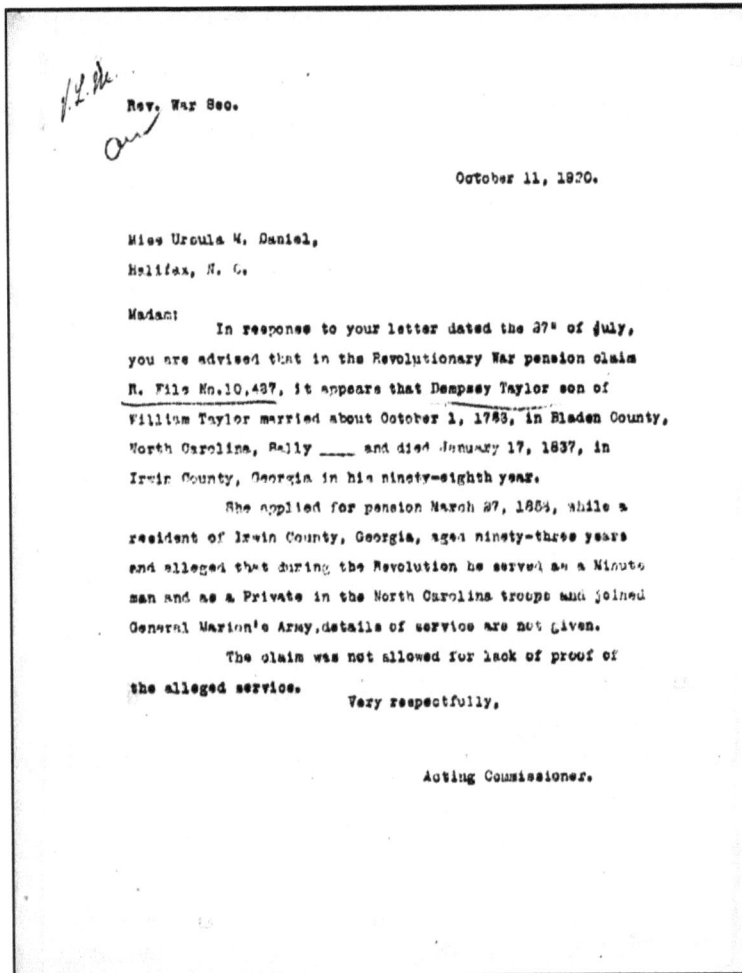

```
                                    Rev. War Sec.

                                        October 11, 1920.

            Miss Ursula M. Daniel,
            Halifax, N. C.

            Madam:
                    In response to your letter dated the 27th of July,
            you are advised that in the Revolutionary War pension claim
            R. File No.10,437, it appears that Dempsey Taylor son of
            William Taylor married about October 1, 1783, in Bladen County,
            North Carolina, Sally ____ and died January 17, 1837, in
            Irwin County, Georgia in his ninety-eighth year.

                    She applied for pension March 27, 1834, while a
            resident of Irwin County, Georgia, aged ninety-three years
            and alleged that during the Revolution he served as a Minute
            man and as a Private in the North Carolina troops and joined
            General Marion's Army, details of service are not given.

                    The claim was not allowed for lack of proof of
            the alleged service.
                                        Very respectfully,

                                        Acting Commissioner.
```

Sarah Sally Swinson was born on 09 Mar 1763 in Sampson, North Carolina, USA as the first child of Theophilus Swinson and Elizabeth Thalley. She had one sibling, namely: Prudence. She died in Aug 1859 in Wilcox, Georgia, USA (lived with son J. Dennis Taylor at time of death). When she was 20, she married Dempsey Taylor, son of William Taylor and Mary Dinah Atherton, on 01 Oct 1783 in Duplin County, North Carolina, USA. Sarah Sally Swinson lived in Irwin County, Georgia, USA in 1850. She lived in Irwin County, Georgia, USA in 1852.

Dempsey Taylor and Sarah Sally Swinson had the following children:

+51. i. JOHN DENNIS[16] TAYLOR was born in 1780 in Duplin County, North Carolina, USA. He died on 31 Oct 1862 in Wilcox County, Georgia, USA. He married (1) Abigail MacNalley in 1805 in North Carolina, USA. She was born in 1790 in North Carolina, USA. She died in 1885 in Irwin, Georgia, USA. He married (2) Margaret "Peggy" Gibbs, daughter of Sampson Gibbs and Ruth Durham, on 03 Dec 1843 in Irwin County, Georgia, USA. She was born on 13 Mar 1829 in Irwin County, Georgia, USA. She died on 19 Sep 1883 in Wilcox County, Georgia, USA.

52. ii. William G. Taylor was born in 1785 in South Carolina, USA. He died in 1859 in Decatur, Georgia, USA (now Grady County).

49. JAMES[15] MADISON SR (Frances[14] Taylor, James Walker[13] Taylor II, James Henry "The Elder"[12] Taylor I, John William "The Immigrant"[11] Taylor, Capt Thomas John[10] Taylor II, Thomas John[9] Taylor I, Rev. Dr. Rowland[8] Taylor, John Thomas[7] Taylor, John William[6] Taylor I, William[5] Taylor II, Sir John[4] Taylor, William[3] Taylor I, Sir John[2] Taylifer, Harger[1] Taylefer, Ambrose) was born on 27 Mar 1723 in Orange County, Virginia, USA. He died on

27 Feb 1801 in Orange County, Virginia, USA (Montpelier Plantation). He married **Eleanor Rose Conway** on 13 Sep 1749. She was born on 09 Jan 1730/31 in King George, Virginia, USA (Port Conway). She died on 11 Feb 1829 in Orange County, Virginia, USA (Montpelier Plantation).

James Madison Sr. and Eleanor Rose Conway had the following child:

53. i. JAMES (4TH PRES)[16] MADISON was born on 16 Mar 1750/51 in King George, Virginia, USA (Belle Grove Plantation, Port Conway). He died on 28 Jun 1836 in Orange County, Virginia, USA (Montpelier Plantation). He married Dorthea "Dolley" Payne on 15 Sep 1794 in Jefferson, West Virginia, USA (Harewood, near Charles Town). She was born on 20 May 1768 in Guilford, North Carolina, USA. She died on 12 Jun 1849 in Washington, District of Columbia, USA.

50. LT. COL. RICHARD LEE[15] TAYLOR (Zachary[14] Sr, James Walker[13] II, James Henry "The Elder"[12] I, John William "The Immigrant"[11], Capt Thomas John[10] II, Thomas John[9] I, Rev. Dr. Rowland[8], John Thomas[7], John William[6] I, William[5] II, Sir John[4], William[3] I, Sir John[2] Taylifer, Harger[1] Taylefer) was born on 03 Mar 1743/44 in Orange County, Virginia, USA. He died on 19 Jan 1829 in Woodford, Kentucky, USA. He married **Sara Dabney Strother** on 20 Aug 1779 in Orange County, Virginia, USA. She was born on 14 Dec 1760 in Orange County, Virginia, USA. She died on 13 Dec 1822 in Woodford, Kentucky, USA.

Lt. Col. Richard Lee Taylor and Sara Dabney Strother had the following child:

+54. i. ZACHARY (12TH PRES)[16] TAYLOR was born on 24 Nov 1784 in Orange County, Virginia, USA (Montebello). He died on 09 Jul 1850 in Washington, District of Columbia, USA (White House). He married Margaret Mackall Smith on 21 Jun 1810 in Louisville, Jefferson, Kentucky, USA. She was born on 21 Sep 1788 in Calvert, Cecil, Maryland, USA. She died on 14 Aug 1852 in Pascagoula, Jackson, Mississippi, USA.

Generation 16

51. JOHN DENNIS[16] TAYLOR (Dempsey[15], William Abraham Lawrence[14], William Nathaniel[13], James Henry "The Elder"[12] I, John William "The Immigrant"[11], Capt Thomas John[10] II, Thomas John[9] I, Rev. Dr. Rowland[8], John Thomas[7], John William[6] I, William[5] II, Sir John[4], William[3] I, Sir John[2] Taylifer, Harger[1] Taylefer) was born in 1780 in Duplin County, North Carolina, USA. He died on 31 Oct 1862 in Wilcox County, Georgia, USA. He married (1) **ABIGAIL MACNALLEY** on 9 Apr 1803 in North Carolina, USA. She was born in 1790 in North Carolina, USA. She died in 1885 in Irwin, Georgia, USA. He married (2) **MARGARET "PEGGY" GIBBS**, daughter of Sampson Gibbs and Ruth Durham, on 03 Dec 1843 in Irwin County, Georgia, USA. She was born on 13 Mar 1829 in Irwin County, Georgia, USA. She died on 19 Sep 1883 in Wilcox County, Georgia, USA.

Known as "JD," and also Dennis, John Dennis Taylor was born in Duplin County, North Carolina, son of Dempsey Taylor and Sally Swinson. Dennis had six children with his first wife Abigail MacNalley. A few months before his second marriage in 1843, Dennis became a member of the New Hope Primitive Baptist Church in Irwin (now Wilcox) County. A church is labeled "primitive" if it has an "anti-missionary" (anti foreign missions vs local missions) policy (McDonald, 1987, p. 111). Dennis added Margaret Gibbs as a second wife that year while his first wife Abbie was still alive and he had another nine children. Church records show he was received and baptized April 1, 1843, before his second marriage, and was excluded three years later on Oct. 31, 1846, after his second marriage.

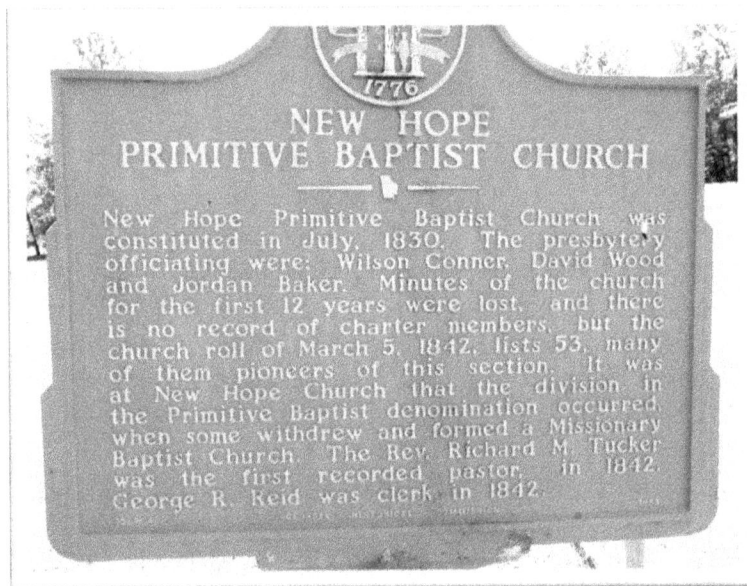

JD Taylor was baptized in 1843 here at the New Hope Primitive Baptist Church and Cemetery south of Abbeville, Georgia. Author photo 17 Apr 2021.

John Dennis Taylor's mother Sarah Sally Swinson Taylor lived her last years in his home and died there in August 1859 according to the mortuary schedule attached to the 1860 Census of Wilcox County, Georgia (Pioneers of Wiregrass Georgia, 1951, p. 443). John Dennis Taylor's great granddaughter Marjorie Taylor said she was told, "He weighed over 200 pounds, and could lift a 300 pound barrel of flour and walk with it."

Abigail "Abbie" MacNalley was born in 1790 in North Carolina, USA. She died in 1885 in Irwin, Georgia, USA. When she was 13, she married John Dennis Taylor, son of Dempsey Taylor and Sarah Sally Swinson, on 09 Apr 1803 in North Carolina, USA. Abigail MacNalley lived in Irwin, Georgia, USA in 1850 (age 60). She was also known as Abbie. One tradition says that the town of Abbeville, founded in 1857 as the seat of newly formed Wilcox County, is named after her as the wife of the original owner. She was affiliated with the Quaker religion. She was buried in Ben Hill, Georgia, USA (Salem Baptist Church Cemetery).

John Dennis Taylor and Abigail MacNalley had the following children:
55.   i.   SEABORN[17] TAYLOR was born in 1805 in Burke, Georgia, USA. He died in 1869 in Georgia, USA.
+56.   ii.   LEMUEL TAYLOR SR was born in 1812 in Burke, Georgia, USA. He died in 1887 in

Wilcox County, Georgia, USA. He married Rebecca Abigail McAnally on 20 Feb 1833 in Irwin, Georgia, USA. She was born in 1815 in Irwin, Georgia, USA. She died about 1859 in Irwin, Georgia, USA.

57.   iii.   EVAN TAYLOR was born in 1813 in Burke, Georgia, USA. He died in 1885 in Charlton, Georgia, USA.
58.   iv.   NANCY TAYLOR was born in 1817 in Telfair, Georgia, USA.
59.   v.   JOSEPH TAYLOR was born in 1825 in Irwin County, Georgia, USA.
60.   vi.   MARGARET TAYLOR was born in 1828 in Georgia, USA.

Margaret "Peggy" Gibbs was born on 13 Mar 1829 in Irwin County, Georgia, USA as the third child of Sampson Gibbs and Ruth Durham. She had three siblings, namely: Catherine, Nathaniel S, and Allen. She died on 19 Sep 1883 in Wilcox County, Georgia, USA. When she was 14, she married John Dennis Taylor, son of Dempsey Taylor and Sarah Sally Swinson, on 03 Dec 1843 in Irwin County, Georgia, USA.

Margaret "Peggy" Gibbs lived in Irwin County, Georgia, USA in 1850 (age 22). She lived in Wilcox, Georgia, USA in 1860 (created from Irwin County in 1857); age 33. She lived in Wilcox, Georgia, USA in 1870 (House Creek; age 41; Cannot Read: Y; Cannot Write: Y; Personal Estate Value: 572; Real Estate Value: 600; Occupation: Keeping House). She lived in District 1171, Wilcox, Georgia, USA in 1880 (age 51; Marital status: Widowed; Relation to Head of House: Self). She was also known as Peggy. FamilySearch ID: (K871-SGP) Race: White. She was buried in Ben Hill, Georgia, USA (Salem Baptist Church Cemetery; Find A Grave #67475277).

Right: Margaret "Peggy" Gibbs gravestone at the Salem Baptist Church Cemetery north of Fitzgerald, Georgia. Courtesy findagrave.com (#67475277).

John Dennis added Margaret "Peggy" Gibbs as his second wife in the mid-1840's while his first wife Abbie was still alive. In 1861 Peggy's younger brother Allen Gibbs, a Confederate soldier, died of typhoid fever in Chimborazo Hospital in Richmond VA (Rigdon, 2002, pp. 273, 274). According to Peggy's descendants Elsie and Nettie Taylor, RT's grandmothers Peggy Gibbs and Jane Land both helped raise him and his siblings after his mother Susannah Young died two days after he was born in 1871. Elsie said Jane was very kind and gentle, and even though she was six feet tall and weighed more than two hundred pounds she could outwork most of the men (Taylor D. , Dennis Taylor email to David G. Conklin, 2022).

John Dennis Taylor and Margaret "Peggy" Gibbs had the following children:
61.   i.   SAMUEL[17] TAYLOR was born in 1844 in Irwin County, Georgia, USA.
+62.   ii.   RICHARD LEMUEL TAYLOR was born in 1846 in Irwinville, Irwin, Georgia, USA. He

died on 20 Apr 1899 in Irwin County, Georgia, USA. He married (1) SUSANNAH YOUNG, daughter of Richard Joseph Young and Jane Jincy Land, in 1861 in Wilcox County, Georgia, USA. She was born in 1839 in Irwin County, Georgia, USA. She died on 26 Sep 1871 in Abbeville, Wilcox, Georgia, USA. He married (2) TEMPERANCE ZEMFA GIBBS, daughter of William Gibbs and Mary Taylor, on 21 Dec 1875 in Wilcox, Georgia, USA. She was born in 1839 in Irwin County, Georgia, USA. She died in 1880 in Wilcox County, Georgia, USA. He married (3) RUTH CLEMENTS, daughter of Eliseh Clements and Elizabeth Turner, after 1881 in Wilcox County, Georgia, USA. She was born in Mar 1851. She died on 26 Feb 1926 in Fitzgerald, Ben Hill, Georgia, USA.

63. iii. JOHN TAYLOR was born in 1847 in Irwin County, Georgia, USA.

64. iv. JAMES LEMUEL TAYLOR was born in Apr 1849 in Irwin County, Georgia, USA. He died on 17 Feb 1930 in Ocilla, Irwin, Georgia, USA. He married ELIZABETH YOUNG. She was born on 05 Dec 1851 in Wilcox, Georgia, USA. She died on 25 Apr 1919 in Irwin County, Georgia, USA.

65. v. SAMPSON TAYLOR was born on 12 Feb 1851 in Irwin County, Georgia, USA. He died on 07 Dec 1913 in Irwin County, Georgia, USA. He married Mary Ann Clements on 22 Jan 1874. She was born in Mar 1846. She died date Unknown.

66. vi. DEMPSEY TAYLOR II was born on 11 Apr 1854 in Irwin County, Georgia, USA. He died on 29 Oct 1885 in Irwin County, Georgia, USA.

+67. vii. JESSE HORTON TAYLOR was born on 22 Mar 1856 in Wilcox, Georgia, USA. He died on 08 Nov 1925 in Williamsons Mill, Ben Hill, Georgia, USA. He married Mary Van Fletcher in 1880 in Worth, GA. She was born on 12 Nov 1861 in Sycamore, Turner, Georgia, USA. She died on 11 Apr 1935 in Georgia USA.

68. viii. SARAH ANN TAYLOR was born in 1859 in Wilcox, Georgia. She died in 1936.

69. ix. JULIA ANN TAYLOR was born on 19 Feb 1861 in Georgia, USA. She died on 02 Dec 1942 in Georgia, USA. She married JOHN TOLIVER LIVINGSTON. He was born on 25 Sep 1857 in Georgia USA.. He died on 18 Apr 1935 in Georgia USA.

54. ZACHARY (12TH PRES)[16] TAYLOR (Col.Richard Lee[15], Zachary[14] Sr, James Walker[13] II, James Henry "The Elder"[12] I, John William "The Immigrant"[11], Capt Thomas John[10] II, Thomas John[9] I, Rev. Dr. Rowland[8], John Thomas[7], John William[6] I, William[5] II, Sir John[4], William[3] I, Sir John[2] Taylifer, Harger[1] Taylefer) was born on 24 Nov 1784 in Orange County, Virginia, USA (Montebello). He died on 09 Jul 1850 in Washington, District of Columbia, USA (White House). He married **Margaret Mackall Smith** on 21 Jun 1810 in Louisville, Jefferson, Kentucky, USA. She was born on 21 Sep 1788 in Calvert, Cecil, Maryland, USA. She died on 14 Aug 1852 in Pascagoula, Jackson, Mississippi, USA.

Zachary (12th Pres) Taylor and Margaret Mackall Smith had the following child:

70. i. SARAH KNOX[17] TAYLOR was born on 06 Mar 1814 in Vincennes, Knox, Indiana, USA (Fort Knox II). She died on 15 Sep 1835 in St Francisville, West Feliciana, Louisiana, USA (malaria). She married Jefferson Finis (CSA Pres) Davis on 17 Jun 1835 in Jefferson, Kentucky, USA. He was born on 03 Jun 1808 in Fairview, Christian, Kentucky, USA. He died on 06 Dec 1889 in New Orleans, Orleans, Louisiana, USA.

Wife of Jefferson Davis, future CSA President, Sarah Knox "Knoxie" Taylor Davis was the daughter of the 12th U.S. President Zachary Taylor and part of the notable Lee Family. She met Jefferson Davis when living with her father and family at Fort Crawford during the Black Hawk War in 1832. They married in 1835 and she died of malaria only three months later.

Generation 17

56. LEMUEL[17] TAYLOR SR (John Dennis[16], Dempsey[15], William Abraham Lawrence[14], William Nathaniel[13], James Henry "The Elder"[12] I, John William "The Immigrant"[11], Capt Thomas John[10] II, Thomas John[9] I, Rev. Dr. Rowland[8], John Thomas[7], John William[6] I, William[5] II, Sir John[4], William[3] I, Sir John[2] Taylifer, Harger[1] Taylefer) was born in 1812 in Burke, Georgia, USA. He died in 1887 in Wilcox County, Georgia, USA. He married **Rebecca Abigail McAnally** on 20 Feb 1833 in Irwin, Georgia, USA. She was born in 1815 in Irwin, Georgia, USA. She died about 1859 in Irwin, Georgia, USA.

Lemuel Taylor Sr. and Rebecca Abigail McAnally had the following children:
71. i. SUSAN[18] TAYLOR was born in 1838 in Irwin, Georgia, USA. She married James D Gibbs, son of John Allen Gibbs and Martha Patsy Smith, on 24 Jan 1861 in Wilcox, Georgia, USA. He was born in 1838 in Abbeville, Wilcox, Georgia, USA. He died on 29 Aug 1862 in Warwick, Virginia, USA (killed in the Civil War).
72. ii. LEMUEL DENNIS TAYLOR was born on 22 Feb 1843 in Irwin, Georgia, USA. He died on 05 Nov 1930 in Coffee, Georgia, USA. He married Elizabeth Cornelia Pate on 08 Jun 1874 in Wilcox Co, GA. She was born on 29 Feb 1856 in Pulaski, Georgia, USA. She died on 28 Oct 1951 in Tift County, Georgia, USA.

62. RICHARD LEMUEL[17] TAYLOR (John Dennis[16], Dempsey[15], William Abraham Lawrence[14], William Nathaniel[13], James Henry "The Elder"[12] I, John William "The Immigrant"[11], Capt Thomas John[10] II, Thomas John[9] I, Rev. Dr. Rowland[8], John Thomas[7], John William[6] I, William[5] II, Sir John[4], William[3] I, Sir John[2] Taylifer, Harger[1] Taylefer) was born in 1846 in Irwinville, Irwin, Georgia, USA as the second child of John Dennis Taylor and Margaret "Peggy" Gibbs. He had eight siblings, namely: Samuel, John, James Lemuel, Sampson, Dempsey, Jesse Horton, Sarah Ann, and Julia Ann. He died on 20 Apr 1899 in Fitzgerald, Irwin County, Georgia, USA. When he was 15, he married (1) **Susannah Young**, daughter of Richard Joseph Young and Jane Land, in 1861 in Wilcox County, Georgia, USA. When he was 29, he married (2) **Temperance Zemfa Gibbs**, daughter of William Gibbs and Mary

Taylor, on 21 Dec 1875 in Wilcox, Georgia, USA. When he was 45, he married (3) **Ruth Clements**, daughter of Eliseh Clements and Elizabeth Turner, on 27 Dec 1891 in Wilcox County, Georgia, USA.

Left: Photo of Richard Lemuel Taylor in about 1871 prior to the birth of his second son Richard Thomas Taylor. From Marjorie Taylor Collection.

Richard Lemuel Taylor lived in Irwin County, Georgia, USA in 1850 (age 5). He lived in Irwin County, Georgia, USA in 1861. He served in the military on 25 Jun 1861 in Co A, 61st GA Infantry Regiment, CSA (Irwin County Cowboys). He served in the military on 27 Aug 1861 in Wilcox County, Georgia, USA (Wilcox Co formed 22 Dec 1857 from parts of Irwin). He lived in Militia District 1158, House Creek, Wilcox, Georgia, USA in 1870 (age 25; Male Citizen Over Twentyone: Y; Personal Estate Value: $249; Real Estate Value: $350; Occupation: Farmer). He lived in District 1171, Wilcox, Georgia, USA in 1880 (age 34; Occupation: Farmer; Enumeration District: 099; Marital Status: Married; Relation To Head: Self). His estate was probated on 05 Jun 1899 in Wilcox, Georgia, USA. He was also known as Lamuel Taylor. His cause of death was cerebral hemorrhage. Race: (White) He was buried in Ben Hill County, Georgia, USA (Morris Hill Ministry Cemetery).

Richard Lemuel (LEM-yule) Taylor went by the name of Lemuel. Unfortunately a number of his Georgia relatives had the same first name or middle name so it is difficult to sort them out if you do not know the family. His youngest son by his second wife he named Francis Lemuel Taylor who was known as "Lamb." His younger brother James' full name was James Lemuel. His youngest brother Jesse's son, Richard Lemuel's nephew, was Albert Lamuel (LAM-yule). His older half-brother was Lemuel Sr.; and Lemuel Sr.'s son, Richard Lemuel's half nephew, was Lemuel Dennis. His son Richard Thomas named one of his sons Richard Lamuel who was known as "Dick." To make matters more confusing, in those days people were often known by their middle names or nicknames rather than by first names.

Richard Lemuel Taylor lived his whole life in Irwin County Georgia as a farmer except for his time in the Civil War. Like most Taylor men of his age he fought for the Confederate Army but did not keep a diary. Records say he was a Private in Co A, 61st GA Infantry Regiment, CSA, known as the Irwin County Cowboys. The Captain of Company A was J. Y. McDuffie (Clements, 1932, p. 523). The 61st Regiment was assembled at Charleston, South Carolina in May 1862. It was formed around the 7th Georgia Battalion. The men were from Irwin, Tattnall, Brooks, Bulloch, Montgomery, Bibb, Quitman, and Wilkes counties. Ordered north in June, the unit arrived at Petersburg VA with 1,000 men. During the war the Regiment was part of the Army of Northern Virginia under Generals Lawton, Gordon, and Evans. The 61st Regiment participated in many engagements including the Seven Days' Battles, Cold Harbor, Shenandoah Valley, and Appomattox. Casualties included 36 at Gaines' Mill, 63 at Second Manassas, 114 at Sharpsburg and 100 at Fredericksburg. At Gettysburg the Regiment lost 37 percent of its strength of 288. At Monocacy the Regiment lost 65 percent of its strength of 150. When they surrendered they had no officers and a strength of only 81 men of which only 49 were armed (Tiegreen C. H., 2012, p. 30).

Just prior to R. Lemuel's enlistment in the Confederate Army, he married Susannah Young, the first of his three marriages (Clements, 1932, p. 518). Susannah died two days after the birth of their youngest child Richard Thomas Taylor. Four years later, in 1875 Lemuel married Temperance "Tempie" Gibbs and they had two more children before she died in 1882. R. Lemuel's last marriage was to Ruth "Ruthie" Clements in 1891, the former wife of John Allen Gibbs. They had no children.

Susannah Young was born in 1839 in Irwin County, Georgia, USA as the first child of Richard Joseph Young and Jane Land. She had ten siblings, namely: James, Millie, Mary, John, Thomas A, Elizabeth, Henry, Georgeann, Martha, and Saraann. She died on 26 Sep 1871 in Abbeville, Wilcox, Georgia, USA. When she was 22, she married Richard Lemuel Taylor, son of John Dennis Taylor and Margaret "Peggy" Gibbs, in 1861 in Wilcox County, Georgia, USA. Susannah Young lived in Irwin, Georgia, USA in 1850 (age 11). She lived in Wilcox, Georgia, USA in 1860 (age 21). She lived in Militia District 1158, House Creek, Wilcox, Georgia, USA in 1870 (age 30; Occupation: Keeping House). She was also known as Susan, Suzanne. She died two days after her youngest son Richard Thomas was born. Race: (White)

Richard Lemuel Taylor and Susannah Young had the following children:

73.   i.   JAMES H.[18] TAYLOR was born on 10 Dec 1867 in Wilcox County, Georgia, USA (Twin to Mary). He died on 15 Oct 1938 in Waycross, Ware, Georgia, USA (age 70). He married Catherine Sarah Jane Hancock on 28 Aug 1895 in Irwin County, Georgia, USA. She was born on 22 Dec 1877 in Irwin County, Georgia, USA. She died on 14 Dec 1947 in Rebecca, Turner, Georgia, USA.

+74.   ii.   MARY ELIZABETH TAYLOR was born on 10 Dec 1867 in Rochelle, Wilcox County, Georgia, USA (Twin to James). She died on 27 Jul 1949 in Wray, Irwin, Georgia, USA. She married Jesse Jackson Luke on 05 Jun 1895 in Wilcox, Georgia, USA. He was born on 15 Mar 1868 in Irwin, Georgia, USA. He died on 14 Dec 1935 in Wray, Irwin, Georgia, USA (stomach cancer).

75.   iii.   MARGARET ABIGAIL TAYLOR was born on 27 Jan 1870 in House Creek, Wilcox, Georgia, USA. She died on 29 Mar 1911 in Ben Hill County, Georgia, USA. She married William Robert Luke on 31 Dec 1889 in Wilcox, Georgia, USA. He was born on 25 Apr 1867 in Irwin, Georgia, USA. He died on 11 Dec 1936 in Ben Hill County, Georgia, USA.

+76.   iv.   RICHARD THOMAS TAYLOR was born on 24 Sep 1871 in Abbeville, Wilcox, Georgia, USA (his mother Susannah died 2 days after his birth). He died on 14 Oct 1963 in Boise, Ada, Idaho, USA (age 92). He married Roxie Ann Gibbs daughter of Isaac Gibbs and Susan Amanda Hancock, on 13 Oct 1896 in Irwin County, Georgia, USA. She was born on 13 May 1880 in Irvin, Wilkes, Georgia, USA. She died on 18 Dec 1956 in Caldwell, Canyon, Idaho, USA.

Temperance Zemfa Gibbs was born in 1839 in Irwin County, Georgia, USA as the first child of William Gibbs and Mary Taylor. She died in 1882 in Wilcox County, Georgia, USA. When she was 36, she married Richard Lemuel Taylor, son of John Dennis Taylor and Margaret "Peggy" Gibbs, on 21 Dec 1875 in Wilcox, Georgia, USA. She lived in Irwin, Georgia, USA in 1850 (age 11). She lived in Wilcox, Georgia, USA in 1860 (age 20; Attended School: Yes; Cannot Read: Y). She lived in Militia District 433, House Creek, Wilcox, Georgia, USA in 1870 (age 30; Cannot Write: Y; Occupation: No Occupation). She lived in District 1171, Wilcox, Georgia, USA in 1880 (age 41; Occupation: Keeping House; Cannot Read: Yes; Cannot Write: Yes; Enumeration District: 099; Marital Status: Married; Relation To Head: Wife). She was also known as Tempie Taylor. Race: (White)

Richard Lemuel Taylor and Temperance Zemfa Gibbs had the following children:

77. i.   WILLIAM MARION[18] TAYLOR was born on 15 Oct 1876 in Wilcox County, Georgia, USA. He died on 25 Oct 1938 in Quitman, Brooks, Georgia, USA (W Gordon St).

78. ii. FRANCIS LEMUEL "LAMB" TAYLOR was born on 15 Nov 1881 in Abba, Irwin, Georgia, USA.

Ruth Clements was born in Mar 1851 as the first child of Eliseh Clements and Elizabeth Turner. She died on 26 Feb 1926 in Fitzgerald, Ben Hill, Georgia, USA (age 75). When she was 26, she married John Allen Gibbs Jr, son of John Allen Gibbs and Martha Patsy Smith, on 09 Dec 1877 in Irwin, Georgia, USA. When she was 40, she married Richard Lemuel Taylor, son of John Dennis Taylor and Margaret "Peggy" Gibbs, on 27 Dec 1891 in Wilcox County, Georgia, USA. Ruth Clements lived in District 1171, Wilcox, Georgia, USA in 1880 (age 29; Occupation: Keeping House; Enumeration District: 099; Marital Status: Married; Relation To Head: Wife). She was buried in 1926 in Irwin County, Georgia, USA (Clements (Ebenezer) Cemetery; Find A Grave #126393649). She was also known as Ruth Gibbs, Ruth Taylor, and "Ruthie". Her cause of death was stomach cancer. FamilySearch ID: (MLTR-9VB) Race: (White).

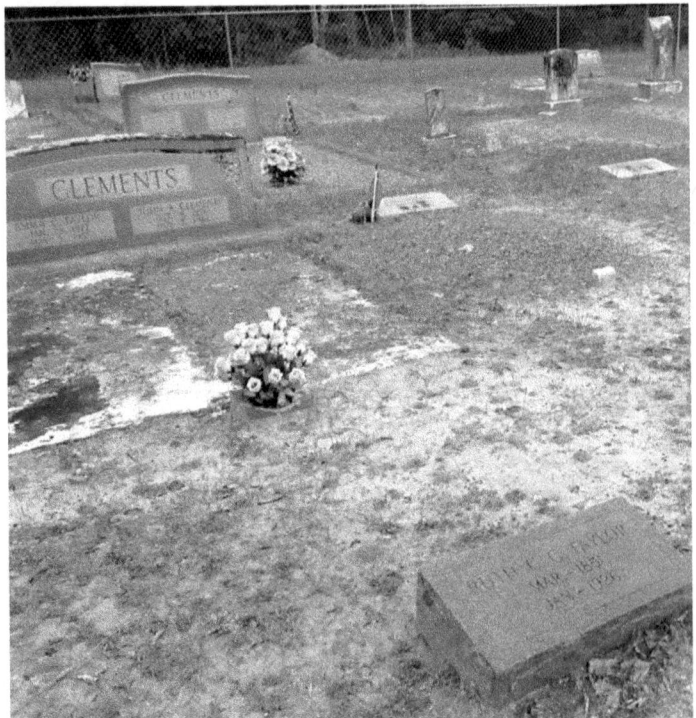

Right: Ruth Clements-Gibbs-Taylor grave (bottom right) in Clements Cemetery on Big Lake Road, north of Irwinville, Georgia. Author photo 17 Apr 2021.

67. JESSE HORTON[17] TAYLOR (John Dennis[16], Dempsey[15], William Abraham Lawrence[14], William Nathaniel[13], James Henry "The Elder"[12] I, John William "The Immigrant"[11], Capt Thomas John[10] II, Thomas John[9] I, Rev. Dr. Rowland[8], John Thomas[7], John William[6] I, William[5] II, Sir John[4], William[3] I, Sir John[2] Taylifer, Harger[1] Taylefer) was born on 22 Mar 1856 in Wilcox, Georgia, USA. He died on 08 Nov 1925 in Williamsons Mill, Ben Hill, Georgia, USA. He married **Mary Van Fletcher** on 7 Dec 1879 in Worth, GA. She was born on 12 Nov 1861 in Sycamore, Turner, Georgia, USA. She died on 11 Apr 1935 in Georgia USA.

Jesse Horton Taylor and Mary Van Fletcher had the following children:

79.   i.   JOHN HORTON[18] TAYLOR was born on 26 Jul 1882 in Wilcox, Georgia. He died on 25 May 1954 in Ben Hill County, Georgia, USA.

80.   ii.   REASON TAYLOR was born on 07 Dec 1886 in Georgia. He died on 23 Aug 1985 in Nassau, Florida, USA.

81.   iii.   IDA CORDELL TAYLOR was born on 09 Feb 1891 in Ben Hill County, Georgia, USA. She died on 09 Oct 1977 in Ben Hill, Georgia, USA.

82.   iv.   NANCY ALICE TAYLOR was born on 19 Dec 1892 in Wilcox, Georgia. She died on 09 Jun 1966 in Ben Hill, Georgia.

83.   v.   ALBERT LAMUEL TAYLOR was born on 22 Mar 1895 in Wilcox, Georgia. He died on 08 Feb 1967 in Jacksonville, Duval, Florida, USA.

84.   vi.   ROSA ELLEN TAYLOR was born on 17 Aug 1898 in Irwin County, Georgia, USA. She died on 11 Feb 1964 in Fitzgerald, Ben Hill County, Georgia, USA.

85.   vii.   RACHEL LILLIAN TAYLOR was born on 22 Nov 1903 in Wilcox, Georgia. She died on 19 Jun 1973 in Abbeville, Wilcox County, Georgia, USA.

Jessie Horton Taylor Family in about 1905.
Front, from left: Rosa Ellen, unknown, Mary Van Fletcher, unknown infant,
Jessie Horton with Rachel Lillian, unknown, Albert Lamuel.
Back, from left: Reason, Ida Cordell, Nancy Alice, John Horton.
Courtesy Tammie Schnall, Ancestry.com. 19 Aug 2011.

Chapter 2. Richard Thomas Taylor and Roxie Ann Gibbs

1. RICHARD THOMAS[18] **TAYLOR** (Richard Lemuel[17], John Dennis[16], Dempsey[15], William Abraham Lawrence[14], William Nathaniel[13], James Henry "The Elder"[12]I, John William "The Immigrant"[11], Capt Thomas John[10] II, Thomas John[9] I, Rev. Dr. Rowland[8], John Thomas[7], John William[6] I, William[5] II, Sir John[4], William[3] I, Sir John[2] Taylifer, Harger[1] Taylefer) was born on 24 Sep 1871 in Abbeville, Wilcox, Georgia, USA (His mother Susannah died 2 days after his birth). He died on 14 Oct 1963 in Boise, Ada, Idaho, USA. He married **Roxie Ann Gibbs**, daughter of Isaac Gibbs and Susan Amanda Hancock, on 13 Oct 1896 in Irwin County, Georgia, USA. She was born on 13 May 1880 in Irvin, Wilkes, Georgia, USA. She died on 18 Dec 1956 in Caldwell, Canyon, Idaho, USA.

Right: Roxie Gibbs and Richard Taylor on their wedding day in Fitzgerald, Georgia 13 Oct 1896. From Marjorie Taylor Collection.

Richard Thomas Taylor lived in District 1171, Wilcox, Georgia, USA in 1880 (age 8; Marital status: Single; Relation to Head of House: Son). He lived in Mystic, Irwin, Georgia, USA in 1900. He lived in Okemah, Okfuskee, Oklahoma, USA in 1910 (Marital Status: Married; Relation to Head of House: Head). He was employed as a Farmer in 1930. He lived in White Cross, Ada, Idaho, USA in 1930 (age 59); Marital Status: Married; Relation to Head of House: Head). He lived in Union, Ada County, Idaho in 1935. He lived in Union Election Precinct, Union, Ada, Idaho, USA in 1940 (age 68; Occupation: Farming; Attended School: No; Class of Worker: Working on own account; Employment Code: 1; Employment Details: No; Employment History: No; Enumeration District: 1-51A; Grade Completed: Elementary school, 4th grade; Home Ownership: Owned; Is Employed: Yes; Owns Farm: Yes; Public Emergency Work: No; Seeking Work: No; Value Of Home: 2,500; Marital Status: Married; Relation To Head: Head). He lived in Boise, Idaho, USA in 1945 (Street Address: 7 W Franklin). He lived in Boise, Idaho, USA in 1948 (Street Address: 113 N Orchard Ave). He lived in Boise, Idaho, USA in 1956 (Street Address: 103 N Orchard Ave; Occupation: Farmer). He was buried on 18 Oct 1963 in Boise, Ada, Idaho, USA (Cloverdale Cemetery (Sec 10VV-23-2); Find A Grave #214874752). His cause of death was cerebral thrombosis from arteriosclerotic heart disease and heart failure. Race: (White)

In 1871 Richard Thomas Taylor became the youngest of four children born to Richard Lemuel Taylor and his first wife Susannah Young in Abbeville, Georgia. He never knew his mother who died two days after his birth. According to Richard's daughter Nettie his grandmother Margaret "Peggy" Gibbs raised him and his older siblings James, Mary (twins), and Margaret at least until Richard Lemuel married his second wife "Tempie" Gibbs four years later in 1875.

RT Taylor as he was known, and his siblings, grew up on his father's farm near Abbeville, Georgia. Like many young men at that time he did not get much if any schooling. His education consisted of working the soil and caring for livestock. He was "street" smart but had no time to learn to read, write, or cypher until his wife taught him after they were married. His son Art remembers that he would listen to the radio to learn commodity prices and could tell you how much a cow or pig would weigh and its value just by looking at it (Taylor D. , Dennis Taylor Family History Video Interview, 2016, p. 44:13). He farmed according to the phases of the moon and the signs of the zodiac. As a young man, he also learned how to catch alligators and sell them for extra money. According to his granddaughter Mary LaVonne Guerra:

> He told me he would tie up his rowboat on the bank, tie a long rope to back of the boat, tie a chicken to the other end, and throw it into the water. The alligator would bite the chicken and roll in the water to pull it loose as they typically did, this wrapped the rope around the gator. Then he would drag the wrapped up alligator onto the bank and kill it" (Guerra M. , 2015).

From left: John Mixon, his wife Sarah Ellen Gibbs (Roxie's sister), and their two children Edna and William in 1902 visit the house RT Taylor built in 1895 for his future wife Roxie on the Taylor farm near Arp, Georgia. From Sara Lucas Gilstrap Collection.

In 1895, as was the custom in Georgia then, RT built a new house on his father's farm in Georgia for his future wife Roxie Gibbs whom he married the following year in 1896. By 1897 their first daughter Elsie was born and they began putting down roots surrounded by family. But all was not well. When his father Richard Lemuel Taylor died in 1899, his brother James H. Taylor, as the oldest son, laid claim to all of the family property. RT's grandson Dennis Raymond Taylor describes the events:

> According to Elsie, James H. thought that everything went to him since he was the oldest son. All the land and livestock (pigs and cattle) that was branded with my grandfather's (R.T.) brand. Evidently James H. took all of the livestock, sold it and kept the money from the sale for himself. My aunt [Elsie] said that Grandad Taylor told her that he was so mad, that if he stayed in Georgia, he would shoot his brother (Taylor D. , Taylor Clan Family History, 2021).

This was no idle threat from this auburn-haired Irishman as even his granddaughter Tecla Guerra described his volatile temper during a later incident on one of his Idaho farms:

> They had a neighbor who would steal their irrigation water. . . He would divert it and take their water. Grandad had talked to him lots about it. Well, one of the boys had discovered this guy had done it again, so told Grandad. Grandad grabbed a shovel and off he went. He was going to kill that guy. Grandma told the boys to go tackle Grandad. . . They got him with a football tackle and carried him back to the house. . . The guy that stole the water was right there and the boys told him, "You don't know how lucky you are. He was about to kill you." Anyway Grandad, when he would get angry, he would get sick afterwards and I guess he was in bed for two or three days after that (Guerra T. , 2018, p. 27:22).

In 1905, three years after their second child Nommie was born, they packed up and left Georgia looking for a farm of their own. They farmed for a few years near Wewahitchka in the Florida panhandle south of Tallahassee where their third child Bessie was born in 1907. Being close to the Gulf of Mexico, RT developed a taste for fresh oysters and would go down the beach and gather oysters and take his pepper sauce and eat them there (Tiegreen C. H., 2012, p. 25). He also bought a fiddle from the Sears & Roebuck catalog in 1906 and taught himself to play. His granddaughter Tecla Guerra also learned to play on this violin and still has it. But by 1908 they were on the move again. As RT's grandson Dennis Raymond Taylor says:

> Grandad Taylor had heard that Oklahoma had better soil to grow crops. Evidently in Florida it required a lot of fertilizer to make things grow. Poor soil [made it] hard to feed your livestock and family. In Oklahoma, Dick was born [in 1909] followed by Art, Nettie and Marge (Taylor D. , Taylor Clan Family History, 2021).

Left: Grandad Richard T. Taylor's catalog-ordered violin. Author photo 17 Aug 2018.

The 1910 U.S. Federal Census shows the Taylor family living in Okemah, Oklahoma. RT Taylor farmed in Oklahoma for nearly 20 years, first on a 320-acre ranch south of Tulsa near Okemah where his four youngest children were born. Then later east of Tulsa near Pryor at the Hawkins Ranch and the 985-acre Three S Ranch. He raised both livestock and crops in Oklahoma. During World War I he contracted with the army to raise and train mules for pulling caissons. He bred mammoth jacks with Percheron mares which he trained as draft mules. According to RT's granddaughter Tecla:

> He had a particular mule [and] could not train him. He would not break for harness. So Grandad who was a fairly decent-sized man balled up his fist and let that mule have it right between the eyes. He broke his hand and thought he'd killed that mule. . . He got back to the house and told the boys "After dinner we'll go out there and drag that mule in and we'll bury him." They went out there to bury that mule and he was up grazing. He turned out to be the best mule he ever had on the place (Guerra T. , 2018, p. 29:26).

His youngest daughter Marjorie also said that he was respected by the farmhands for how he treated them:

> Dad had sharecroppers there (colored people). I can still hear dad talk about those people. They called him Mr. Rich and he treated them with great respect. He planted watermelons in the cotton fields for them to eat when they were hot and tired. He said one of the men saved his life when a centipede bit his foot through a slit in his shoe. It was almost dark and the chickens were going to roost; and the colored man heard about Mr. Rich getting bit. So he ran and grabbed a chicken and cut it open and wrapped it around his foot. Dad said the chicken was green when they removed it later (Tiegreen C. H., 2012, p. 24).

Pre-1920 photo of the Taylor family at their farm near Pryor, Oklahoma.
Top row, from left: Elsie, Artice, Roxie, Richard T, unknown.
Bottom row, from left: unknown, unknown, Bessie, Nettie, Marjorie, Lamuel (Dick).
From Dennis R. Taylor Collection.

But again fate brought him trouble. In September 1919 he traded his Okemah property for the Three S Ranch. The farmer who traded the property made a deal with a local attorney to make up two deeds to the property, and when RT Taylor began making serious money the lawyer asserted his interest in the ranch. The court ruled for the swindlers and RT was forced to pay rent to keep his family in their own house. He fell into a deep depression and with the help of a friend temporarily occupied himself with trapping and selling animal pelts (Tiegreen C. H., 2012, p. 24).

To make matters worse, RT was told by a doctor that the lung problems he was having would get worse if he did not move to a drier climate. A neighbor who had sold their farm and moved to Farmington, New Mexico wrote back that the climate was dry and the land was very productive. So in about 1925, the Taylor family sold the Hawkins Ranch and headed west. Art and Dick drove a truck loaded with their belongings while RT drove a new car with his wife Roxie and daughters Nettie (age 10) and Marge (age 9). The older daughters stayed in Oklahoma where Elsie and Nommie were now married and Bessie was enrolled in school (Taylor D. , Taylor Clan Family History, 2021).

After arriving in Farmington, New Mexico in 1926 RT heard that the government was building a new dam and irrigation canals nearby and they were paying top dollar for skilled workmen and trucks. So he got himself and his oldest son Dick jobs as carpenters and hired out his 15-year-old son Art to drive their own truck hauling dirt and equipment. They worked there for almost a year before RT decided to move again in about 1927. Grandson Dennis continues his story:

Dad (Art) said that in a very short time they had built up a good nest egg for buying a farm. Some of the workers were from Boise, Idaho. They told my Grandad that the land was a very rich soil (no fertilizer needed) and that they had lots of water in Boise. This was what Grandad Taylor was looking for! Since they had almost finished the work at the dam, the family set off for Idaho. It was late in December... They went up through Utah, then to Idaho. Dad [Art] remembers staying at camp grounds in Provo, Salt Lake City and Logan, Utah. While in Salt Lake they saw the Christmas lights... Dad said it was very cold in Utah and they had to drive in lots of snow. They arrived in Boise, Idaho the first of January (Taylor D. , Taylor Clan Family History, 2021).

Right: Roxie Taylor is at the gate by the barn and RT Taylor is in the doorway of the shed at Eagle Ranch about 1940. From Marjorie Taylor Collection.

After arriving in Boise in 1928, RT Taylor rented rooms in a two-story boarding house for his family (the 1883 Onweiler house, 3080 Meridian Road, which is still occupied today) and then rented Brookover Farm out on the "Boise bench" at Ustick and South Cole roads. This was the first of RT's three farms in the Boise Valley. He next rented the Limp Ranch, about 3 miles north of Meridian. Then about 1933, RT purchased 200 acres of bottomland on the banks of the Boise River near Eagle and named it the Eagle Ranch. RT raised his youngest four children here and worked his Boise farms with the help of his two sons for another ten years until he retired at the age of 72. He auctioned off his property and equipment in February 1943. In the late 1990s the Eagle Ranch and its three artesian wells was subdivided and developed into 22 estates called Moon Lake Ranch.

But before he retired, RT returned to visit Georgia in 1941, but only after his brother James had passed away. Wife Roxie and daughter Nettie accompanied him to celebrate his 70th birthday and visit relatives they had never met in their 36-year absence, including RT's only surviving sister Mary Elizabeth and half-brother Francis Lemuel "Lamb" Taylor. The local Fitzgerald, Georgia newspaper featured photos and articles about the visit (Brown, 1941, p. 2).

THE LEADER-ENTERPRISE & PRE$

Richard Taylor Home After 36 Years Away

Richard Taylor, standing left, is "home" in the Abba-Arp section of Ben Hill and Irwin counties for his 70th birthday after 36 years away—farming near Eagle, Idaho. He is meeting young kinfolks he never had seen and having a good time generally. At his right is his lovely daughter, Nettie, R. N. of Oklahoma City. Next to her is Lamb Taylor, of Ocilla, his only surviving brother. Seated left is Mrs. Taylor. Center is Mrs. Mary Taylor Luke, of Wray, only surviving sister, the mother of Mrs. C. D. Green, The Leader's Wray correspondent. At right is Mrs. Ellen Mixon at whose lovely home in Arp the Taylor clan and its Luke, Gibbs, Minchew, Tomberlin, Williamson and other connections gathered last Sunday to welcome Mr. Taylor back to his buyhood stomping grounds.

Richard Taylors Meeting Kin They Never Saw Before

ABBA-ARP NEWS

By MRS. NANCY BROWN
Leader Staff Correspondent

Going to Valdosta Friday were Mr. and Mrs. Richard Taylor, visiting home after 36 years in Eagle, Idaho, Nettie Tavior, Mrs. Mary Luke and Mr. and Mrs. A. J. Brown. They visited relatives in Valdosta and drove back by Quitman Saturday, spending a while with some of Mr. Taylor's nieces and nephews that he had never seen. They were born after he left the Wiregrass to make his home in Idaho .

Mr. and Mrs. Richard Taylor and daughter, Nettie, Mrs. Mary Luke, Mr. F. L. Taylor and Mr. and Mrs. A. J. Brown attended church at Salem Sunday and were the guests of Mr. and Mrs. Allen Williamson for the rest of the day.

Mr. and Mrs. Floyd McElmurray, of Crossroads, visited his parents in Rebecca Sunday afternoon.

Mr. L. Gentry, of Crossroads, has returned from a trip to Gulfport, Miss.

Mr. and Mrs. A. J. Brown had as their guests Thursday night Mr. and Mrs. Richard Taylor and daughter, Nettie, F. L. Taylor, Misses Mamie, Mary and Ida Luke, Mr. and

Mrs. Edd Whitaker and daughter, Frances, Mrs. Mary Luke and Mr. and Mrs. Alvah Brown and son, Bobby. They all enjoyed a grand fish supper.

Mr. and Mrs. Tommy Brown, of Crossroads, were the guests of her parents, Mr. and Mrs. T. D. Fuller, of Sibbie, Sunday.

Mrs. Henry Land, Jr., and Mrs. Alice Land, of Crossroads, drove to Ocilla Friday to the funeral of Mrs. Nancy Mixon.

Mr. and Mrs. Charles D. Greer, The Leader's Wray correspondent, Mr. Kenneth Luke and Mary Lena Green, all of Wray, visited relatives in Abba Sunday afternoon.

Everyone is glad to know that Mr. C. F. Dement is up again after having a stroke.

Mr. and Mrs. Thurman Braham are the proud parents of a fine baby boy.

Miss Aldine Crews, of Crossroads, is visiting her sister in Cordele.

Pine Level Pastor Urges Wholesome Outlets for Youth

ASHTON NEWS

By MRS. J. D. BISHOP
Leader Staff Correspondent

Rev. W. H. Wilcox delivered a stirring sermon at Pine Level Sun-

RT Taylor (center back row) and Roxie Gibbs (right front) visit
Charley Green's family turpentine still near Irwinville, GA, Sep 1941.
From Marjorie Taylor Collection.

RT Taylor and Roxie Gibbs visit the Taylor family farm near Arp, Georgia, Sep 1941.
From Marjorie Taylor Collection.

After retiring, RT and Roxie bought a house at 103 N. Orchard Avenue, just west of Boise. Soon RT had a garden, roses and fruit trees at the new house and his grandchildren remember him teaching them all about farming well into his 80s. Grandson Dennis Raymond Taylor remembered his visits vividly:

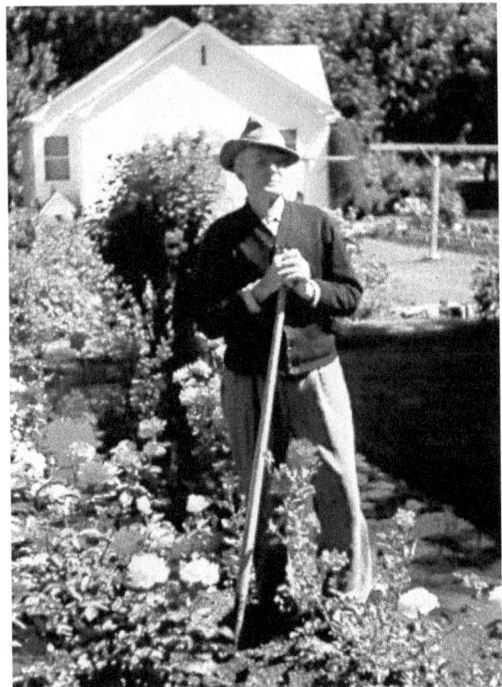

He could go down a row of vegetables and could weed or pick the vegetables without bending his knees. It made my back hurt but didn't seem to bother him. What I remember about Grandad Taylor was watching him grow vegetables and fruit on his place at Orchard Avenue in Boise. He had a small house and was on about 2-3 acres of ground. It was flood irrigated and he grew his garden, grapes, apples and had some chickens in the back. . . We would stay with Grandad and Grandma Taylor. In December it would be cold at night because they only had a heater in the living room. We would be sent to bed with a heated rock and sleep on a feather bed mattress (Taylor D. , Taylor Clan Family History, 2021).

Right: RT Taylor in his rose garden on Orchard Avenue in Boise, Idaho about 1956. From Sara Lucas Gilstrap Collection.

PUBLIC SALE!

As I Have Rented My Ranch, I Will Hold a Public Auction at the Place Located

2¼ Miles East of Star on High. 44

OR 4 MILES WEST OF EAGLE

Thurs. Feb. 25 '43

ONE O'CLOCK

16 HEAD HOLSTEIN CATTLE

11 Good Young Holstein Cows. Test and Production Given Day of Sale.
1 Holstein Bull, Purebred.   3 Yearling Holstein Heifers.
4 Holstein Bull Calves.

4 HEAD OF HORSES

1 Mare, Weight 1700 Pounds, 7 Years Old.
1 Mare, Weight 1700 Pounds, 6 Years Old.
1 Mare, Weight 1400 Pounds,11 Years Old.
1 Horse, Weight 1400 Pounds, 7 Years Old.

150 White Leghorn Pullets

85 HEAD OF HOGS

5 White Sows, all Bred, 4 to Farrow in March.
1 Purebred White Boar.   75 Weaner Pigs.

FARM IMPLEMENTS

1 DeLaval Two-Unit Milking Machine.
12 Milk Cans.
1 McCormick - Deering Feed Grinder.
1 Rubber Tired Wagon and Box.
1 Good Stock Trailer.   1 New Truck Bed.
1 McCormick - Deering Drill, 8 foot.
150 Sacks.   2 Sets Harness.
1 Three Section Harrow.   1 Gang Plow.
1 Fresno.   1 Disc.
2 Good Iron Wheel Wagons and Racks.
1 Two Foot Hay Rake.   1 Spring Tooth Harrow.
1 Walking Plow.   1 Good Land Leveler.
1 Clutton Ditcher.   1 Tumble Bug Fresno, New.
1 Buzz Saw.   1 Grindstone.
1 Complete Blacksmith Outfit.
1 Sup.   Some 2 Inch Pipe.
1 Cook Stove.   1 Heater.
Other Articles Too Numerous to Mention Here.

50 TONS HAY.   1400 BUSHELS BARLEY.
500 BUSHELS WHEAT. 200 BUSHELS SEED OATS.

TERMS:—CASH. No Property to Be Removed Until Settled For.

FREE COFFEE   LUNCH BY LADIES

R. T. TAYLOR

OWNER

Leo Marsters, Newell Wheeler,   Harry Bruce, Clerk

AUCTIONEERS

Meridian Times Quick Sale Bill Printing

Left: At the age of 72 RT Taylor auctioned off his Eagle Ranch property, equipment and livestock and retired on 25 Feb 1945. From Marjorie Taylor Collection.

He was also an avid fisherman and hunter. He loved venison and was a very good shot. He enjoyed fishing for trout in the rivers and lakes in the mountains north of Boise, but his favorite fishing was catching gunnysack loads of catfish with his granddaughters Tecla and Mary Guerra near Nampa, Idaho. As Tecla recalls:

One of the fun things we used to do with Grandad Taylor is they [Dad and Grandad] would go to Lake Lowell and they would rent a boat, just a row boat. And grandad would have a whole stack of gunnysacks. And he nailed the gunnysacks to the gunnels of the boat. And we would fish until those gunnysacks were full of catfish . . . hundreds of them (Guerra T. , 2018, p. 13:39).

ROXIE ANN[11] GIBBS (Isaac[10], John Allen[9], Thomas Anderson[8], John[7] II, George T[6], George[5], Thomas Kent[4], Robert John[3] Gibbes, Stephen Matthew[2] Gibbes, William Thomas[1] Gibbes) was born on 13 May 1880 in Irvin, Wilkes, Georgia, USA as the tenth child of Isaac Gibbs and Susan Amanda Hancock. She had nine siblings, namely: Joseph II, James Monroe, John J, Mary A, Martha Jane, Jacob Jackson, Isabel Frances, Sarah Ellen, and Suson E. She died on 18 Dec 1956 in Caldwell, Canyon, Idaho, USA (age 76). When she was 16, she married Richard Thomas Taylor, son of Richard Lemuel Taylor and Susannah Young, on 13 Oct 1896 in Irwin County, Georgia, USA.

Roxie Ann Gibbs lived in Mystic, Irwin, Georgia, USA in 1900. She lived in Okemah, Okfuskee, Oklahoma, USA in 1910 (Marital Status: Married; Relation to Head of House: Wife). She lived in White Cross, Ada, Idaho, USA in 1930 (age 49; Marital Status: Married; Relation to Head of House: Wife). She lived in Union, Ada, Idaho in 1935. She lived in Union Election Precinct, Union, Ada, Idaho, USA in 1940 (Age 59; Attended School: No; Employment Code: 5; Employment Details: Home Housework; Employment History: No; Enumeration District: 1-51A; Grade Completed: Elementary school, 8th grade; Is Employed: No; Public Emergency Work: No; Seeking Work: No; Marital Status: Married; Relation To Head: Wife). She lived in Boise, Idaho, USA in 1948 (Street Address 113 N Orchard Ave). She lived in Boise, Idaho, USA in 1956 (Street Address: 103 N Orchard Ave). She was buried on 22 Dec 1956 in Boise, Ada, Idaho, USA (Cloverdale Cemetery (Sec 10VV-23-1); Find A Grave #214875255). Her cause of death was Cystitis. Race: (White).

The Isaac Gibbs family at their farm near Fitzgerald, Georgia in 1895.
Sitting, from left: Isaac Gibbs and his wife Susan Amanda Hancock
Standing, from left: Joseph, Roxie Ann, Sarah Ellen (for whom Marjorie Ellen Taylor is
named), and Martha Jane Gibbs. From Marjorie Taylor Collection.

In 1880 Roxie Ann Gibbs became the youngest of ten children born to Civil War veteran and Appomattox surrender survivor Isaac Gibbs and Susan Amanda "Mandy" Hancock. Descendant James W. King of Albany, GA says the Gibbs family is said to be descended from two brothers who came from Cork Ireland to the Carolinas in the 1600s. Roxie was named after her father's sister and it is likely that she and Richard Taylor grew up together as RT's paternal grandmother Margaret "Peggy" Gibbs raised him from an infant after his mother died.

Left: Undated portrait of Richard Thomas Taylor and Roxie Ann Gibbs. From Marjorie Taylor Collection.

According to Roxie's granddaughter Tecla Guerra, the Gibbs family lived on a plantation and the ten Gibbs children including Roxie attended school and could read and write. However, Roxie apparently had very little practical knowledge. She was raised by a "mammie" (a black woman employed as a nurse or servant to a white family). As her granddaughter says:

> How or why she got involved with a poor uneducated farmer is beyond me. She did not know how to dress herself, the mammie always did it. She did not know how to fix her hair. She did not know how to wash anything. She didn't know how to boil water. Nothing. She knew nothing [about housekeeping]. . . Grandad had to teach her everything. One time she had invited some friends over and said, "I'll cook." She baked some biscuits, and she had some gravy, and I don't know what all she did but she had worked long and hard on this meal. They came in and sat at the table, and Grandad took a biscuit. It was like a hockey puck. He couldn't even split it apart. He threw it against the wall and it bounced! (Guerra T. , 2018, p. 58:29).

Nevertheless, she ended up becoming a farmer's wife and raising seven children, despite several miscarriages and stillbirths. Roxie was only sixteen years old when she married RT. She had her first child Elsie only a year later and her father Isaac Gibbs helped care for the new arrival (Tiegreen C. H., 2012, pp. 26, 34). Roxie lost her first boy by miscarriage before Nommie was born in 1902. Then she lost twin boys before Art was born in 1911. Roxie's daughter Elsie said they were buried on the farm in Okemah. According to Roxie's granddaughter Tecla Guerra, "She had smallpox and the babies delivered early and the babies were covered with smallpox, and they were born alive but they couldn't keep them alive." (Guerra T. , 2018, p. 1:01:30).

She lost another boy before Nettie was born in 1915. As Granddaughter Mary Guerra recalled:

> She had a Spina Bifida baby that Aunt Elsie said she would carry the baby from the cradle to Grandma. Grandma was very, very ill after the baby was born and the baby lived for about ten days. She would have to carry the baby to Grandma to nurse the baby and she went in one day and the baby was dead (Guerra T. , 2018, p. 1:02:30).

But all of the children that survived were educated. That was very important to Roxie. RT had only completed 1st grade and 3 weeks of 2nd grade before his father pulled him out to work on the farm (Guerra T. , 2018, p. 1:04:05). Roxie also read the newspaper to RT every night and later taught him to read and write. As grandson Dennis Raymond Taylor said, "She worked very hard at being a mother and a farmer's wife. . . an excellent cook. . . Roxie ran a tight ship around the family farm. Cooking for farm hands and a large family was not easy in those days. Hard work from dawn to dusk" (Taylor D. , Taylor Clan Family History, 2021).

Richard Thomas Taylor and Roxie Ann Gibbs had the following children:

+2. i. ELSIE BLANCHE[19] TAYLOR was born on 27 Oct 1897 in Fitzgerald, Ben Hill, Georgia, USA. She died on 29 Jan 1995 in Dallas, Dallas, Texas, USA (age 97). She married James Glenn Porter on 04 Feb 1920 in Muskogee, Muskogee, Oklahoma, USA. He was born on 15 Feb 1900 in Grady Indian Territory, Oklahoma, USA. He died on 04 Apr 1984 in Marathon, Monroe, Florida, USA.

+3. ii. NOMMIE LEE TAYLOR was born on 18 Oct 1902 in Wilcox County, Georgia, USA. She died on 11 Nov 1993 in Santa Fe, New Mexico, USA (age 91). She married Elmer Lawrence Lucas on 18 Dec 1925 in Enid, Garfield, Oklahoma, USA (in the First Christian Church). He was born on 22 Mar 1898 in Owensville, Gibson, Indiana, USA. He died on 05 Nov 1966 in Norman, Cleveland, Oklahoma, USA.

+4. iii. BESSIE AMANDA TAYLOR was born on 03 Jul 1907 in Wewahitchka, Gulf, Florida, USA. She died on 21 Apr 1997 in Carrollton, Collin, Texas, USA (age 88). She married Carl Mandeville Tiegreen, son of Otto Fredrick Johansson Tiegreen and Elisabeth Engmark Johansdotter, on 17 Jun 1929 in Pocatello, Bannock, Idaho, USA. He was born on 03 Dec 1898 in Ganado, Jackson, Texas, USA. He died on 11 Jun 1983 in Biloxi, Harrison, Mississippi, USA.

5. iv. RICHARD LAMUEL TAYLOR was born on 17 May 1909 in Okemah, Okfuskee, Oklahoma, USA. He died on 30 May 2001 in Boise, Ada, Idaho, USA (age 92). He married Mabel Ruth Crone on 10 Jan 1942 in Boise, Ada, Idaho, USA. She was born on 12 Jul 1918 in Stanton, Blaine, Idaho, USA (Little Wood River). She died on 08 Dec 2008 in Boise, Ada, Idaho, USA.

+6. v. ARTICE RAYMOND TAYLOR was born on 13 Oct 1911 in Okemah, Okfuskee, Oklahoma, USA. He died on 02 May 2006 in Boise, Ada, Idaho, USA (age 94). He married Hazel Florence McClure, daughter of Joseph Taylor McClure and Thursa Henry, on 02 Mar 1935 in Meridian, Ada, Idaho, USA. She was born on 05 Oct 1910 in Harrison, Boone, Arkansas, USA. She died on 02 Jul 1990 in Boise, Ada, Idaho, USA.

+7. vi. NETTIE LAVONNE TAYLOR was born on 03 Feb 1915 in Okemah, Okfuskee, Oklahoma, USA. She died on 28 Apr 2002 in Boise, Ada, Idaho, USA (age 87). She married Guadalupe Filiberto Guerra, son of Jose Antonio Guerra and Tecla Guerra de Guerra, on 18 Apr 1945 in Boise, Ada, Idaho, USA (First Christian Church). He was born on 16 Mar 1900 in Roma, Starr, Texas, USA (Rancho El Colorado). He died on 27 Dec 1982 in Boise, Ada, Idaho, USA (age 82).

+8. vii. MARJORIE ELLEN TAYLOR was born on 27 Dec 1916 in Okemah, Okfuskee, Oklahoma, USA. She died on 03 Mar 2016 in Boise, Ada, Idaho, USA (age 99). She married Allen Rayburne Lievsay on 31 May 1941 in Ada, Pontotoc, Oklahoma, USA. He was born on 02 Sep 1914 in Caddo, Bryan, Oklahoma, USA. He died on 22 Nov 2005 in Boise, Ada, Idaho, USA.

A separate chapter is written for each of Richard Thomas's children that lived to be adults.

1921 --Richard Thomas Taylor family in Oklahoma. Front, from left: Nettie LaVonne, Elsie Blanche, Elsie Christine Porter (Elsie's daughter), Artice Raymond, Marjorie Ellen, Roxie Ann Gibbs, Richard Lamuel. Back, from left: Bessie Amanda, Richard Thomas, Nommie Lee. From Marjorie Taylor Collection.

1930s --Richard Thomas Taylor family in Boise, Idaho. Front, from left: Artice (Art), Roxie Gibbs, Richard Thomas, Richard (Dick). Back, from left: Nettie, Marjorie, Bessie, Nommie (Tomi), Elsie. From Marjorie Taylor Collection.

1956 –Richard Thomas Taylor family at Roxie Gibbs funeral in Boise, Idaho.
Sitting, from left: Nommie (Tomi), Richard Thomas, Elsie.
Standing, from left: Bessie, Nettie, Richard (Dick), Marjorie, Artice (Art).
From Marjorie Taylor Collection.

1950s –Richard Thomas Taylor children in Boise, Idaho. From left:
Nommie (Tomi), Elsie, Artice (Art), Marjorie, Richard (Dick), Bessie, Nettie.
From Marjorie Taylor Collection.

1975 –Richard Thomas Taylor children at Palisades Lake, Idaho. Front, from left: Richard (Dick), Nommie (Tomi), Nettie. Back, from left: Artice (Art), Elsie, Bessie, Marjorie. Author photo Aug 1975.

1988 –Richard Thomas Taylor children in Boise, Idaho. From left: Bessie, Elsie, Richard (Dick), Marjorie, Nommie (Tomi), Nettie, Artice (Art). From Marjorie Taylor Collection.

Chapter 3. Elsie Blanche Taylor and James Glenn Porter

Elsie & Glenn

Generation 1

1. ELSIE BLANCHE^I TAYLOR (Richard Thomas^A, Richard Lemuel^B, John Dennis^C, Dempsey^D, William Abraham Lawrence^E, William Nathaniel^F, James Henry "The Elder"^{G} I, John William "The Immigrant"^{H}, Capt Thomas John^I II, Thomas John^J I, Rev Dr Rowland^K, John Thomas^L, John William^M I, William^N II, Sir John^O, William^P I, Sir John^Q Taylifer, Harger^R Taylefer) was born on 27 Oct 1897 in Fitzgerald, Ben Hill, Georgia, USA as the first child of Richard Thomas Taylor and Roxie Ann Gibbs. She had six siblings, namely: Nommie Lee, Bessie Amanda, Richard Lamuel, Artice Raymond, Nettie LaVonne, and Marjorie Ellen. She died on 29 Jan 1995 in Dallas, Dallas, Texas, USA (age 97). She married **James Glenn Porter** on 04 Feb 1920 in Muskogee, Oklahoma, USA. He was born on 15 Feb 1900 in Grady Indian Territory, Oklahoma, USA. He died on 04 Apr 1984 in Marathon, Monroe, Florida, USA.

Portraits of Elsie Blanche Taylor and James Glenn Porter in 1979.
From Marjorie Taylor Collection.

Elsie Blanche Taylor lived in Mystic, Irwin, Georgia, USA in 1900. She lived in Okemah, Okfuskee, Oklahoma, USA in 1910 (Marital Status: Single Relation to Head of House: Daughter). She lived in Ada, Oklahoma, USA in 1934. She lived in Ada, Pontotoc, Oklahoma, USA in 1935. She lived in Ada, Pontotoc, Oklahoma, USA on 01 Apr 1940 (age 42; Occupation: Teacher; Attended School: No; Class of Worker: Wage or salary worker in private work; Employment Code: 1; Employment Details: No; Employment History: No; Enumeration

District: 62-1; Grade Completed: College, 5th or subsequent year; Hours Worked: 40; Income: 1500; Income Other Sources: No; Is Employed: Yes; Public Emergency Work: No; Respondent: Yes; Seeking Work: No; Weeks Worked: 52; Marital Status: Married; Relation To Head: Wife). She lived in Oklahoma City, Oklahoma, USA in 1952 (Street Address: 1206 SW 32nd). She had a medical condition of arthritis and high blood pressure in 1976 in Marathon, Monroe, Florida, USA. She had a medical condition of shingles on her face and neck in 1983. She was buried on 01 Feb 1995 in Park City, Sedgwick, Kansas, USA (Kechi Township Cemetery [section 7, 4th row from west]; Find A Grave #5679778). Her cause of death was pneumonia and congestive heart problems. Race: (White).

Right: This portrait of Elsie (on left) and her sister Nommie was made in about 1916. From Sara Lucas Gilstrap Collection.

In 1897 Elsie Taylor became the first born of Richard and Roxie Taylor's seven children. It would be another 19 years before her youngest sister Marjorie was born in Oklahoma, and 97 years before she passed on. As her daughter-in-law Virginia Quillin Porter said, "From horse and buggy to 'virtual reality,' Elsie did not just live those days' she loved and experienced life as few people do" (Porter V. Q., 1995). Her mother was only seventeen when Elsie was born, so her Grandfather Isaac Gibbs helped care for her during her first few years in Georgia. By the time the family arrived in Oklahoma Elsie was eleven years old and soon became a second mother to her six younger sisters and brothers. Elsie's youngest sister Marjorie said, "Elsie was my mother. [She was] 19 years older" (Taylor M. , 2015, p. 6:50).

Left: Elsie (3rd from left) and her sister Nommie (far right) played basketball during high school in Okemah, OK, about 1916. From Sara Lucas Gilstrap Collection.

When she was 23 years old Elsie married Glenn Porter and started her own family in Ada, Oklahoma. Like her mother, Elsie valued education and even with two children she finished college and went on for a master's degree. She taught Home Economics for a number of years at East Central State College. Then Elsie managed the glove and blouse department in Brown's Department Store in Oklahoma City. Later she owned a maternity shop. After Glenn retired they bought a summer residence in the Sister's Creek trailer park on Grand Lake near Grove, Oklahoma where they celebrated their 50th wedding anniversary. By 1980 Elsie and Glenn had moved further south to Marathon, in the Florida Keys where they celebrated their 60th wedding anniversary.

Elsie soon became a dedicated artist. Like her younger sisters, she favored flower and landscape themes and painted primarily with oils. Elsie also made pottery, was a seamstress, and a wonderful cook. At age 89, Elsie said she was enrolled in a church exercise class with her sister Bessie because, "Old people sit and do nothing too much. I'm the kind that likes to be up and going. It keeps people alive" (Harding, 1987, p. 2). Her Daughter-in-law Virginia Quillin Porter recalled:

> One of my favorite memories of Elsie was her excitement on the occasion of hers and Glenn's 60th wedding anniversary. Dressed in a lovely blue formal, with an orchid on her shoulder, she was the bell of the ball. She saw that everyone's cup was full; she bubbled and shone, and out-danced us all (Porter V. Q., 1995).

James Glenn Porter was born on 15 Feb 1900 in Grady Indian Territory, Oklahoma, USA as the first child of James Lee Porter and Leona Neomi McNatt. He died on 04 Apr 1984 in Marathon, Monroe, Florida, USA. When he was 19, he married Elsie Blanche Taylor, daughter of Richard Thomas Taylor and Roxie Ann Gibbs on 04 Feb 1920 in Muskogee, Muskogee, Oklahoma, USA.

James Glenn Porter and Elsie Blanche Taylor at the Taylor
Family Reunion at Palisades Lake, Idaho. Author photo Aug 1975.

James Glenn Porter lived in Wetumka, Hughes County, Oklahoma, USA in 1910. He lived in Okfuskee, Okfuskee, Oklahoma, USA on 12 Sep 1918 (Street Address: #2 Wetumka). He lived in Ada, Pontotoc, Oklahoma, USA in 1934 and in 1935. He lived in Marathon, FL in 1935. He lived in Ada, Pontotoc, Oklahoma, USA in 1940 (Age: 40; Occupation: Manager; Attended School: No; Class of Worker: Wage or salary worker in private work; Employment Code: 1;

Employment Details: No; Employment History: No; Enumeration District: 62-1; Grade Completed: High School, 3rd year; Home Ownership: Rented; Hours Worked: 48; Income: 1940; Income Other Sources: No; Is Employed: Yes; Owns Farm: No; Public Emergency Work: No; Seeking Work: No; Value of Home: 32; Weeks Worked: 52; Marital Status: Married; Relation To Head: Head). He was employed as a National Supply Company in 1942 in Seminole, Seminole, Oklahoma, USA. He lived in Ada, Pontotoc, Oklahoma, USA in 1942. He was described as age 42; Complexion: Ruddy; Eye Color: Blue; Hair Color: Brown; Height: 5' 10"; Weight: 199 on 15 Feb 1942. He lived in Oklahoma City, Oklahoma, USA in 1952 (Street Address: 1206 SW 32nd; Occupation: Manager). He had a medical condition of arthritis and high blood pressure in 1976 in Marathon, Monroe, Florida, USA. He was also known as Glenn. Race: (White). He was buried in Park City, Sedgwick, Kansas, USA (Kechi Township Cemetery).

Since Glenn's father and his son's first name was also James, his friends and family always called him Glenn. He was born in Oklahoma in what was known as Grady Indian Territory. Beyond that we do not have much firsthand knowledge of Glenn. We know that he wrote a family biography in 1982 (*The Porters*, J. Glenn Porter) which was distributed to several family members at that time but we have not yet been able to find a copy. We also know Glenn lived in Ada, Oklahoma for many years and had been a salesman for the National Supply Company for 40 years before retiring with Elsie in the 1960s. He was an avid fisherman and taught his children how to fish. He was also a tinkerer and passed on his knowledge of how to fix almost anything.

Elsie (Taylor) Porter (on left) with two of her children, James Laddie and Virginia Josephine in Wetumka, Oklahoma about 1926. From Marjorie Taylor Collection.

James Glenn Porter and Elsie Blanche Taylor had the following children:

2. i.   ELSIE CHRISTINE[2] PORTER was born on 25 Dec 1920. She died on 09 Jan 1922.

+3. ii.   JAMES LADDIE PORTER was born on 24 Aug 1922 in Pryor, Mayes, Oklahoma, USA.

He died on 05 Feb 1997 in Cedar Hill, Dallas County, Texas, USA. He married Virginia Beth Quillin on 13 Nov 1948 in Seminole, Oklahoma, USA. She was born on 29 Nov 1921 in Cruce Steven, Oklahoma. She died on 04 Jul 2007 in Valley Center, Sedgwick County, Kansas, USA.

+4.   iii.   VIRGINIA JOSEPHINE PORTER was born on 01 Feb 1924 in Oklahoma, USA. She died on 28 Jan 1986 in Marathon, Monroe, Florida, USA. She married Ferdinand Winfield Scott II on 05 Aug 1944 in San Antonio, Bexar, Texas, USA. He was born on 02 Mar 1921 in Morenci, Michigan, USA. He died on 25 Jan 1993.

Generation 2

3. JAMES LADDIE² PORTER (Elsie Blanche¹ Taylor, James Glenn) was born on 24 Aug 1922 in Pryor, Mayes, Oklahoma, USA as the second child of James Glenn Porter and Elsie Blanche Taylor. He had two siblings, namely: Elsie Christine, and Virginia Josephine. He died on 05 Feb 1997 in Cedar Hill, Dallas County, Texas, USA. He married **Virginia Beth Quillin** on 13 Nov 1948 in Seminole, Oklahoma, USA. She was born on 29 Nov 1921 in Oklahoma City, Oklahoma, Oklahoma, USA. She died on 04 Jul 2007 in Washington, Franklin, Missouri, USA.

Ray Lievsay visits his wife's nephew "Laddie" Porter at his home in Oklahoma, 1994.
From left: Virginia Quillin, James "Laddie" Porter, Allen "Ray" Lievsay.
From Marjorie Taylor Collection.

James Laddie Porter lived in Ada, Pontotoc, Oklahoma, USA in 1935. He lived in Ada, Pontotoc, Oklahoma, USA on 01 Apr 1940 (Age 17; Attended School: Yes; Employment Code: 6; Employment Details: School; Employment History: No; Enumeration District: 62-1; Grade Completed: High School, 3rd year; Is Employed: No; Public Emergency Work: No;

Seeking Work: No; Marital Status: Single; Relation To Head: Son). He lived in Ada, Pontotoc, Oklahoma, USA in 1942 (age 20; Relation To Head: Self). He was described as age 19; Occupation: Student; Complexion: Light; Eye Color: Blue; Hair Color: Blonde; Height: 5' 10"; Weight: 170 lbs. on 30 Jun 1942. He lived in Oklahoma in 1951 (age 29). He lived in Cedar Hill, Dallas County, Texas, USA in 1997. He was also known as Jim or Laddie. Race: (White). He was buried in Park City, Sedgwick, Kansas, USA (Kechi Township Cemetery [section 7, 4th row from west]; Find A Grave #5679780).

According to his son James Paul Porter, Laddie went to college and became a geologist for the Shell Oil Company. Then during World War II he was a pilot, nearly being killed three different times in training accidents. After the war he married Virginia and they raised six children. Then sometime afterwards he began seriously studying the Bible and along the way immersing himself in it. He decided that God wanted him to keep the Sabbath, which ended his career with Shell Oil. Then the local church kicked him out due to doctrinal differences. But the family survived hard times and when his oil well finally came in, he was able to move into a handsome house, and he had the three things he valued most in his life: his family, his home, and his spiritual journey (Porter J. P., 1997, p. 2).

Virginia Beth Quillin was born on 29 Nov 1921 in Oklahoma City, Oklahoma. She died on 04 Jul 2007 in Washington, Franklin, Missouri, USA. When she was 26, she married James Laddie Porter, son of James Glenn Porter and Elsie Blanche Taylor, on 13 Nov 1948 in Seminole, Oklahoma, USA.

Virginia Beth Quillin lived in Konawa, Seminole, Oklahoma, USA in 1930. She lived in Konawa, Seminole, Oklahoma, USA in 1935. She lived in Konawa, Seminole, Oklahoma, USA in 1940. Race: (White). She was buried in Park City, Sedgwick, Kansas, USA (Kechi Township Cemetery; Find A Grave #23119255).

Right: Virginia Beth Quillin about the year she was married in 1948. From Marjorie Taylor Collection.

Virginia was always the consummate communicator for the Porter family. No wonder she was the executive secretary for the Coleman Corporation in Wichita, Kansas before retirement. All the letters I read from her in the 1990s were nicely printed out on her "word processor" as she called her computer. Not only did we get the Porter family news, but almost always an attached photo, news clipping, or in the case of a funeral, a copy of the announcement, obituary and eulogy. For 72 years she also sent a "round robin" family letter to keep her family informed, and during World War II she started one to her four brothers in the military. She detailed her approach in a "Dear Ann Landers" column (Landers, A. 1996) in which she said she came from a long line of "persistent communicators."

James Laddie Porter and Virginia Beth Quillin had the following children:

+5.   i.   QUILLIN FORD *3* PORTER was born on 27 Sep 1945 in Ada, Pontotoc, Oklahoma, USA. He died on 03 Jul 2010 in Kansas City, Clay, Missouri, USA.

6.   ii.   JAN ELIZAETH PORTER was born in 1951. She married Stephen Turner Gerdel on 06 Jun 1971 in Valley Center, Sedgwick, Kansas, USA.

7.   iii.   JAMES PAUL PORTER was born in Feb 1952. He married JOAN PORTER.

8.   iv.   KIMBERLY PORTER was born on 23 Jun 1954. She married RANDY OTT.

9.   v.   SCOTT PORTER.

10.   vi.   WHITNEY PORTER. She married ROBERT LUTZ.

Virginia Quillin Porter's letter to Ann Landers.
(Landers, 1996, p. 3D)

4. VIRGINIA JOSEPHINE*2* PORTER (Elsie Blanche*1* Taylor, James Glenn) was born on 01 Feb 1924 in Pryor, Mayes, Oklahoma, USA as the third child of James Glenn Porter and Elsie Blanche Taylor. She had two siblings, namely: Elsie Christine, and James Laddie. She died on 28 Jan 1986 in Marathon, Monroe, Florida, USA. She married **Ferdinand Winfield Scott II** on 05 Aug 1944 in San Antonio, Bexar, Texas, USA. He was born on 02 Mar 1921 in Morence, Michigan, USA. He died on 25 Jan 1993.

Virginia Josephine Porter lived in Marathon, FL in 1935. She lived in Ada, Pontotoc, Oklahoma, USA in 1940. She lived in Owosso, Michigan, USA in 1948 (Street Address: 3 N Ball Apt #3). She was also known as Josie and Jo. Her cause of death was the result of a diabetic coma. She was employed as a Fishermen's Hospital Counselor in Marathon, Monroe, Florida, USA. She lived in Marathon, Monroe, Florida, USA (Street Address: 1571 Overseas Hwy). Race: (White).

Ferdinand Winfield Scott II was born on 02 Mar 1921 in Morence, Michigan, USA. He died on 25 Jan 1993 (age 71). When he was 23, he married Virginia Josephine Porter, daughter of James Glenn Porter and Elsie Blanche Taylor, on 05 Aug 1944 in San Antonio, Bexar, Texas, USA.

Ferdinand Winfield Scott II was employed as a Crowley Milner and Co buyer; Complexion: Dark; Eye Color: Brown; Hair Color: Brown; Height: 5' 11" Weight: 168 on 16 Feb 1942 in Detroit, Wayne, Michigan, USA. He lived in Owosso, Michigan, USA in 1948 (Street Address: 3 N Ball Apt #3; Occupation: Buyer). He lived in Michigan in 1951 (age 30). He lived in Schaumburg, Cook, Illinois, USA in 1993. Race: (White).

Ferdinand Winfield Scott II and Virginia Josephine Porter had the following children:
- 11. i.   JOLANDA TRACY³ SCOTT was born on 22 Jul 1945.
- 12. ii. KORDAYA LEIGH SCOTT was born on 21 Aug 1948. She married GARY L MICHELOTTI. He was born on 14 Oct 1953.
- 13. iii. W. BRADFORD SCOTT was born on 10 Mar 1954.

Generation 3

5. QUILLIN FORD³ PORTER (James Laddie², Elsie Blanche¹ Taylor, James Laddie², James Glenn, James Lee) was born on 27 Sep 1945 in Konawa, Seminole, Oklahoma, USA. He died on 03 Jul 2009 in Wichita, Sedgwick, Kansas, USA. He married **YOLANDA PORTER**.

Quillin Ford Porter and Yolanda Porter had the following children:
- 14. i.   TIFFANY LYNN⁴ PORTER was born on 05 Apr 1968 in Kansas City, Clay, Missouri, USA. She died on 09 Jun 2003.
- 15. ii. ALEXIS PAINTER PORTER.
- 16. iii. TRACI HUDDLESTON PORTER.
- 17. iv. CHAD PORTER.
- 18. v.   KEN PORTER.

Left: Elsie (Taylor) Porter (on left), nephew Donald Tiegreen, and sister Bessie (Taylor) Tiegreen at Fort Worth Botanical Garden 31 Aug 1986. A note was attached by Sara that read, "A rare picture of Elsie smiling!" From Sara Lucas Gilstrap Collection.

Chapter 4. Nommie Lee Taylor and Elmer Lawrence Lucas

Tom

Generation 1

1. NOMMIE LEE[1] TAYLOR (Richard Thomas[A], Richard Lemuel[B], John Dennis[C], Dempsey[D], William Abraham Lawrence[E], William Nathaniel[F], James Henry "The Elder"[G] I, John William "The Immigrant"[H], Capt Thomas John[I] II, Thomas John[J] I, Rev. Dr. Rowland[K], John Thomas[L], John William[M] I, William[N] II, Sir John[O], William[P] I, Sir John[Q] Taylifer, Harger[R] Taylefer) was born on 18 Oct 1902 in Wilcox County, Georgia, USA as the second child of Richard Thomas Taylor and Roxie Ann Gibbs. She had six siblings, namely: Elsie Blanche, Bessie Amanda, Richard Lamuel, Artice Raymond, Nettie LaVonne, and Marjorie Ellen. She died on 11 Nov 1993 in Santa Fe, New Mexico, USA (age 91). She married **Elmer Lawrence Lucas**, son of Jessie E. Lucas and Martha Wilmina Knowles, on 18 Dec 1925 in Enid, Garfield, Oklahoma, USA (First Christian Church). He was born on 22 Mar 1898 in Owensville, Gibson, Indiana, USA. He died on 05 Nov 1966 in Norman, Cleveland, Oklahoma, USA.

Left: Portrait of Nommie Lee Taylor about 1940. From Sara Lucas Gilstrap Collection.

Nommie Lee Taylor lived in Okemah, Okfuskee, Oklahoma, USA in 1910 (age 7; Marital Status: Single; Relation to Head: Daughter). She was employed as a Spanish lecturer at the University of Oklahoma in 1925. She lived in Enid, Oklahoma, USA in 1928 (Street Address: 2202 E Maple Ave). She lived in Enid, Garfield, Oklahoma, USA in 1930 (Street Address: East Randolph; age 27; Able to Speak English: Yes; Attended School: No; Can Read Write: Yes; Enumeration District: 0021; Homemaker: Yes; Registration District: 0021; Marital Status: Married; Relation to Head: Wife). She lived in Enid, Oklahoma, USA in 1940 (Street Address: 2230 E Randolph). She lived in Oklahoma in 1958 (Age: 56). She lived in Santa Fe, Santa Fe, New Mexico, USA in 1984. She was also known as Tomi. Race: (White). She was buried in Oklahoma City, Cleveland County, Oklahoma USA (Resthaven Gardens Cemetery [section 4]; Find A Grave #82967883).

Nommie Taylor was born in Georgia, five years after her older sister Elsie, leading to speculation that her mother Roxie may have had a stillborn son during one of her three earlier miscarriages. She never did like her name and later changed it to "Tomi." Her daughter Sara Lucas tells us who named her mother:

They had a black maid who helped with the work around the house back in Georgia and she named my mother Nommie. . . Mother was never very happy with her name and later in life she changed it to Tomi" (Lucas S. , 2019, p. 31:24).

Left: Elmer Lucas and his bride Nommie Taylor on their wedding day in Enid, Oklahoma 18 Dec 1925. From Sara Lucas Gilstrap Collection.

Tomi was very close to her older sister Elsie. They attended school together, were both on the Okemah High School basketball team, and both stayed in Oklahoma starting their own families when the Taylor family moved on to Idaho. Following her older sister, Tomi also valued education and earned a Bachelor's degree at Phillips University in Enid and later a Master's degree at Oklahoma University in Norman. In fact it was as a geology student at Phillips University that she met her future husband Elmer Lucas who got his first job there as a geology teacher (Lucas S. , 2019, p. 14:34).

Tomi and Elmer raised their three daughters in Enid while Elmer taught geology. But even with a job, raising a family during the depression was not easy. Daughter Sara remembers, "Somedays daddy didn't even get paid teaching at Phillips University" (Lucas S. , 2019, p. 26:40). But she enjoyed the eight summers the family spent at Yosemite and other western national parks in the late 1930s where Elmer was a Ranger Naturalist during the summer.

Tomi's oldest daughter Wanda says, "She was still the best mother. She really cared what we did. She watched our romancing years too, because we would go out on a date and were sitting in the car in front and the porch light was flashing" (Lucas W. , 2017, p. 20:40). But she was also a lover of all things beautiful and enjoyed flower gardening, arranging, painting, and eventually judging. Tomi became a Master Gardener, an International Rose Judge, and organized a local chapter of the Ikebana oriental flower arranging school. Like her sisters she was an extremely talented artist. Tomi's niece Mary Guerra recounted a visit to her home in Oklahoma in 1983:

> She had that beautiful Chinese ink painting in the garbage and didn't want me to have it because it was not perfect and I took it anyway. I said I'm taking this out of your garbage and she says "I don't have anything perfect enough to give to people" (Lucas W. , 2017, p. 45:04).

Elmer Lawrence Lucas was born on 22 Mar 1898 in Owensville, Gibson, Indiana, USA as the first child of Jessie E. Lucas and Martha Wilmina Knowles. He had three siblings, namely: Hazel L, Ethel, and Ralph J. He died on 05 Nov 1966 in Norman, Cleveland, Oklahoma, USA. When he was 27, he married Nommie Lee Taylor, daughter of Richard Thomas Taylor and Roxie Ann Gibbs, on 18 Dec 1925 in Enid, Garfield, Oklahoma, USA (First Christian Church).

Right: During the summer when not teaching Geology at Phillips University, Elmer Lucas took his family and became a Ranger-Naturalist at Yosemite National Park in the 1930s. From Sara Lucas Gilstrap Collection.

Elmer Lawrence Lucas lived in Montgomery, Gibson, Indiana, USA in 1900 (StreetAddress: Walnut; age 2; EnumerationDistrict: 0008; MaritalStatus: Single; RelationToHead: Son). He lived in Montgomery, Gibson, Indiana, USA in 1910 (age 12; Marita lStatus: Single; Relation To Head: Son). He lived in Gibson, Indiana, USA in 1917. He lived in Gibson, Indiana, USA on 12 Sep 1918 (Street Address: 1 Cynthiana). He lived in Montgomery, Gibson, Indiana, USA in 1920 (age 21; Occupation: None; Able To Speak English: Yes; Attended School: yes; Can Read: Yes; Can Write: Yes; Enumeration District: 189; Marital Status: Single; Relation To Head: Son). He received a BA degree in 1922 at Indiana University. He received an MA degree in 1924 at Indiana University. He lived in Enid, Oklahoma, USA in 1925 (Street Address: 2212 E Maple; Occupation: Professor). He received a PhD (Geology) degree in 1926 at the University of Oklahoma. He was employed as an Assistant Professor of Geology in 1927 at Phillips

University. He lived in Enid, Oklahoma, USA in 1928 (StreetAddress: 2202 E Maple Ave; Occupation: Assistant Professor). He lived in Enid, Garfield, Oklahoma, USA in 1930 (StreetAddress: East Randolph; AbleToSpeakEnglish: Yes; AttendedSchool: No; CanReadWrite: Yes; ClassofWorker: Wage or salary worker; HomeOwnership: Rented; IsEmployed: Yes; LiveOnFarm: No; OwnedRadio: Yes; RegistrationDistrict: 0021; ValueOfHome: 35; Veteran: Yes; War: WWI; MaritalStatus: Married; RelationToHead: Head; Occupation: Professor). He lived in Enid, Garfield, Oklahoma in 1935. He lived in Enid Twp, Enid, Garfield, Oklahoma, USA in 1940 (StreetAddress: East Randolph; Age: 42; Occupation: Teacher; CityWard: 4; ClassofWorker: Wage or salary worker in private work; EmploymentCode: 1; EmploymentDetails: No; EmploymentHistory: No; EnumerationDistrict: 24-20; GradeCompleted: College, 5th or subsequent year; HomeOwnership: Rented; HoursWorked: 45; Income: 480; IncomeOtherSources: No; Industry: Philips University; IsEmployed: Yes; OwnsFarm: No; PublicEmergencyWork: No; SeekingWork: No; ValueOfHome: 15; WeeksWorked: 52; Married Marital Status: Married; Head RelationToHead: Head). He lived in Enid, Garfield, Oklahoma, USA in 1940 (StreetAddress: 2230 E Randolph; Occupation: Teacher). He was employed as a Professor of Geology in 1941 at the University of Oklahoma. He was described on 14 Feb 1941 as Complexion: Light; EyeColor: Hazel; HairColor: Gray; Height: 5 6; Weight: 185; missing part thumb and index finger. He lived in Norman, Cleveland, Oklahoma, USA in 1942 (age 44; RelationToHead: Self). He lived in Norman, Cleveland, Oklahoma, USA in 1950. Age: 52; AttendedSchool: 30 or over; ClassofWorker: Government; Enumeration District: 14-28; Grade Completed: No; Income: 66; Income Other Sources: 0; LiveOnFarm: No; OccupationCategory: Working; OtherIncomeSupplement: 600; SchoolYearsCompleted: O; Head RelationToHead: Head; MaritalStatus: Married). He lived in Norman, Cleveland, Oklahoma, USA in 1966. Race: (White) Ethnicity: (American) He was buried in Oklahoma City, Oklahoma, USA (Resthaven Gardens Cemetery (Sec 4, Lot 35. Grave 1); Find A Grave #82967918).

Left: Portrait of Elmer Lucas when he was the 1922 "Big Ten" Conference Wrestling Champion. From Sara Lucas Gilstrap Collection.

Elmer Lucas grew up on his father Jessie's farm near Owensville, Indiana. He served in the Army in World War I and afterwards decided to become a geologist instead of a farmer. Elmer used his Army pay and worked hard to finance his education at Indiana University during the 1920s. Apparently later, as a veteran, he was able to use the federal "G.I. Bill" to help fund his advanced studies. He was a strapping young man and joined the Indiana University Wrestling Team, becoming the "Big Ten" Conference Champion in 1922. Elmer's daughter Sara said that his roommate at Indiana University was none other than future singer-song writer Hoagy Carmichael. (Lucas S. , 2019, p. 14:28).

He met his future wife Nommie Taylor when he was teaching geology at Phillips University in Enid, Oklahoma. They were married in 1925 and had three daughters. But during the summer Elmer was gone and raising the children and managing the household was primarily left to Nommie. According to daughter Sara, during the summer when not teaching, her father:

> . . . worked for an oil company in the geology area doing reconnaissance work in Idaho, Wyoming, Utah. . . My mother's mother and father lived in Boise, Idaho. So we would go during the summer and visit them and see our father during the summertime (Lucas S. , 2019, p. 05:00).

During the 1930s, Elmer was one of twenty scientists chosen by the National Park Service to become a summer Ranger Naturalist. Elmer was assigned to Yosemite National Park in California. So for the next eight years, the entire Lucas family was able to stay together during the summers. They would pack the car and drive to California, each year taking a different scenic route, and do the same thing when returning to Oklahoma at the end of the summer. Daughter Wanda Lucas commented, "Yosemite was a great experience. Oh what a good childhood. My sister Sara and I talked so many times about we had the best childhood of anybody on earth." (Lucas W. , 2017, p. 19:10).

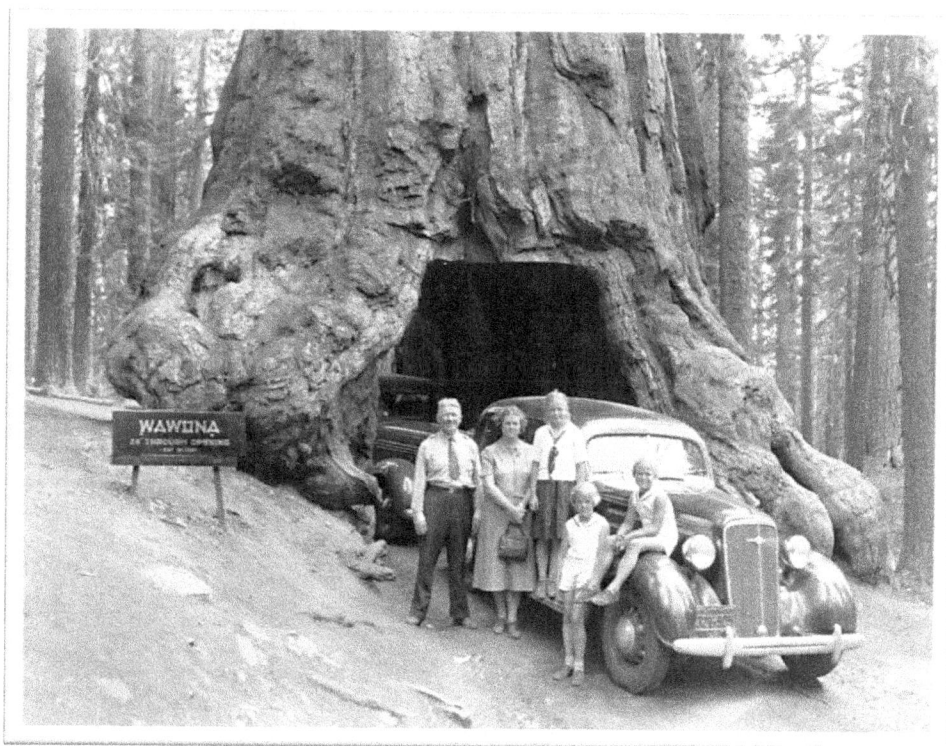

The Lucas family stops for a photo in the Wawona Tree in Yosemite National Park, about 1939. From left: Elmer, Nommie, Wanda, and twins Sara and Sue.
From Sara Lucas Gilstrap Collection.

In 1941 Elmer became Professor of Geology at Oklahoma University and the family moved to Norman, where he spent the remainder of his career and life teaching, working as a consultant for oil companies, and as a visiting professor.

Elmer Lawrence Lucas and Nommie Lee Taylor had the following children:

+2.   i.   WANDA LEE² LUCAS was born on 14 Feb 1927 in Enid, Garfield, Oklahoma, USA. She married Robert Maxwell Stofer on 17 Jul 1949 in Norman, Cleveland, Oklahoma, USA (in the First Christian Church). He was born on 01 Sep 1913 in Columbus, Bartholomew, Indiana, USA. He died on 13 Mar 1978 in Kettering, Montgomery, Ohio, USA.

+3.   ii.   MARTHA SUE LUCAS was born on 13 Aug 1930 in Enid, Garfield, Oklahoma, USA (Twin to Sara). She died on 22 Oct 1970 in Palwal, Haryana, India. She married Oliver Gene Abston on 07 May 1950 in Norman, Cleveland, Oklahoma, USA. He was born on 24 Jul 1928 in Muskogee, Muskogee, Oklahoma, USA. He died in Mar 2020 in Winter Haven, Polk, Florida, USA.

+4.   iii.   SARA ANN LUCAS was born on 13 Aug 1930 in Enid, Garfield, Oklahoma, USA (Twin to Sue). She married Billy Bert Gilstrap, son of Bertrum Bernard Gilstrap and Mayme Lee Clark, on 31 Jul 1948 in Norman, Cleveland, Oklahoma, USA (in the First Christian Church). He was born on 13 May 1924 in Ardmore, Carter, Oklahoma, USA. He died on 30 Oct 2003 in Colorado Springs, El Paso, Colorado, USA (ashes at spouse Sara's house).

Generation 2

2. WANDA LEE² LUCAS (Nommie Lee¹ Taylor, Elmer Lawrence) was born on 14 Feb 1927 in Enid, Garfield, Oklahoma, USA as the first child of Elmer Lawrence Lucas and Nommie Lee Taylor. She had two siblings, namely: Martha Sue, and Sara Ann. She married **Robert Maxwell Stofer** on 17 Jul 1949 in Norman, Cleveland, Oklahoma, USA (First Christian Church). He was born on 01 Sep 1913 in Columbus, Bartholomew, Indiana, USA. He died on 13 Mar 1978 in Kettering, Montgomery, Ohio, USA.

Right: Wanda Lee Lucas in 2011. From Wanda Lucas Stofer Collection.

Wanda Lee Lucas lived in Enid, Garfield, Oklahoma, USA in 1930 (Street Address: East Randolph; age 3; Able to Speak English: Yes; Attended School: No; Enumeration District: 0021; Registration District: 0021; Marital Status: Single; Relation to Head: Daughter). She lived in Norman, Oklahoma, USA in 1948 (University of Oklahoma). She lived in Dayton,

Ohio, USA in 1959 (Street Address: 939 Renwood Dr). She was employed as a Musician and Educator between 1966 and 1989 in Dayton, Montgomery, Ohio, USA. She lived in Dayton, Ohio, USA in 1993 (Street Address: 939 Renwood Dr); Race: (White).

Wanda is the oldest of the three Lucas sisters and grew up first in Enid, then in Norman, Oklahoma where her father was a geology professor. Like her sisters and mother, Wanda became a talented artist and musician, but not without some encouragement from Nommie. Wanda still recalls some 70 years later:

> My mother was very adamant that the three girls study piano. Everybody else was taking tap dancing. So we all took piano lessons at 50 cents an hour. I seemed to be the one of the three that went the farthest and maybe did the best and I remember wanting to quit along the way because there were a lot more interesting things, and I can [still] feel her hot breath on my neck saying, "You will keep playing." (Lucas W. , 2017, p. 02:34).

Wanda did keep playing and when in the tenth grade, Nommie arranged for her to take organ lessons at the university from Mildred Andrews, the best organist in the country. Little did Wanda know that she would soon meet her future husband at a national music workshop in Colorado during her junior year at Oklahoma University. Wanda and Bob Stofer were married a year later and she moved to Cleveland with Bob. He was the choir director for the Presbyterian Church of the Covenant and chorus director for the Cleveland Orchestra. She says, "I didn't go back to Oklahoma or see my folks for a year and you know, I didn't really miss them." Their first two children, Robert Jr. and Sara Ann, were born during their eight years in Cleveland.

In 1956, an opportunity arose for Bob at the Westminster Presbyterian Church in Dayton, Ohio. It was an opportunity to have a better life in a smaller city and provide a better family life for the children. Larry was born there in 1957. Wanda attended two universities to obtain a Music Teaching Certificate beyond her Bachelor of Music degree (in organ). She then taught in a Junior High School for 20 years, followed by playing the organ for the Christian Science Church for many years. Wanda also studied Watercolor Painting at Sinclair College for 15 years. Now she is a retired music educator, artist, and member of many groups, both music and art. She is also known for her beautiful flower paintings. "It's been a happy life, and I am so blessed to have had three kids that turned out, every one, so well." (Lucas W. , 2017, p. 24:26).

Mary (Guerra) Conklin (left) and Wanda Lucas pose with one of Wanda's paintings. Author photo 23 Aug 2017.

Robert Maxwell Stofer was born on 01 Sep 1913 in Columbus, Bartholomew, Indiana, USA. He died on 13 Mar 1978 in Kettering, Montgomery, Ohio, USA (age 65). When he was 35, he married Wanda Lee Lucas, daughter of Elmer Lawrence Lucas and Nommie Lee Taylor, on 17 Jul 1949 in Norman, Cleveland, Oklahoma, USA (First Christian Church).

Robert Maxwell Stofer lived in German, Bartholomew, Indiana, USA in 1920 (Age: 6; AbleToSpeakEnglish: Yes; AttendedSchool: yes; EnumerationDistrict: 13; MaritalStatus: Single; RelationToHead: Son). He lived in Columbus, Columbus, Bartholomew, Indiana, USA in 1930 (StreetAddress: Franklin; Age: 16; AbleToSpeakEnglish: Yes; AttendedSchool: Yes; CanReadWrite: Yes; EnumerationDistrict: 0004; RegistrationDistrict: 4; MaritalStatus: Single; RelationToHead: Son). He graduated in 1931 in Columbus, Bartholomew, Indiana, USA (Columbus High School). He lived in Columbus, Bartholomew, Indiana, USA in 1935. He received a BA degree in 1940 in Wabash College, Indiana. He lived in Columbus, Columbus, Bartholomew, Indiana, USA in 1940 (StreetAddress: Owenty Fifth; Age: 26; AttendedSchool: No; EmploymentCode: 7; EmploymentDetails: Unable to Work; EmploymentHistory: No; EnumerationDistrict: 3-11; GradeCompleted: College, 2nd year; IncomeOtherSources: No; IsEmployed: No; PublicEmergencyWork: No; SeekingWork: No; MaritalStatus: Married; RelationToHead: Son). He received a Master of Music degree about 1942 from Union Theological Sacred Seminary. He was employed as a organist-choirmaster at the Church of the Covenant in 1948 in Cleveland, Cuyahoga, Ohio, USA. He lived in Cleveland, Cuyahoga, Ohio, USA in 1949. He lived in Indiana in 1951. StreetAddress: 939 Renwood Dr; Occupation: Choir Director and Organist in 1959 in Kettering, Montgomery, Ohio, USA. He lived in Dayton, Ohio, USA in 1959. He lived in Kettering, Montgomery, Ohio, USA in 1978. He was cremated in Mar 1978 in Kettering, Montgomery, Ohio, USA (Wright

State University Cemetery). He was also known as Bob. His cause of death was rheumatoid arthritis. Race: (White)

Left: Wanda Lucas stands next to a portrait of her late husband Robert Stofer. Author photo 23 Aug 2017.

Robert's early life showed a lot of promise. At the age of 14 he was hired as the organist-choir director of the First Baptist Church in Columbus, Indiana. In 1940 he was offered a four-year free scholarship to Wabash College in Crawfordsville, Indiana, if he would be the Chapel Organist. Since it was a Liberal Arts college no music classes were offered so he regularly studied with a top Indianapolis organist. After graduating from Wabash College, he went to New York City to enroll in the Union Theological Sacred Seminary, where he received his Master of Music degree. He studied with all the top organists, and from there he received a job offer from the Church of the Covenant. Wanda recalls, "He was organist-choirmaster at the Church of the Covenant in Cleveland," when she met him at the Colorado workshop in 1948. (Lucas W. , 2017, p. 4:47). A year later, this "Okie" girl was married to him and had moved to Cleveland, Ohio. At the time, Robert was also directing the Cleveland Men's Chorus and Wanda loved going to the many performances during the eight years they lived in Cleveland. Soon Bob applied for and became the choir director and organist for Westminster Church in Dayton, Ohio where the pay was better, the schools were closer, and the air was cleaner. Wanda recalls, "We used to hang out clothes on a line and in Cleveland I had to clean the lines all the time because of the smoke and soot" (Lucas W. , 2017, p. 6:33).

When his younger son Larry showed an interest in music, Robert not only found time to teach him how to play the organ, but also how to design and build one. In fact Robert himself designed the Wright State University concert hall organ when he was an organ teacher there. As if completing his legacy, years later his son Larry took the organ apart, repaired it and put it back together again when the concert hall was remodeled. Truth be known, Larry Stofer built, rebuilt, and repaired many of the church organs in Dayton, Ohio, just as his father taught him.

Robert Maxwell Stofer and Wanda Lee Lucas had the following children:

+5. i.   ROBERT MAXWELL³ STOFER JR was born on 13 Apr 1952 in Cleveland, Cuyahoga, Ohio, USA. He died on 08 Apr 2020 in Jacksonville, Duval, Florida, USA (Fernandina Beach Baptist Hospital). He married Brenda Straley in Jun 1980 in Dayton, Montgomery, Ohio, USA (Westminster Presbyterian Church). She was born on 16 Jun 1957.

6.   ii. SARA ANN STOFER was born on 12 Oct 1954 in in Cleveland, Cuyahoga, Ohio, USA. She married Mark Vincent Skripsak on 14 Dec 1979.

7. iii.   LAWRENCE EDWARD STOFER was born on 03 Jul 1957 in Dayton, Montgomery, Ohio, USA. He married (1) ANGELA M MENDELL on 01 May 1993. She was born in 1965. She died on 29 Jun 1997 in Dayton, Montgomery, USA. He married (2) CAROLE WERK-MEISTER on 04 Feb 2001. She was born in 1944. He died on 07 Apr 2013. His cause of death was complications from rheumatoid arthritis. He was buried in Fairborn, Greene County, Ohio, USA (Rockafield Cemetery; Find A Grave #200720745).

3. MARTHA SUE^2 LUCAS (Nommie Lee^1 Taylor, Elmer Lawrence) was born on 13 Aug 1930 in Enid, Garfield, Oklahoma, USA (Twin to Sara as the second child of Elmer Lawrence Lucas and Nommie Lee Taylor). She had two siblings, namely: Wanda Lee, and Sara Ann. She died on 22 Oct 1970 in Palwal, Haryana, India. She married **Oliver Gene Abston** on 07 May 1950 in Norman, Cleveland, Oklahoma, USA. He was born on 24 Jul 1928 in Muskogee, Muskogee, Oklahoma, USA. He died in Mar 2020 in Winter Haven, Polk, Florida, USA.

Martha Sue Lucas, or Sue as she liked to be called, lived in Enid Twp, Enid, Garfield, Oklahoma, USA in 1940. She lived in Enid Twp, Enid, Garfield, Oklahoma, USA in 1940 (Street Address: East Randolph; 9 Age: 9; CityWard: 4; Enumeration District: 24-20; GradeCompleted: Elementary school, 4th grade; Marital Status: Single; RelationToHead: Daughter). She lived in Norman, Cleveland, Oklahoma, USA in 1946 (Age: Abt 16). She graduated in 1948 in Norman, Cleveland, Oklahoma, USA (Norman High School). She lived in Oklahoma City, Oklahoma, USA in 1949 (StreetAddress: 425 SB 16th; Occupation: Saleswoman). She lived in Norman, Cleveland, Oklahoma, USA in 1950 (Age: 19; Enumeration District: 14-28; IsEmployed: No; Occupation Category: Other; Seeking Work: No; Worked Last Week: No; Relation To Head: Daughter; MaritalStatus: Single). She lived in New Delhi, Delhi, India in 1970 (Age: 40). She was cremated on 23 Oct 1970 in New Delhi,

Delhi, India. She was also known as Sue. Her cause of death was an automobile accident. Race: (White). She was buried in Oklahoma City, Oklahoma, USA (Resthaven Gardens Cemetery (Sec 4, Lot 35. Grave 3); Find A Grave #82967806).

Right: The Lucas sisters show off their Christmas presents at home in Enid, Oklahoma in 1934. From left: Wanda, twins Sue and Sara. From Sara Lucas Gilstrap Collection.

Sue was Sara's "younger" twin and they grew up together as the Lucas' younger daughters in Norman, Oklahoma. As sister Sara explained, "I was five minutes older than Sue. . . That's why I am the middle child." (Lucas S. , 2019, p. 15:45). Growing up together, the sisters attended Norman High School as did Sue's future husband Gene Abston who graduated two years ahead of Sue. When she was younger Sue taught synchronized swimming and was also attracted to art and flower arranging.

After her marriage to Gene Abston in 1950, she raised two boys and accompanied husband Gene as he worked for the U.S. State Department at Embassies in exotic places like Tokyo and New Delhi. Tragically, her life was cut short at age 40 when she died in an automobile accident in October 1970 near New Delhi in Palwal, Haryana, India.

According to Sue's older sister Wanda, also killed was a Japanese woman, Mia Strommaul, who was married to a white and lived in Washington D.C., and an Indian student who was a daughter of the Maharajah. The only survivor was an Indian student who was the sister of a member of the Indian Parliament.

Oliver Gene Abston was born on 24 Jul 1928 in Denton, Denton, Texas, USA. He died on 10 Jan 2020 in Winter Haven, Polk, Florida, USA. When he was 21, he married Martha Sue Lucas, daughter of Elmer Lawrence Lucas and Nommie Lee Taylor, on 07 May 1950 in Norman, Cleveland, Oklahoma, USA. When he was 66, he married Margaret Allen Toepfer on 28 Nov 1994 in Monroe, Florida.

Left: Newlyweds Sue Lucas and Gene Abston pose with young cousins Mary Guerra (left) and Tecla Guerra (right) in 1950. From Sara Lucas Gilstrap Collection.

Gene Abston, as he was known, lived in Sulphur, Murray, Oklahoma, USA in 1935. He lived in Jacobs Township, Holdenville, Hughes, Oklahoma, USA in 1940 (Street Address: South Oak; Age: 11; Attended School: Yes; Enumeration District: 32-17; Grade Completed: Elementary school, 5th grade; Residence Farm; Marital Status: Single; Relation To Head: Son). He lived in Norman, Cleveland, Oklahoma, USA in 1946 (Age: 18; Relation To Head: Self). He was described as Complexion: Ruddy; Eye Color: Gray; Hair Color: Brown; Height: 5 9; Weight: 185 in 1946. He lived in Norman, Oklahoma in 1954 (University of Oklahoma; Age: Abt 20). He served in the military in 1970 in Palwal, Haryana, India (Lt. Col. US Army). He was employed as a Bureau of Alcohol, Tobacco and Firearms agent in 1973 in Arlington, Arlington, Virginia, USA. He lived in Falls Church, Fairfax, Virginia, USA in 1986 (Street Address: 3701 S George Mason Drive Unit 112n; Age: 58). He lived in Fernandina Beach, Nassau, Florida, USA in 1987 (Postal Code: 33881-8741 (1987); Street Address: 196 Fairway Cir; Age: 59). He lived in Winter Haven, Polk, Florida, USA in 1996 (Street Address: 196

Fairway Cir; Phone Number: 941-294-2208). He was buried on 28 Apr 2021 in Arlington, Arlington County, Virginia, USA (Arlington Cemetery; Columbarium Court 11-EE Column 18 Niche 1; Find A Grave #225971521). He was also known as Gene. Race: (White)

We believe that Gene joined the U.S. Army Air Forces just before it was renamed the U.S. Air Force in 1947 based on the couple's engagement notice in the Norman Oklahoma newspaper in 1950. At any rate, by the time he graduated from college, he became a U.S. Army officer, later attaining the rank of Lieutenant Colonel. He was a quiet man and worked for the U.S. government for most of his career, both in the U.S. and overseas. My wife Mary Guerra and I stayed with him for three months in his house in Arlington, Virginia while I was attending the Army officer basic course at Fort Belvoir in early 1973. He had only lost his wife less than two years earlier. At that time he was working as a Bureau of Alcohol, Tobacco, Firearms and Explosives (ATF) agent. Due to our hectic schedules we did not see him much then and unfortunately never saw him afterwards. After Gene retired, he moved to Florida, where he died in 2020.

Oliver Gene Abston and Martha Sue Lucas had the following children:

8.   i.   DAVID ALAN[3] ABSTON was born on 31 May 1951. He died on 18 Dec 2006 (age 56).
9.   ii.   RICHARD LUCAS ABSTON was born on 28 Oct 1952.

4. SARA ANN[2] LUCAS (Nommie Lee[1] Taylor, Elmer Lawrence) was born on 13 Aug 1930 in Enid, Garfield, Oklahoma, USA (Twin to Sue, as the third child of Elmer Lawrence Lucas and Nommie Lee Taylor). She had two siblings, namely: Wanda Lee, and Martha Sue. When she was 17, she married **Billy Bert Gilstrap**, son of Bertrum Bernard Gilstrap and Mayme Lee Clark, on 31 Jul 1948 in Norman, Cleveland, Oklahoma, USA (First Christian Church). He was born on 13 May 1924 in Ardmore, Carter, Oklahoma, USA. He died on 30 Oct 2003 in Colorado Springs, El Paso, Colorado, USA (ashes at spouse Sara's house).

Right: Twins Sara Lucas (left) and Sue Lucas (right) posed for their portraits in Enid, Oklahoma in about 1950. From Sara Lucas Gilstrap Collection.

Sara Lucas graduated in 1948 in Norman, Oklahoma, USA (Norman High School). She received a BFA (bachelor of fine arts) degree in 1968 at the University of Oklahoma. She received a MFA (master of fine arts) degree in 1970 in University of Oklahoma. She lived in Colorado Springs, El Paso, Colorado, USA in 1998 (Street Address: 6584 Bull Hill Ct). She was employed as a weaving, metal design, and pottery instructor at the University of Texas in Midland, Midland, Texas, USA.

Sara grew up during the Great Depression of the 1930s and says she will always remember how hard it was for her parents to save money to buy clothes for her and her sisters. She remembers the day that she finally got a pair of new white shoes for Easter and what happened to them:

> I remember I found this old galosh and went over to where this old filling station was and put my foot down into a bucket of oil to test that shoe, and the galoshes had holes in them. I remember I got a spanking for that –coming home with one oily-white shoe. . . I'm probably five years old and testing this galosh [with my] brand new white Easter shoes. (Lucas S. , 2019, p. 26:45).

Sara still vividly remembers the summers she spent from age 5 to age 10 with her family in Yosemite National Park where her father was a ranger-naturalist. She even remembers climbing Half Dome Mountain with her family. She recalled that a few years later her family spent the summers with her grandparents in Boise, Idaho so they could see their father Elmer Lucas who was doing geology reconnaissance in Idaho, Wyoming and Utah for the oil companies.

The Lucas family climbing Half Dome Mountain in 1937.
From left: Elmer, Sue, Sara, Nommie, Wanda.
From Wanda Lucas Stofer Collection.

Sara says, "I took an art class in high school and I really, really liked that class." (Lucas S. , 2019, p. 11:00). But other things had a priority at the time. Like her mother Nommie, Sara met her future husband at the University. In 1948 she met Bill Gilstrap, a young geology student who was in her father's geology class at the University. They were married soon after and upon graduation he began working as a geologist in Buffalo, Wyoming for Carter Oil Company, which later became Exxon. Although she has both Bachelor's and Master's degrees in art, she did not finish college until after she was married. But once she found she liked working with the visual arts, there was no stopping her, despite raising three children at the same time.

At age 91, Sara still works almost daily in her workshop and has developed her skills in clay, fiber, metal and graphic arts over the years to the point that she not only makes and exhibits her creations, but has become a teacher and lecturer as well. The easiest way to appreciate her wide-ranging skills is to log-on to her website (http://saragilstrap.com), where you can see a photo of her workshop and view the many pieces of her original creations on display.

Billy Bert Gilstrap was born on 13 May 1924 in Ardmore, Carter, Oklahoma, USA as the first child of Bertrum Bernard Gilstrap and Mayme Lee Clark. He died on 30 Oct 2003 in Colorado Springs, El Paso, Colorado, USA (ashes at spouse Sara's house). When he was 24, he married Sara Ann Lucas, daughter of Elmer Lawrence Lucas and Nommie Lee Taylor, on 31 Jul 1948 in Norman, Cleveland, Oklahoma, USA (First Christian Church).

Right: Bill Gilstrap in 1987. From Sara Lucas Gilstrap Collection.

Billy Bert Gilstrap lived in Ardmore, Ardmore, Carter, Oklahoma, USA in 1930 (Street Address: F Street North West; age 5; Attended School: No; Enumeration District: 0005; Registration District: 0005; Marital Status: Single; Relation to Head: Son). He lived in Ardmore, Carter, Oklahoma, USA in 1935. He lived in Ardmore Township, Ardmore, Carter, Oklahoma, USA on 01 Apr 1940 (Street Address: 417 5th St N W; Age: 15; Occupation: Student; Attended School: Yes; Employment Code: 6; Employment Details: School; Employment History: No; Enumeration District: 10-4; Grade Completed: High School, 1st year; Income: 0; Income Other Sources: No; Is Employed: No; Public Emergency Work: No; Residence Farm Nineteen Thirty Five: No; Seeking Work: No; Weeks Worked: 0; Marital Status: Single; Relation to Head: Son). He lived in Ardmore, Oklahoma, USA in 1941 (age 16, Ardmore High School). He lived in Ardmore, Carter, Oklahoma, USA in 1942 (age 18; Relation to Head: Self). He was described as Occupation: Student; Complexion: Dark; Eye Color: Brown; Hair Color: Brown in 1942. He lived in Ardmore, Oklahoma, USA in 1946 (Street Address: 417 5th Ave NW; Occupation: Student). He received a BS degree from Oklahoma University about 1948 in Norman, Cleveland, Oklahoma, USA. He was employed with Carter Oil (now Exxon) about 1948 in Buffalo, Johnson, Wyoming, USA. He lived in Santa Fe, Santa Fe, New Mexico, USA in 1993. He lived in Colorado Springs, Colorado, USA in 1998 (Street Address: 6584 Bull Hill CT). He was also known as Bill. Race: (Indian-mother) Race: (White-father).

Left: Sara Lucas with two of her children in Colorado Springs, Colorado. From left: Christine, Sara, Paul. Author photo 9 May 2019.

Billy Bert Gilstrap and Sara Ann Lucas had the following children:

+10.   i.   STEPHEN LAWRENCE³ GILSTRAP was born on 02 Jun 1949 in Norman, Cleveland, Oklahoma, USA. He married Mary Kathryn Sawyers on 24 Jun 1978 in Midland, Texas, USA. She was born in 1951.

11.   ii.   CHRISTINE SUZANNE GILSTRAP was born on 24 Apr 1951 in Norman, Cleveland, Oklahoma, USA. She married William David Beadles on 07 Sep 2010 in Hot Springs, Fall River, South Dakota, USA. He was born on 16 Aug 1952 in Normal, McLean, Illinois, USA.

12.   iii.   JAMES PAUL GILSTRAP was born on 09 Oct 1954 in Tulsa, Creek, Oklahoma, USA. He died on 24 Dec 2021 in Colorado Springs, CO

Generation 3

5. ROBERT MAXWELL³ STOFER JR (Wanda Lee² Lucas, Nommie Lee¹ Taylor, Robert Maxwell) was born on 13 Apr 1952 in Cleveland, Cuyahoga, Ohio, USA as the first child of Robert Maxwell Stofer and Wanda Lee Lucas. He had two siblings, namely: Sara Ann, and Lawrence Edward. He died on 08 Apr 2020 in Jacksonville, Duval, Florida, USA (Fernandina Beach Baptist Hospital). When he was 28, he married **Brenda Straley** in Jun 1980 in Dayton, Montgomery, Ohio, USA (Westminster Presbyterian Church).

Robert Maxwell Stofer Jr lived in Dayton, Montgomery, Ohio, USA in 1955 (age 3).He graduated in 1970 in Dayton, Montgomery, Ohio, USA (Fairmont West High School).He received a BS Dentistry degree in 1974 in Ohio State University. He received a Doctorate of Dental Surgery degree in 1977 in Ohio State University. He was cremated in Apr 2020 in Florida, USA. He was also known as Rob. His cause of death was Arthritis complications leading to Peritonitis. He was employed as an Associate Professor of Dentistry in Ohio State University.

Right: Rob Stofer Jr. with his wife Brenda Straley, Christmas, 2005. From Marjorie Taylor Collection.

Rob was born in Cleveland and grew up in Dayton. He loved music, and in his earlier years, Rob played keyboard in several rock 'n roll bands. He was a multi-talented go-to guy who would do anything for his friends and neighbors. In fact, his friends had nicknamed him "MacGyver" knowing he could probably fix it, no matter what it was.

Rob worked as a page in the Ohio State Legislature to help pay for college at the Ohio State University. He became a dentist, soon earning a doctorate of dental surgery and later becoming an associate professor of dentistry at Ohio State. Rob started a private and group practice, establishing Centerville Family Dental, where he practiced dentistry for 42 years. During those years he completed the Midwest Implant Institute Program and taught in several dental school programs.

He met his wife **Brenda Straley** at the university cafeteria where she was studying to become a nurse. They married, and she had two children when she became Mrs. Ohio. She even started a karaoke business on the side where her children enjoyed helping. Rob's mother Wanda says that Brenda's nursing skills have been of great help to the family. Unfortunately, the Stofer men have all battled arthritis, and Rob passed in 2020 from arthritis complications leading to peritonitis.

Robert Maxwell Stofer Jr and Brenda Straley had the following children:

13. i.   BRITTANY ANN⁴ STOFER was born in Oct 1982 in Dayton, Montgomery, Ohio, USA.
14. ii. ROBERT MAXWELL STOFER III was born on 30 Apr 1984 in Dayton, Montgomery, Ohio, USA.

7. **LAWRENCE EDWARD³ STOFER** (Wanda Lee² Lucas, Nommie Lee¹ Taylor, Robert Maxwell) was born on 03 Jul 1957 in Dayton, Montgomery, Ohio, USA. He married (1) ANGELA M MENDELL on 01 May 1993. She was born in 1965. She died on 29 Jun 1997 in Dayton, Montgomery, USA. He married (2) CAROLE WERK-MEISTER on 04 Feb 2001. She was born in 1944. He died on 07 Apr 2013. His cause of death was complications from rheumatoid arthritis. He was buried in Fairborn, Greene County, Ohio, USA (Rockafield Cemetery; Find A Grave #200720745).

Left: Larry Stofer with his wife Carole Werk-Meister, Christmas, 2005. From Marjorie Taylor Collection.

After he married Carole they lived in the Huffman Historic District of the city of Dayton prior to moving to Beavercreek. Larry was the owner of the Rainbow Pipe Organ Company. He built and updated many of the remarkable pipe organs located in the city of Dayton, including those at Holy Angels Church, St John's Lutheran Church, the Wright State University Concert Hall, and Dayton Westminster Presbyterian Church. He also worked on many private home pipe organ installations to include Ridgeleigh Terrance, the home of philanthropist Virginia Kettering in Dayton, Ohio.

10. **STEPHEN LAWRENCE**[3] **GILSTRAP** (Sara Ann[2] Lucas, Nommie Lee[1] Taylor, Billy Bert, Bertrum Bernard) was born on 02 Jun 1949 in Norman, Cleveland, Oklahoma, USA. He married Mary Kathryn Sawyers on 24 Jun 1978 in Midland, Texas, USA. She was born in 1951.

Right: Stephen (on left), Christine, and Paul Gilstrap read together in Tulsa, Oklahoma in 1959. From Sara Lucas Gilstrap Collection.

Stephen Lawrence Gilstrap and Mary Kathryn Sawyers had the following child:

15.   i.   STEPHEN DAVID[4] GILSTRAP was born on 26 Jun 1979 in Odessa, Ector, Texas, USA. He died on 30 Jun 1979 in Odessa, Ector, Texas, USA (meningitis).

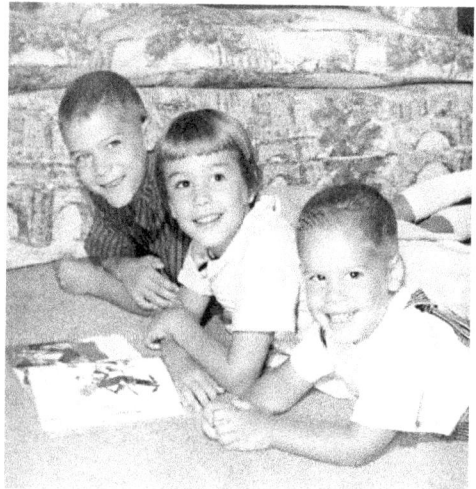

Chapter 5. Bessie Amanda Taylor and Carl Mandeville Tiegreen

Generation 1

1. BESSIE AMANDA[I] TAYLOR (Richard Thomas[A], Richard Lemuel[B], John Dennis[C], Dempsey[D], William Abraham Lawrence[E], William Nathaniel[F], James Henry "The Elder"[G] I, John William "The Immigrant"[H], Capt. Thomas John[I] II, Thomas John[J] I, Rev. Dr. Rowland[K], John Thomas[L], John William[M] I, William[N] II, Sir John[O], William[P] I, Sir John[Q] Taylifer, Harger[R] Taylefer) was born on 03 Jul 1907 in Wewahitchka, Gulf, Florida, USA. She had six siblings, namely: Elsie Blanche, Nommie Lee, Richard Lamuel, Artice Raymond, Nettie LaVonne, and Marjorie Ellen. She died on 21 Apr 1997 in Carrollton, Dallas, Texas, USA (age 89). She married **Carl Mandeville Tiegreen**, son of Otto Fredrick Johansson Tiegreen and Elisabeth Engmark Johansdotter, on 17 Jun 1929 in Pocatello, Bannock, Idaho, USA. He was born on 03 Dec 1898 in Ganado, Jackson, Texas, USA. He died on 11 Jun 1983 in Biloxi, Harrison, Mississippi, USA.

Right: Bessie Taylor and Carl Tiegreen at the Taylor Family Reunion at Palisades Lake, Idaho. Author photo Aug 1975.

Bessie Amanda Taylor lived in Okemah, Okfuskee, Oklahoma, USA in 1910. She received a Business degree about 1928 at State College. She was employed as a Steam Railroad Stenographer in 1930 in Pocatello, Bannock, Idaho, USA. She lived in Pocatello, Bannock, Idaho, USA in 1930 (Street Address: N. Garfield; Age: 22; Able To Speak English: Yes; Attended School: No; CanReadWrite: Yes; ClassofWorker: Wage or salary worker; EnumerationDistrict: 0012; Homemaker: Yes; HomeOwnership: Rented; IsEmployed (yesterday): No; LiveOnFarm: No; OwnedRadio: Yes; RegistrationDistrict: 12; ValueOfHome: 30; MaritalStatus: Married; RelationToHead: Wife; Occupation: Stenographer). She lived in Orchard, Ada, Idaho, USA on 20 Sep 1932. She lived in Election Precinct, outside Boise, Ada, Idaho, USA on 01 Apr 1940 (StreetAddress: Resseguie Street; Age: 32; AttendedSchool: No; EmploymentCode: 5; EmploymentDetails: Home Housework; EmploymentHistory: No; EnumerationDistrict: 1-26; GradeCompleted: High School, 4th year; Income: 0; IncomeOtherSources: No; IsEmployed: No; PublicEmergencyWork: No; Respondent: Yes; SeekingWork: No; WeeksWorked: 0;

MaritalStatus: Married; RelationToHead: Wife). She was employed as a Bank of Mississippi Branch Manager between 1953 and 1983 in Biloxi, Harrison, Mississippi, USA. She was buried on 25 Apr 1997 in Biloxi, Harrison, Mississippi, USA (Southern Memorial Park, 2076 Beach Blvd; Find A Grave #114356095). She was affiliated with the Baptist (First Baptist Church of Biloxi) religion. She lived in Oklahoma. Race: (White)

Bessie Amanda Taylor was Richard Thomas and Roxie Ann's third child and their first child born after the Taylor family left Georgia. She was born five years after her older sister Nommie. It is believed that her mother Roxie had one of her miscarriages with stillborn twins after she had Bessie and they moved to Oklahoma. We believe she was named after her mother Roxie's brother James Gibbs' daughter Bessie Gibbs, born in 1898. Her middle name comes from her maternal grandmother, Susan Amanda Hancock. (Tiegreen C. H., 2012, p. 9).

Left: Typical homestead house in Wewahitchka, Florida, where Bessie Taylor was born. The area is known for its Bass fishing and Tupelo Honey. Author photo 12 Apr 2021.

In 1908 when Bessie was barely a year old, Richard packed up the family and moved from Florida to Oklahoma where they farmed for the next twenty years. Bessie was raised here where her four younger brothers and sisters were born. In 1925 when the family moved west again, Bessie elected to stay in Pryor, Oklahoma, moving in with her oldest sister Elsie to finish school and get a business degree at the local state college. She moved to Wewoka, Oklahoma with her sister Elsie and husband Glen and was living with them when she met her future husband Carl Tiegreen. In 1929, Carl moved to Pocatello, Idaho to become a materials accountant for the Union Pacific Railroad. Meanwhile, Bessie finished her studies and took the train to marry him there and work for the same industry as a stenographer. In 1930, they rented an apartment at 522 North Garfield Street for $30 per month. (Tiegreen C. H., 2012, p. 9).

In 1933, Carl started working for the Veterans Administration in Boise, where their children Don and Alan were born and Bessie became the Postmaster for Orchard, Idaho in 1932, moving to Boise the next year. Later the family moved to Ohio and in 1953 he was transferred to the VA Center in Biloxi, where Bessie went back to work after raising their two children. She became the Branch Manager for the Bank of Mississippi. Carl retired in 1965 and Bessie lived in Biloxi until 1993.

Everyone loved Bessie. In 2009 her youngest sister Marjorie summed up her feelings in an email to Bessie's grandson Carl H. Tiegreen as follows:

I remember Bess, your grandmother, talking to me about you years ago. She loved her grandchildren very much and was so proud of all of you. . . I am 92 years old and the youngest of 7 children and last one remaining as your dad and Uncle Don has probably told you. As the old saying goes—a lot of water has gone under the bridge, and I don't remember as I'd like to. I can tell you now that your grandmother was the most wonderful person I ever knew. I don't ever remember her saying anything bad about anything or anybody. I always said she was a 'Saint.' She was so intelligent and could do the most beautiful things with her hands. I could go on about her, but you can guess how I feel" (Tiegreen C. H., 2012, p. 10).

Carl Mandeville Tiegreen was born on 03 Dec 1898 in Ganado, Jackson, Texas, USA as the sixth child of Otto Fredrick Johansson Tiegreen and Elisabeth Engmark Johansdotter. He had six siblings, namely: Hillel Ivan, Leonas J, Althea, Addiel, Francis Clara, and Arnold Fredrick. He died on 11 Jun 1983 in Biloxi, Harrison, Mississippi, USA. When he was 30, he married Bessie Amanda Taylor, daughter of Richard Thomas Taylor and Roxie Ann Gibbs, on 17 Jun 1929 in Pocatello, Bannock, Idaho, USA

Right: Bessie Taylor and Carl Tiegreen celebrate their 50th Wedding Anniversary in Biloxi, Mississippi in June 1979. From Marjorie Taylor Collection.

Carl Mandeville Tiegreen lived in Ganado, Jackson, Texas, USA in 1900. He lived in Tioga, Neosho, Kansas, USA on 01 Mar 1905. He lived in Chanute, Neosho, Kansas, USA in 1910 (Age: 11; MaritalStatus: Single; RelationToHead: Son). He lived in Chanute, Neosho, Kansas, USA in 1915. He lived in Chanute, Neosho, Kansas, USA on 18 Sep 1918 (StreetAddress: 516 N Grant; RelationToHead: Son). He lived in Chetopa, Neosho, Kansas, USA in 1920 (StreetAddress: N Grant; Age: 21; Occupation: Clerk; AbleToSpeakEnglish: Yes; AttendedSchool: No; CanRead: Yes; CanWrite: Yes; EnumerationDistrict: 208; Industry: AT and SF; IsEmployed: Wage or Salary; MaritalStatus: Single; RelationToHead: Son). He was employed as a Steam Railroad Materials Accountant in 1929 in Pocatello, Bannock, Idaho, USA. He lived in Pocatello, Bannock, Idaho, USA in 1930. He lived in Boise, Ada, Idaho, USA in 1935 (1306 N 12th). He lived in Ada, Idaho, USA in 1940 (StreetAddress: Resseguie Street; Age: 41; Occupation: Procurement Clerk; AttendedSchool: No; ClassofWorker: Wage or salary worker in Government work; EmploymentCode: 1; EmploymentDetails: No; EmploymentHistory: No; EnumerationDistrict: 1-26; GradeComplete). He was employed as a Veterans Admin clerk on

16 Feb 1942 in Boise, Ada, Idaho, USA. He was described as Age 43; Complexion: Light; Eye Color: Other; Hair Color: Brown; Height: 5' 8'; Weight: 144 lbs. on 16 Feb 1942 in Boise, Ada, Idaho, USA. He was employed as a Veterans Admin finance clerk and auditor between 1953 and 1965 in Biloxi, Harrison, Mississippi, USA. Race: (White) Ethnicity: (American) He was buried in Biloxi, Harrison, Mississippi, USA (Southern Memorial Park, 2076 Beach Blvd; Find A Grave #52616423).

The Otto Tiegreen family in 1901 with son Carl at age 2. Hjalmar, Julia, and Julius are from Otto's first wife. Front, from left: Addiel, Otto, Carl, Elisabeth, Francis. Back, from left: Hillel, Hjalmar, Julia, Julius, Althea, Leonas. Not Shown: Arnold, who was not born until 1903. Courtesy of Mary Tiegreen via Ancestry.com.

Although Carl was born in Texas, at age 2 he and his family traveled by covered wagon to southeastern Kansas. His father Otto with second wife Elisabeth finally put down roots in the town of Chanute after emigrating from Sweden. Carl grew up in Chanute where he played semi-pro baseball during his youth and could still throw a mean fastball when he was in his 70's according to his son Alan (Tiegreen C. H., 2012, p. 6).

"He was always interested in math and figures and things like that so he naturally gravitated toward accounting" said his son Alan (Tiegreen A. F., 2021, p. 11:54). After high school Carl worked for seven years for the Santa Fe Railroad in Chanute as an office worker and later report clerk. Soon after that he opened a grocery store with his younger brother Arnold. After selling the store in 1919, Carl got a job with Prairie Oil and Gas; and in 1925 joined the Union Pacific Railroad in Wewoka, Oklahoma where he met his future wife Bessie Taylor. Carl then moved to Pocatello, Idaho where Bessie joined him in 1929 where they were married.

Carl became a clerk and later auditor for the Veterans Administration and by 1932 they were in Boise, Idaho where Bessie's father and younger brothers and sisters lived. This was a wonderful reunion for Bessie and her two sons were born here. In 1944 however they transferred to Lincoln, Nebraska then; in 1945 to Montgomery, Alabama; followed by Chillicothe, Ohio in 1945 and the Biloxi VA Center in 1953. He retired in 1965 on a salary of $11,723 per year (Tiegreen C. H., 2012, p. 5).

It is said that Carl loved being a grandfather. Grandson Carl Hurt Tiegreen recalled he always enjoyed visiting the grandchildren:

> Being young, I could never understand why Grandma was the one driving when they arrived and not Grandad. I was told that it was because he was [8 years] "older" and having her drive was "safer." Also, I can remember sitting on Grandad's lap in the family rocking chair, while he sang me silly songs, many of which were in Swedish. He was also adept at container puzzles and would solve difficult ones while I was out for the morning (Tiegreen C. H., 2012, p. 8).

He was also an amateur writer of poems and prose, tackling subjects as complicated as his analysis of the 23rd Psalm Bible passage in 1972, or as simple as a short poem to congratulate Bessie's younger brother Art on his marriage in 1935.

```
    For days and weeks and months galore
    And many years to come
    We wish you joy and contentment
    In your new and happy home.

    Thru all the time that before you lies
    Thru all joys and sadness too
    We know that one great thought of love
    Will live between you two.

    If two good friends can help you on
    To achieve that which is best
    We trust that you will not forget
    The Good Will of Carl and Bess.

By-Carl Tiegreen          to Hazel & Art
                             1935
```

Carl Mandeville Tiegreen and Bessie Amanda Taylor had the following children:

+2. i.   DONALD RICHARD[2] TIEGREEN was born on 03 Mar 1933 in Boise, Ada, Idaho, USA. He married (1) NANCY J FOX on 27 Dec 1958. She was born on 23 Jun 1936 in Hancock, Ohio, USA. He married (2) MARY SANDRA HOGAN on 16 Jun 1984 in Houston, Texas, USA. She was born on 24 Oct 1937. She died in 2020 in Corpus Christi, Nueces, Texas USA.

+3. ii.   ALAN FREDERICK TIEGREEN was born on 06 Jul 1935 in Boise, Ada, Idaho, USA.

He married (1) HELEN HURT, daughter of Walter Harvey Hurt Jr. and Stella Wolverton Dyess, on 14 Jun 1958 in Waynesboro, Wayne, Mississippi, USA (First Baptist Church). She was born on 18 Jun 1937 in Waynesboro, Wayne, Mississippi, USA. He married (2) JUDITH TATUM on 17 Dec 1982 in Decatur, De Kalb, Georgia, USA. She was born on 13 Nov 1944 in Atlanta, De Kalb, Georgia, USA. She died on 21 Jul 1989 in Atlanta, De Kalb, Georgia, USA. He married (3) NANCY HOPPER DOBY on 11 Jul 1992 in Atlanta, De Kalb, Georgia, USA. She was born on 27 May 1948 in Corbin, Knox, Kentucky, USA.

Generation 2

2. DONALD RICHARD[2] TIEGREEN (Bessie Amanda[1] Taylor, Carl Mandeville, Otto Fredrick Johansson) was born on 03 Mar 1933 in Boise, Ada, Idaho, USA. He married (1) **NANCY J FOX** on 27 Dec 1958. She was born on 23 Jun 1936 in Hancock, Ohio, USA. He married (2) **MARY SANDRA HOGAN** on 16 Jun 1984 in Houston, Texas, USA. She was born on 24 Oct 1937. She died in 2020 in Corpus Christi, Nueces, Texas USA.

Left: Donald Richard Tiegreen in Fort Worth, Texas, 1986. From Sara Lucas Gilstrap Collection.

Donald Richard Tiegreen lived in Ada, Idaho, USA in 1935. He lived in Election Precinct outside Boise City, Ada, Idaho, USA in 1940 (Street Address: Resseguie Street; Age: 7; Attended School: Yes; Enumeration District: 1-26; Grade Completed: None; Marital Status: Single; Relation To Head: Son). He lived in Chillicothe, Ross, Ohio, USA in 1949 (Age: Abt 16). He lived in Chillicothe, Ohio in 1951 (Age: 16). He graduated in Jun 1951 in Chillicothe, Ross, Ohio, USA (Chillicothe High School). He lived in Chillicothe, Ross, Ohio, USA in 1952 (StreetAddress: 622 Allen 4682; United States Navy Occupation: United States Navy). He served in the military between 1952–1956 in San Diego, San Diego, California, USA (US Navy Electronics Technician; USS Albany, CA-123; USS Columbus; Ship Classification: CA-74). He lived in Chillicothe, Ross, Ohio, USA in 1952 (StreetAddress: 622 Allen 4682; United States Navy Occupation: United States Navy). He served in Biloxi, Harrison, Mississippi, USA in 1954 (StreetAddress: VA Cen 5472; Occupation: United States Navy). He lived in West Lafayette, Tippecanoe, Indiana, USA in 1960 (Occupation: Student). He received a Bachelor of Science (Chemical Engineering) degree in May 1960 at Purdue University, Indiana. He lived in Dallas, Dallas County, Texas, USA between 1969 and 1983 (StreetAddress: 7731 Briaridge Rd; Occupation: Chemical Engineer). He lived in Carrollton, Dallas County, Texas, USA in 1985. He lived in Carrollton, Dallas County, Texas, USA in 1993 (StreetAddress: 2103 Teton Pl). He lived in Richmond, Madison, Kentucky, USA in 2005 (StreetAddress: 2012 Deerfield Ln; Age: 72). He lived in Corpus Christi, Nueces County, Texas, USA in 2018 (7731 Cedar Creek Circle). He lived in Plano, Collin County, Texas, USA in 2020 (moved here after death of spouse Mary Sandra). He was also known as Don. Race: (White).

Although Don was two years older than his brother, Alan remembers, "We did have a lot of fun [together in Boise] playing in the hills, flying kites, and even trying to learn how to ski down our street which was not easy." (Tiegreen A. F., 2021, p. 03:16). Also according to his brother Alan, he had an engineer's mind. After graduating from Chillicothe High School in Chillicothe, Ohio in 1951, Don joined the US Navy and served as an electronics technician for four years from 4 March 1952 to 12 July 1956. He served in San Diego, San Francisco (Treasure Island) and on board the USS Albany out of Norfolk, VA (Class CA-123), and the USS Columbus out of Boston, MA and Long Beach, CA (Class CA-74). Then he used the G.I. Bill to study at Purdue University in West Lafayette, Indiana, where he received a Bachelor of Science degree in Chemical Engineering in 1960.

He was soon working as an engineer and production manager for Corning Glassworks in New York before moving to West Virginia to work for a subsidiary. Don also worked for Texas Instruments in Dallas, Texas as a production manager from 1969 to 1983. Always looking for new products to develop, he then formed his own company with a business partner specializing in pneumatic instrumentation for oil and gas companies. He grew his new company and later was able to sell it and retire. (Tiegreen A. F., 2021, p. 14:53).

Donald Richard Tiegreen and Nancy J. Fox had the following children:
+4. i.   MICHAEL RICHARD[3] TIEGREEN was born on 31 May 1959. He married Debra K Swygert on 23 May 1992 in Dallas, Texas, USA. She was born on 24 Mar 1954.
 5. ii.   KRISTIN ELIZABETH TIEGREEN was born on 04 Aug 1961. She married Dean A Ramseyer on 30 Aug 2008 in Dallas, Dallas, Texas, USA.
 6. iii. SUSAN AMANDA TIEGREEN was born on 18 Jan 1964 in Jefferson, Kentucky, USA. She died on 16 Oct 1992 in Dallas, Texas. She married Leslie C Cooper on 15 Aug 1982 in Dallas, Texas, USA. He was born on 02 May 1955.
+7. iv.   CATHERINE MARIE TIEGREEN was born on 08 Nov 1966. She married Mark Stuart Seymour on 13 Aug 1988 in Dallas, Texas, USA. He was born on 29 Oct 1962.

Donald Richard Tiegreen and Mary Sandra Hogan had no children.

Right: Mary (Guerra) Conklin with Cousin Alan Tiegreen and wife Nancy at his home in Atlanta, Georgia. From left: Nancy Doby, Alan, Mary, Dave Conklin. Author photo 18 Apr 2021.

3. ALAN FREDERICK[2] TIEGREEN (Bessie Amanda[1] Taylor, Carl Mandeville, Otto Fredrick Johansson) was born on 06 Jul 1935 in Boise, Ada, Idaho, USA as the second child of Carl Mandeville Tiegreen and Bessie Amanda Taylor. When he was 22, he married (1) **HELEN HURT**, daughter of Walter Harvey Hurt Jr. and Stella Wolverton Dyess, on 14 Jun 1958 in Waynesboro, Wayne, Mississippi, USA (First Baptist Church). She was born on 18 Jun 1937 in Waynesboro, Wayne, Mississippi, USA. He married (2) **JUDITH TATUM** on 17 Dec 1982 in Decatur, De Kalb, Georgia, USA. She was born on 13 Nov 1944 in Atlanta, De Kalb, Georgia, USA. She died on 21 Jul 1989 in Atlanta, De Kalb, Georgia, USA. He married (3) **NANCY HOPPER DOBY** on 11 Jul 1992 in Atlanta, De Kalb, Georgia, USA. She was born on 27 May 1948 in Corbin, Knox, Kentucky, USA.

Alan Frederick Tiegreen lived in Election Precinct, Outside Boise City, Ada, Idaho, USA in 1940 (Street Address: Resseguie Street; Age: 4; Attended School: No; Enumeration District: 1-26; Grade Completed: None; Marital Status: Single; Relation To Head: Son). He lived in Chillicothe, Ross, Ohio, USA in 1950 (Age: Abt 16). He graduated in Jun 1953 in Chillicothe, Ross, Ohio, USA (Chillicothe High School). He lived in Biloxi, Harrison, Mississippi, USA in 1954 (Street Address: 3003 Corley St; Occupation: Student). He received a Bachelor of Arts degree in 1957 from the University of Southern Mississippi. He served in the military in 1960 in Los Angeles, California, USA. Employer: U. S. Army Reserve (light aircraft maintenance). He received a Bachelor of Professional Arts degree in 1961 from the Art Center of Design in Los Angeles. He was employed as a teacher of painting, drawing, and illustration in 1965 at Georgia State University, Atlanta, GA. He was employed as an illustrator of children's books in 1977 in Decatur, De Kalb, Georgia, USA. He lived in Atlanta, Fulton, Georgia, USA in 1978 (Georgia State University). He lived in Roswell, Fulton, Georgia, USA in 1985. He lived in Atlanta, Fulton, Georgia, USA in 1989 (Street Address: 220 Skyland Dr). He lived in Atlanta, Fulton, Georgia, USA in 1993 (Street Address: 4279 Wieuca Rd NE). Race: (White)

Alan was the younger of Bessie's two boys. He fondly remembers his childhood growing up with his brother Don near his grandfather Richard Taylor's farm in Boise, Idaho, "[Ours was] the third house from the end on a brand new dirt street leading up into the foothills. It was a great place to play, sagebrush and grass, some caves to explore. They said they were gold miner's caves. It was a lot of fun." (Tiegreen A. F., 2021, p. 02:17).

But these days did not last long due to his father's job with the Veterans Administration. Frequent transfers required the family to move across the country. By the time Alan had graduated from high school, he had lived in Idaho, Nebraska, Alabama and Ohio. But they still took summer vacations from Ohio to visit the grandparents' farm in Boise. Alan remembers:

> Back in the 40s and 50s we drove cross country to Boise from Chillicothe in a 1937 Ford with no air conditioning. I remember we got into Idaho along the Snake River and it was too hot to roll the windows down because the air was so hot and if you rolled the windows up and put paper over them you were in an oven. You couldn't win. (Tiegreen A. F., 2021, p. 18:55).

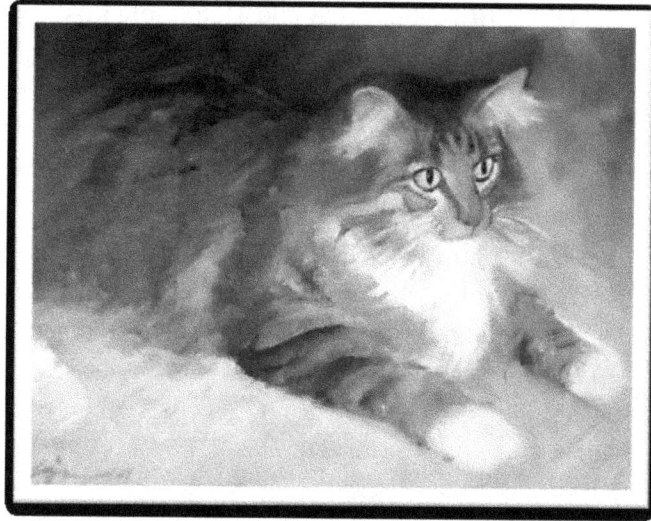

Above: Alan Tiegreen cat painting, about 2007. From Alan Tiegreen Collection.

Alan showed an early interest in both music and art, but his talent for drawing prevailed. He said, "I always liked art. I liked music too, but I didn't have the patience or the discipline. . . I enjoy music, but I've always liked making things, making pictures, and I was entranced by a magazine illustration and that's why I went to art school." (Tiegreen A. F., 2021, p. 08:10). When his father was transferred to Biloxi, Mississippi, Alan enrolled in the University of Southern Mississippi, receiving a Bachelor of Arts degree in 1957, meeting his first wife Helen there, and serving in the U.S. Army Reserve while at school. Alan continued his studies at the Art Center of Design in Los Angeles, earning a Bachelor of Professional Arts degree in 1961. Their first child Karen was born in Los Angeles.

Tiegreen's paintings have been exhibited at the Smithsonian Institution in Washington, D. C., the Knoxville World's Fair, New York City, Atlanta, and Los Angeles. He and one of his former students, Nena Allen, painted a 112 by 14-foot mural for the Grant Simmons plant in Atlanta, Georgia. Among the honors and awards he has received are the Boston Globe Horn Book fiction honor and Newbery honor award in 1978 and the Young Readers Choice in 1980, all for *Ramona and Her Father* by Beverly Cleary; and the American Book Awards children's fiction paperback award in 1981 for *Ramona and Her Mother* by Beverly Cleary. He also received the New York Times Notable in 1984 and the Parents' Choice literature award in 1984 for *Ramona Forever* by Beverly Cleary; the Buckeye (3-5) in 1985, the Newbery honor award in 1982, the Charlie May Simon for 1983-1984, and the Sunshine (runner-up) in 1984 all for *Ramona Quimby, Age 8* by Beverly Cleary; and the Golden Archer in 1977 and the Mark Twain in 1978 for *Ramona the Brave* by Beverly Cleary. He is also a member of the Society of

Illustrators (Jones, 1994, p. 530). After Alan and Helen left Los Angeles and moved back to Mississippi Alan's intention was to become an illustrator for an ad agency or magazine in New York. But Helen's uncle raved about Atlanta where he lived. Nevertheless, Alan attempted to carry out his plan saying, "I stayed with a friend in New Jersey and commuted into New York and Manhattan with my portfolio on three different subways and a bus, and after two weeks I said, 'I think Atlanta sounds a lot better.' " (Tiegreen A. F., 2021, p. 07:46). So in 1965 he became a teacher of painting, drawing, and illustration at Georgia State University's urban campus in Atlanta where his younger children Christopher and Carl were born. He has since become a published author and an illustrator of children's books and young adult books.

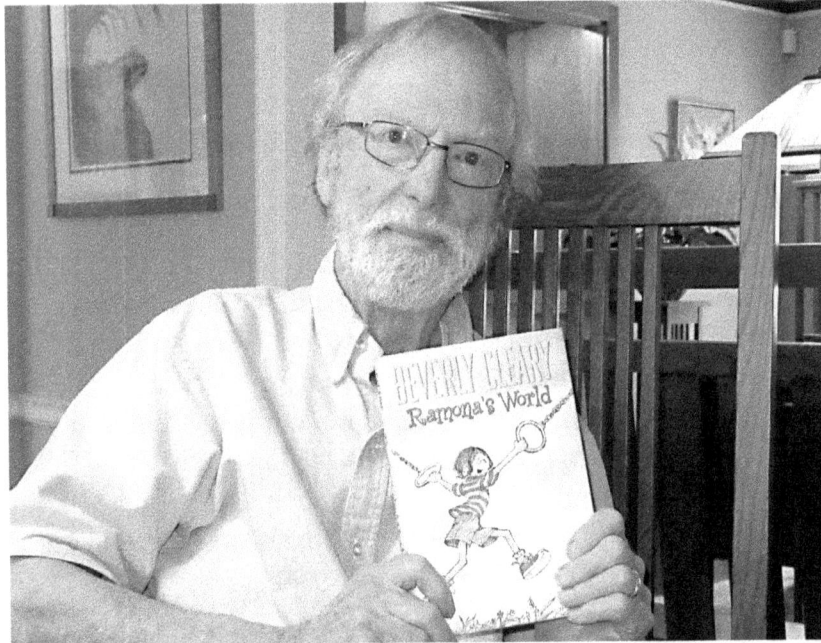

Left: At home in Atlanta Alan Tiegreen holds a children's book he illustrated in 1999, Ramona's World. Author photo 18 Apr 2021.

Alan's first wife **Helen Hurt** was born in Waynesboro, Mississippi on 18 Jun 1937. She is a descendant of four generations of journalists. Her great-grandfather, Walter Nesbitt Hurt, was editor and co-owner of the Hattiesburg American newspaper. Helen married Alan in Waynesboro in 1958 when she was twenty-one. Their first child Karen was born while they were living in Los Angeles. Their other children Christopher and Carl were born after they had moved to Atlanta. When their youngest child Carl was four years old in 1972, she wrote the children's book *Carter Rabbit*, which Alan illustrated, for their three children. Carter Rabbit is the story of a rabbit who is unhappy because he can't make noises like other animals. He is cheered, however, when he learns some of the special things rabbits do. She also published *Welty's Revisions of the Optimist's Daughter* in 1985. Their marriage ended in divorce.

Alan Frederick Tiegreen and Helen Hurt had the following children:

8. i. KAREN ELISE [3] TIEGREEN was born on 13 Dec 1959 in Los Angeles, California, USA.
+9. ii. CHRISTOPHER ALAN TIEGREEN was born on 06 Aug 1963 in Decatur, De Kalb, Georgia, USA. He married (1) LAURA BENNETT on 30 Jan 1985 in Athens, GA. He married (2) HANNAH HINLEY in 1996 in Decatur, De Kalb, Georgia, USA. She was born on 28 Apr 1973 in Decatur, De Kalb, Georgia, USA.
+10. iii. CARL HURT TIEGREEN was born on 06 May 1968 in Decatur, De Kalb, Georgia,

USA. He married Wendy Bridget White on 28 Sep 1996 in Atlanta, Fulton, Georgia, USA (Lutheran Church of the Redeemer). She was born on 06 Jun 1969 in Spartanburg, Spartanburg, South Carolina, USA (Mary Black Hospital).

Alan Frederick Tiegreen and Judith Tatum had no children.
Alan Frederick Tiegreen and Nancy Hopper Doby had no children.

Right: Alan Tiegreen and his children at an exhibition of his work in Atlanta, 6 Jun 2016. From left: daughter Karen, Alan, sons Carl, Christopher. From Alan Tiegreen Collection.

Generation 3

4. MICHAEL RICHARD[3] **TIEGREEN** (Donald Richard[2], Bessie Amanda[1] Taylor, Donald Richard[2], Carl Mandeville, Otto Fredrick Johansson) was born on 31 May 1959. He married Debra K Swygert on 23 May 1992 in Dallas, Texas, USA. She was born on 24 Mar 1954.

Michael Richard Tiegreen and Debra K. Swygert had the following child:
  11. i.   ALEXANDER RICHARD[4] TIEGREEN was born on 24 Jul 1997 (adopted from Russia).

7. CATHERINE MARIE[3] **TIEGREEN** (Donald Richard[2], Bessie Amanda[1] Taylor, Donald Richard[2], Carl Mandeville, Otto Fredrick Johansson) was born on 08 Nov 1966. She married Mark Stuart Seymour on 13 Aug 1988 in Dallas, Texas, USA. He was born on 29 Oct 1962.

Mark S. Seymour and Catherine Marie Tiegreen had the following children:
+12. i.   RACHEL ALLYSA[4] SEYMOUR was born on 28 Oct 1988 in Dallas, Texas, USA. She married Gunnar Hencmann on 25 May 2019. He was born on 16 Mar 1975.
  13. ii. SARA ELIZABETH SEYMOUR was born on 11 Oct 1990.

9. CHRISTOPHER ALAN³ TIEGREEN (Alan Frederick², Bessie Amanda¹ Taylor, Alan Frederick², Carl Mandeville, Otto Fredrick Johansson) was born on 06 Aug 1963 in Decatur, De Kalb, Georgia, USA. He married (1) **LAURA BENNETT** on 30 Jan 1985 in Athens, GA. He married (2) **HANNAH HINELY** in 1996 in Decatur, De Kalb, Georgia, USA. She was born on 28 Apr 1971 in Decatur, De Kalb, Georgia, USA.

Christopher Alan Tiegreen and Laura Bennett had the following children:

+14. i.   JONATHAN REPPARD⁴ TIEGREEN was born on 17 Jul 1987 in Jefferson, Kentucky, USA. He married MATTIE.

15. ii.   CHRISTOPHER TIEGREEN.

Christopher Alan Tiegreen and Hannah Hinely had the following child:

16. i.   TIMOTHY⁴ TIEGREEN was born on 01 Nov 1998 in Decatur, De Kalb, Georgia, USA.

Above: Timothy Tiegreen in 2013.
From Alan Tiegreen Collection.

10. CARL HURT³ TIEGREEN (Alan Frederick², Bessie Amanda¹ Taylor, Alan Frederick², Carl Mandeville, Otto Fredrick Johansson) was born on 06 May 1968 in Decatur, De Kalb, Georgia, USA. He married Wendy Bridget White on 28 Sep 1996 in Atlanta, Fulton, Georgia, USA (Lutheran Church of the Redeemer). She was born on 06 Jun 1969 in Spartanburg, Spartanburg, South Carolina, USA (Mary Black Hospital).

Carl Hurt Tiegreen and Wendy Bridget White had the following children:

17. i.   MADISON⁴ TIEGREEN was born on 13 Jul 2000 in Lilburn, Gwinnett, Georgia, USA.

18. ii.   REILLY SIMS TIEGREEN was born on 24 Jun 2003 in Lilburn, Gwinnett, Georgia, USA.

Left: Sisters Madison and Reilly Tiegreen pose together in 2015. From Alan Tiegreen Collection.

12. Rachel Allysa⁴ Seymour (Catherine Marie³ Tiegreen, Donald Richard² Tiegreen, Bessie Amanda¹ Taylor, Mark Stuart) was born on 28 Oct 1988 in Dallas, Texas, USA. She married Gunnar Hencmann on 25 May 2019. He was born on 16 Mar 1975.

Gunnar Hencmann and Rachel Allysa Seymour had the following child:
19. i. Luke James⁵ Hencmann was born on 25 Oct 2021.

14. Jonathan Reppard⁴ Tiegreen (Christopher Alan³, Alan Frederick², Bessie Amanda¹ Taylor, Christopher Alan³, Alan Frederick², Carl Mandeville, Otto Fredrick Johansson). He married **Mattie**.

Jonathan Tiegreen and Mattie had the following children:
20. i. Arlo Grey⁵ Tiegreen was born in Jun 2020.
21. ii. Zuri Tiegreen.

Chapter 6. Richard Lamuel Taylor and Mabel Ruth Crone

Richard L. Taylor

Generation 1

1. **RICHARD LAMUEL**[1] **TAYLOR** (Richard Thomas[18], Richard Lemuel[17], John Dennis[16], Dempsey[15], William Abraham Lawrence[14], William Nathaniel[13], James Henry "The Elder"[12] I, John William "The Immigrant"[11], Capt. Thomas John[10] II, Thomas John[9] I, Rev. Dr. Rowland[8], John Thomas[7], John William[6] I, William[5] II, Sir John[4], William[3] I, Sir John[2] Taylifer, Harger[1] Taylefer) was born on 17 May 1909 in Okemah, Okfuskee, Oklahoma, USA. He died on 30 May 2001 in Boise, Ada, Idaho, USA (age 92). He married Mabel Ruth Crone, daughter of Thomas Otha Crone and Carrie May Martin, on 10 Jan 1942 in Boise, Ada, Idaho, USA. She was born on 12 Jul 1918 in Stanton, Blaine, Idaho, USA (Little Wood River Valley). She died on 08 Dec 2008 in Boise, Ada, Idaho, USA.

Left: Portrait of "Dick" Taylor in Boise, Idaho about 1930. From Marjorie Taylor Collection.

Richard Lamuel Taylor lived in Okemah, Okfuskee, Oklahoma, USA in 1910 (Marital Status: Single; Relation to Head of House: Son). He was employed as a Farmer in 1930. He lived in White Cross, Ada, Idaho, USA in 1930 (Age: 20; Marital Status: Single; Relation to Head of House: Son). He lived in Union, Ada, Idaho, USA in 1940 (Age: 30; Occupation: Farming; Attended School: No; Class of Worker: Working on own account; Employment Code: 1; Employment Details: No; Employment History: No; Enumeration District: 1-51A; Grade Completed: Elementary school, 3rd grade; Is Employed: Yes; Public Emergency Work: No; Seeking Work: No; Marital Status: Married; Relation To Head: Son). He lived in Eagle, Ada, Idaho, USA in 1940 (Age: 31; Relation To Head: Self). He was described as Occupation: Self; Complexion: Ruddy; Eye Color: Blue; Hair Color: Brown; Height: 6'; Weight: 190 lbs on 16 Oct 1940. He was employed as a technician for Sea-Tac during WW II from 1942 to 1945 in Tacoma, Pierce, Washington, USA. He lived in Boise, Idaho, USA in 1950 (Street Address: 4702 Albion; Occupation: Salesman). He lived in Idaho Falls, Bonneville, Idaho, USA in 1951 (Age: 42). He lived in Boise, Ada, Idaho, USA in 1956. He lived in Boise, Ada, Idaho, USA in 2001. He was buried on 04 Jun 2001 in Boise, Ada, Idaho, USA (Morris Hill Cemetery, (Plot R-29-2); Find A Grave #55599360). He was also known as Dick. He was employed as an Electronics Technician, Mountain Home AFB in Elmore, Idaho, USA. Race: (White)

Richard Lamuel Taylor was named after his grandfather Richard Lemuel Taylor, with two significant differences. First of all, Richard always used his first name or his nickname "Dick," and his middle name Lamuel was spelled with an "a." Secondly his grandfather never used his first name, always using his middle name "LEM-uel," and was nicknamed "LAM." Dick was Richard Thomas and Roxie Ann's fourth child, their first boy, and the first of four children born in Oklahoma.

Right: Dick Taylor holds his twin nieces, Sara and Sue Lucas, at the Taylor's Brookover Farm in Boise, Idaho about 1935. From Marjorie Taylor Collection.

Dick grew up in Oklahoma helping his father on the farm. When he was 16 years old the family moved west and he and his younger brother Artice drove the truck with all their belongings, arriving in Boise, Idaho in 1928. Dick and Art continued to help their father work his Brookover Farm, Limp Ranch, and Eagle Ranch properties until their father retired in 1943 and auctioned off all his property and equipment.

Dick met his future wife Mabel Crone at the Cash Bazaar in Boise, where she worked, and they married in 1942. During World War II, Dick was a technician for Sea-Tac in Tacoma, Washington and for the last 25 years before retirement was an Electronics Technician at Mountain Home Air Force Base in southern Idaho. Early in their marriage they saved to build a home. As Mabel's Nephew Dave Crone explained:

> They lived frugally on Mabel's salary and used Dick's salary to build the house. When it was complete they moved in . . . no mortgage. Then a few years later, and I believe Mabel was now working for Pacific Finance, they decided to start another house right next door. The same thing again . . . no mortgage, and then they sold their original home . . . (Crone, 2008, p. 2).

Left: Dick and his father RT Taylor (right) return from fishing with Dick's nieces, Sara (left), Wanda and Sue Lucas, at the Taylor's Eagle Ranch near Boise, Idaho 1937. From Sara Lucas Gilstrap Collection.

After they retired, Dick and his wife Mabel spent many summers traveling the northwest and western Canada with their camp trailer, where they enjoyed fishing and rock hounding. In the winter they would travel to Arizona to rockhound near Quartzite and Yuma. They worked side-by-side polishing, cutting, and faceting prize-winning gemstones and jewelry. Many family members and friends received beautiful items of jewelry as gifts. Dick and Mabel became life members of the Idaho Gem Club, Idaho Wood Carvers, and Capital Gypsies Chapter of the Good Sam RV Club.

At home in Boise, Dick had the perfect workshop and was always making home improvements. His sister Marjorie remembered, "He built his own first radio, and everybody came and listened; the neighbors and everybody" (Taylor M. , 2015, p. 34:21). They enjoyed their bountiful flower and vegetable gardens. Dick and Mabe were always together, enjoying each other, two but really one. After 59 years with his wife Mabel, Dick passed on in 2001.

Mabel Ruth Crone was born on 12 Jul 1918 in Stanton, Blaine, Idaho, USA (Little Wood River Valley) as the third child of Thomas Otha Crone and Carrie May Martin. She had three siblings, namely: Lena May, Thomas Arthur, and Capt. William Delbert. She died on 08 Dec 2008 in Boise, Ada, Idaho, USA. When she was 23, she married Richard Lamuel Taylor, son of Richard Thomas Taylor and Roxie Ann Gibbs, on 10 Jan 1942 in Boise, Ada, Idaho, USA.

Right: *Mabel Crone and Dick Taylor at the Taylor Family Reunion at Palisades Lake, Idaho. Author photo Aug 1975.*

Mabel Ruth Crone lived in Stanton, Blaine, Idaho, USA in 1920 (Age: 1; Enumeration District: 92; Marital Status: Single; Relation To Head: Daughter). She lived in Franklin, Ada, Idaho, USA in 1930 (Street Address: 2nd St; Age: 11; Able To Speak English: Yes; Attended School: Yes; Can Read Write: Yes; Enumeration District: 0034; Registration District: 34; Marital Status: Single; Relation To Head: Daughter). She lived in Franklin, Ada, Idaho, USA in 1935. She graduated in 1936 in Boise, Ada, Idaho, USA (Franklin High School). She graduated in 1936 in Boise, Ada, Idaho, USA (Boise Secretarial School). She lived in Franklin, Ada, Idaho, USA in 1940 (StreetAddress: 2nd St South; Age: 21; Occupation: Clerk; AttendedSchool: No; ClassofWorker: Wage or salary worker in private work; EmploymentCode: 1; Employment Details: No; Employmen tHistory: No; EnumerationDistrict: 1-34B; GradeCompleted: High School, 4th year; Hours Worked: 48; Income: 650; IncomeOtherSources: No; IsEmployed: Yes; PublicEmergencyWork: No; SeekingWork: No; WeeksWorked: 49; MaritalStatus: Single; RelationToHead: Daughter). She lived in Boise, Ada, Idaho, USA in 1941

(StreetAddress: 2nd St South; Occupation: Saleswoman). She lived in Boise, Ada, Idaho, USA in 1950 (StreetAddress: 4702 Albion). She lived in Ada, Idaho, USA in 1950 (StreetAddress: Albion; Age: 39; Occupation: Clerk; ApartmentNumber: Grandon; ClassofWorker: Private; EnumerationDistrict: 1-76B; HoursWorked: 40; Industry: Dept Store; LiveOnFarm: No; OccupationCategory: Working; ThreeOrMoreAcres: No; RelationToHead: Wife; MaritalStatus: Married). She was employed as a Pacific Finance Mortgage Company employee in 1960 in Boise, Ada, Idaho, USA. She was buried on 12 Dec 2008 in Boise, Ada, Idaho, USA (Morris Hill Cemetery, (Plot R-29-2); Find A Grave #55599302). She was also known as Mabe. Race: (White).

Left: Dick Taylor and Mabel Crone (Dick and Mabe) in the second house they built in Boise, Idaho, 2000. From Marjorie Taylor Collection.

Mabel or "Mabe" as she was known, was born on a farm in south central Idaho's Little Wood River Valley. In 1929 when she was 9 years old the family moved to the city of Boise where she graduated in 1936 from Franklin High School. That same year Mabe also graduated from the Boise Secretarial School. A few years later, when she was working for the Cash Bazaar she met her future husband Richard Taylor whom she married in 1942, a marriage that would last for 59 years until Dick's death in 2001.

Their marriage could have ended abruptly as Mabe soon found that she could not have children and had to have a hysterectomy when she was about age 23. Nevertheless, misfortune just seemed to strengthen Dick and Mabe's relationship. Whether it was camping, fishing, rock hounding, gardening or jewelry making, Mabe was always there to assist and support as her nephew Dave Crone tells us in the following story:

When they went on a Jamboree in later years Dick thought he was still a good driver. But he scared the b-Jesus out of Mabe so she would drive. But when she got within two miles of the rendezvous she would pull over and have Dick get behind the wheel and drive on in. That gesture says a lot about their relationship and the respect they had for one another. (Crone, 2008, p. 3).

Right: This photo of Dick Taylor, Mabel Crone, and Dick's sister Nettie Taylor (on right) was taken the same year that Dick and Mabe were married, 1942. From Marjorie Taylor Collection.

Mabe grew up with an older sister Lena and two brothers, Thomas Arthur "Art," and William Delbert "Del" Crone. Del enlisted in the Army during World War II and became a fighter pilot and captain with the 334th Fighter-Interceptor Squadron during the Korean War. In 1951 his plane was shot down over North Korea and for the next seven years he was listed as missing in action (MIA) before being declared killed in action (KIA). After Mabe's husband Dick passed on, she starting working with her nephew's son Del to determine the history of her brother Captain Del Crone's death in the Korean War. Mabe even sent a DNA sample to the U.S. Defense Department's POW/MIA Accounting Agency. But that was Mabe. Always helping, always assisting, always supporting.

Richard Lamuel Taylor and Mabel Ruth Crone had no children.

Chapter 7. Artice Raymond Taylor and Hazel Florence McClure

Artice R Taylor

Generation 1

1. ARTICE RAYMOND[1] TAYLOR (Richard Thomas[A], Richard Lemuel[B], John Dennis[C], Dempsey[D], William Abraham Lawrence[E], William Nathaniel[F], James Henry "The Elder"[G] I, John William "The Immigrant"[H], Capt. Thomas John[I] II, Thomas John[J] I, Rev. Dr. Rowland[K], John Thomas[L], John William[M] I, William[N] II, Sir John[O], William[P] I, Sir John[Q] Taylifer, Harger[R] Taylefer) was born on 13 Oct 1911 in Okemah, Okfuskee, Oklahoma, USA. He died on 02 May 2006 in Boise, Ada, Idaho, USA (age 94). He married **Hazel Florence McClure**, daughter of Joseph Taylor McClure and Thursa Henry, on 02 Mar 1935 in Meridian, Ada, Idaho, USA. She was born on 05 Oct 1910 in Harrison, Boone, Arkansas, USA. She died on 02 Jul 1990 in Boise, Ada, Idaho, USA.

Right: Art Taylor's high school graduation portrait, May 1933. From Art Taylor Collection.

Artice Raymond Taylor lived in White Cross, Ada, Idaho, USA in 1930 (Age: 18; Marital Status: Single; Relation to Head of House: Son). He graduated in Jun 1933 in Boise, Ada, Idaho, USA (Franklin High School with his younger sister Nettie). He lived in Boise, Ada, Idaho, USA in 1935 (Fairgrounds Manager). He lived in Ada, Idaho, USA in 1940 (Age: 28; Occupation: Salesman; Attended School: No; Class of Worker: Wage or salary worker in private work; Employment Code: 1; Employment Details: No; Employment History: No; Enumeration District: 1-32; Grade Completed: High School, 4th year; Home Ownership: Owned; Hours Worked: 63; Income: 1320; Income Other Sources: No; Is Employed: Yes; Owns Farm: No; Public Emergency Work: No; Seeking Work: No; Value Of Home: 1900; Weeks Worked: 52; MaritalStatus: Married; RelationToHead: Head). He was employed as a Western Auto Supply Salesman on 16 Oct 1940 in Boise, Ada, Idaho, USA. He was described as Complexion: Ruddy; EyeColor: Brown; HairColor: Brown; Height: 5' 10"; Weight: 190 lbs on 16 Oct 1940 in Boise, Ada, Idaho, USA. He lived in Ogden, Weber, Utah, USA in 1950 (StreetAddress: Washington; Age 38; Store Supervisor Occupation: Store Supervisor; ApartmentNumber: Office; ClassofWorker: Private; EnumerationDistrict: 29-86;

Hours Worked: 60; Industry: General Hardware and Merchandize; Live On Farm: No; Occupation Category: Working; Three Or More Acres: No; Head Relation To Head: Head; Marital Status: Married). He lived in Idaho, USA in 1951. He lived in Idaho Falls, Bonneville, Idaho, USA in 1954 (Occupation: Manager). He was employed as a KOA Campground Landman in 1966 in Billings, Yellowstone, Montana, USA. He lived in Billings, Yellowstone, Montana, USA in 1966 (185 Valleyview Drive). He was buried on 05 May 2006 in Meridian, Ada, Idaho, USA (Meridian Cemetery (Sec B, Blk 305, Lot 4); Find A Grave #67111788). He was also known as Art, Patrice. His cause of death was cancer. Race: (White).

From left: Dick and Art Taylor stand in front of their 1931 Model A Ford at the Limp Ranch near Meridian, Idaho while RT Taylor looks on from the porch. From Marjorie Taylor Collection.

Art was born in Oklahoma in 1911, two years after Richard Thomas and Roxie Ann Taylor's older son Richard Lamuel (Dick) Taylor. He grew up fast, learning to drive a tractor at about eight or nine years old. When the family moved west from Oklahoma, Art helped his older brother Dick drive their 3-ton truck with all their belongings to the Boise Valley in 1928. On the way, they spent almost a year in Farmington, New Mexico, working for the government building a dam. Art's son Dennis says, "They were hired to work on the dam and my Dad, at age 15, was hired to drive their own truck to haul dirt and equipment. They were paid top dollar for those days." (Taylor D. , Taylor Clan Family History, 2021).

Left: Art Taylor holding Pacific salmon. From Marjorie Taylor Collection.

When they reached Idaho in 1928 Art and his older brother Dick continued to work with their father on the family farm. After the farm started producing, Art was able to attend Meridian High School, where he met his future wife Hazel McClure. Hazel, like Art, had moved to Idaho in the late 1920s. After dropping out again to work on the farm, Art returned to high school, and in 1933 he graduated with his younger sister Nettie from Franklin High School. Two years later, Art and Hazel were married, a union that gave them two children and lasted for the next 55 years until Hazel died at age 79.

One of Art's first jobs off the farm was managing the county fairgrounds. But Art also loved to meet people and was a natural salesman. So, in 1935 he became a sales agent and later a district manager for Western Auto Supply for the next 16 years with Hazel as his secretary while they raised their children in Boise, Idaho Falls, and Ogden, Utah. In 1948, Art and Hazel purchased the Ogden Motor Lodge. Hazel managed the Lodge until 1951, while Art traveled for Western Auto. They then sold the lodge and moved back to Idaho Falls to become the owners of the Desoto/Plymouth automobile dealership, which later failed due to a recession. In 1958 they purchased the International Harvester Dealership in Jackson Hole, Wyoming (Taylor D. , Dennis Taylor Family History Video Interview, 2016, p. 25:48). Upon selling this dealership in 1961, they moved to Pocatello, Idaho, where Art continued working in the automobile industry with Hazel as his secretary.

In 1966, Art joined the KOA (Kampgrounds of America) Sales Department as a franchise salesman. In 1974, he moved to the KOA headquarters in Billings, Montana to begin selling existing campgrounds under the KOA option system. He was recognized as the $6 million dollar man for selling $6 million in operating campgrounds within one year.

Left: Art (left) and his father RT Taylor (right) with a stringer of trout at Art and Hazel's home in Idaho Falls in about 1945. From Dennis R. Taylor Collection.

Art and Hazel decided it was time to enjoy the things they loved. So Art retired and in 1979 they returned to the Boise Valley to be close to family and friends. Art loved the outdoors and spent his free time riding his favorite horse, Smoky, fishing in mountain lakes and streams, and trailering one of his many boats named Roamer to the northern tip of Vancouver Island, British Columbia to fish for Pacific salmon. Like his father, he loved to fish and tend his rose garden. Art held a lifetime membership in the Elks Club and was an active member of the U.S. Coast Guard Auxiliary in Boise. A highlight of his time in Boise was meeting with the Downtowner Coffee Bunch several times a week.

Hazel Florence McClure was born on 05 Oct 1910 in Harrison, Boone, Arkansas, USA as the first child of Joseph Taylor McClure and Thursa Henry. She died on 02 Jul 1990 in Boise, Ada, Idaho, USA. When she was 24, she married Artice Raymond Taylor, son of Richard Thomas Taylor and Roxie Ann Gibbs on 02 Mar 1935 in Meridian, Ada, Idaho, USA.

Hazel Florence McClure lived in Cowan, Lincoln, Colorado, USA in 1920. She lived in Meridian, Ada, Idaho, USA in 1930. She graduated in 1931 in Meridian, Ada, Idaho, USA (Meridian High School). She lived in Boise, Ada, Idaho, USA in 1935 (Fairgrounds employee). She lived in Boise, Idaho, USA in 1936. She lived in Fairgrounds Precinct, Ada, Idaho, USA in 1940 (Age 29; Attended School: No; Employment Code: 5; Employment Details: Home Housework; Employment History: No; Enumeration District: 1-32; Grade Completed: High School, 4th year; Income: 0; Income Other Sources: No; Is Employed: No; Public Emergency Work: No; Respondent: Yes; Seeking Work: No; Weeks Worked: 0; Marital Status: Married; Relation To Head: Wife). She lived in Ogden, Weber, Utah, USA in 1950 (Street Address: Washington; Age 39; Manager Occupation: Manager; Apartment Number: Office; Classo fWorker: Own Business; Enumeration District: 29-86; Hours Worked: 60; Industry: Motel; Live On Farm: No; Occupation Category: Working; ThreeOrMoreAcres: No; Wife RelationToHead: Wife; MaritalStatus: Married). She lived in Idaho Falls, Bonneville, Idaho,

USA in 1954. She was employed as a secretary/office manager in 1966. She was buried on 06 Jul 1990 in Meridian, Ada, Idaho, USA (Meridian Cemetery (Sec B, Blk 305, Lot 3); Find A Grave #67111777). Race: (White).

Left: Hazel McClure portrait from the 1950s. From Marjorie Taylor Collection.

Hazel McClure was one of four children born to Joe McClure and Thursa Henry. Although she was born in Arkansas, she spent her younger years on the cattle ranch the family homesteaded about 60 miles east of Colorado Springs, Colorado. In a handwritten letter Hazel later described her life on the Colorado plains:

Our lives in the high desert country was at times lonely but for the most part we really enjoyed good neighbors and everyone entered in to the effort to keep things going. We had Sunday school . . . We also had Sunday after noon baseball games; and about once a month we would have an all nite dance in someone's new barn loft or in the two-room school house. . . We had our own music made up by some of our family members. My dad on the violin, one aunt on the piano, 2 uncles on guitars and a Bohemian man on the accordion. I filled in on the piano when my Aunt could not be there . . . Those dances sometimes lasted until 4 o'clock in the morn. Every one would bring a covered dish and at midnite we would eat. (Taylor D. , Taylor Clan Family History, 2014).

After five years of drought turning farms into dustbowls, most of these homesteaders moved on. In 1926, Hazel moved with her family to Meridian, Idaho just west of Boise. In 1931 Hazel graduated from Meridian High School, then LaSalle Business School and began working for the Meridian Creamery.

In 1935, she married Art Taylor and soon began helping Art as his secretary, office manager, and even managing their motel in Ogden, Utah; all while raising their two children. By 1951 Hazel was on the Board of Directors of the Idaho Motel and Hotel Association. In 1958 when the family moved to Jackson, Wyoming, she managed Art's farm machinery business office. In 1966, she was Art's secretary in his association with the KOA campground headquarters and traveled throughout the United States for several years.

Right: Art and Hazel Taylor (on left) with son Dennis and daughter Arlene at the Taylor Family Reunion at Palisades Lake, Idaho. Author photo Aug 1975.

Hazel retired with Art in 1979 and moved back to Boise, Idaho. By then she was a member of the Idaho Falls Business Women's Association and the Jackson Women's Business Association.

Artice Raymond Taylor and Hazel Florence McClure had the following children:

+2. i.   DENNIS RAYMOND² TAYLOR was born on 29 Aug 1937 in Boise, Ada, Idaho, USA. He married Lela Kaye Waddoups, daughter of Ralph Owen Waddoups and Nancy Fern Whiting, on 13 Sep 1957 in Idaho Falls, Bonneville, Idaho, USA (Idaho Falls LDS Temple). She was born on 14 Mar 1937 in Idaho Falls, Bonneville, Idaho, USA.

+3. ii. ARLENE HAZEL TAYLOR was born on 27 Jun 1942 in Idaho Falls, Bonneville, Idaho, USA. She died on 23 Nov 2019 in Boise, Ada, Idaho, USA. She married (1) DONALD DELL EVANS on 22 Aug 1964 in Idaho Falls, Bonneville, Idaho, USA. He was born in 1940 in Lewistown, Fergus, Montana, USA. She married (2) NEIL JEROME PARISOT, son of Albert Holland Parisot Sr and Elizabeth Patricia Mooney, on 15 Jul 1966 in Coeur d'Alene, Kootenai County, Idaho, USA. He was born on 24 Apr 1940 in Butte, Silver Bow, Montana, USA. He died on 22 Mar 2018 in Helena, Lewis and Clark, Montana, USA (St. Peter's Hospital).

Right: Dennis R. Taylor's children and grandchildren celebrate with their parents Lela and Dennis R. Taylor (sitting) and Grandad Art Taylor (on right) in 1993. From Art Taylor Collection.

Generation 2

2. DENNIS RAYMOND[2] TAYLOR (Artice Raymond[1], Richard Thomas[A], Richard Lemuel[B], John Dennis[C], Dempsey[D], William Abraham Lawrence[E], William Nathaniel[F], James Henry "The Elder"[G] I, John William "The Immigrant"[H], Capt. Thomas John[I] II, Thomas John[J] I, Rev. Dr. Rowland[K], John Thomas[L], John William[M] I, William[N] II, Sir John[O], William[P] I, Sir John[Q] Taylifer, Harger[R] Taylefer) was born on 29 Aug 1937 in Boise, Ada, Idaho, USA. He married **Lela Kaye Waddoups** on 13 Sep 1957 in Idaho Falls, Bonneville, Idaho, USA (Idaho Falls LDS Temple). She was born on 14 Mar 1937 in Idaho Falls, Bonneville, Idaho, USA.

Dennis Raymond Taylor lived in Fairgrounds Precinct, Fair Grounds, Ada, Idaho, USA in 1940 (Age: 2; Attended School: No; Enumeration District: 1-32; Grade Completed: None; Income: 0; Income Other Sources: No; Weeks Worked: 0; Marital Status: Single; Relation To Head: Son). He lived in Ogden, Weber, Utah, USA in 1950 (Street Address: Washington; 12 Age: 12; Apartment Number: Office; Enumeration District: 29-86; Live On Farm: No; Three Or More Acres: No; Son RelationToHead: Son; Never Married MaritalStatus: Single). He lived in Boise, Ada, Idaho, USA in 1979. He lived in Bountiful, Davis, Utah, USA in 1984. He lived in Salt Lake City, Utah, USA about 1990 (StreetAddress: 660 S 200 E). He lived in Bountiful, UT in 1994; StreetAddress: 958 Chelsea Dr; age 57). He lived in Las Vegas, Clark, Nevada, USA in 2004 (StreetAddress: 10636 Mission Lakes Ave; Age: 67; StreetAddress: 3712 W Teton St; StreetAddress: 958 Chelsea Dr). He tested his DNA on 22 Nov 2018 (Mary Guerra Shared DNA: 1,001 cM across 38 segments). DNA Match: 07 Jan 2017 (1st cousin to Mary Guerra). Race: (White).

Left: Dennis (center) visits Grandad RT Taylor in Boise, Idaho with his parents Hazel and Art Taylor about 1941. From Art Taylor Collection.

Dennis was the first of Art and Hazel Taylor's two children, born in Boise, Idaho while Art was managing the county fairgrounds. The family soon moved to Idaho Falls, where Dennis grew up and where his future wife Lela was born. But Dennis has many memories as a child of their visit every summer and again at Christmas to grandfather RT Taylor's house on Orchard Street in Boise. As Dennis recalled:

> I remember him always having at back of the stove a pot of green beans with bacon and good stuff in there, and he never refrigerated it, it just sat at the back and he'd warm it up and put some of that stuff in different food, and that was just kind of probably a Georgia thing (Taylor D. , Dennis Taylor Family History Video Interview, 2016, p. 11:11).

Dennis graduated from Utah State University in 1959, the first in his family to go to college. His father soon talked him into coming to Jackson, Wyoming to help him run his International Harvester Dealership. However, less than two years later in 1961 they lost the lease on the building. Art had to close the business and moved to Pocatello to run the GMC dealership. Dennis, meanwhile, followed a career path with Bell Telephone Company for whom he worked until his retirement.

Among Dennis' hobbies is genealogy, which he became interested in while they were living in Boise about 1975. Fortunately during a family reunion at his father's summer home on Palisades Reservoir that year, he was able to finally find out from his older aunts that the RT Taylor family left Georgia because RT had a run-in with his older brother James H. Taylor. Today, Dennis Raymond Taylor has a family history website that presents photos and information about the four family lines that make up the ancestry of the Dennis Raymond Taylor family (Taylor D. , Taylor Clan Family History, 2021).

Dennis Taylor and Lela Waddoups
Above left: 1956 portrait. Above right: 1957 wedding.
Above: 2016 portrait. From Marjorie Taylor Collection.

Lela Kaye Waddoups was born on 14 Mar 1937 in Idaho Falls, Bonneville, Idaho, USA. When she was 20, she married Dennis Raymond Taylor, son of Artice Raymond Taylor and Hazel Florence McClure, on 13 Sep 1957 in Idaho Falls, Bonneville, Idaho, USA (Idaho Falls LDS Temple).

Lela Kaye Waddoups lived in Menan Precinct (Outside of Village of Menan), Menan, Jefferson, Idaho, USA in 1940 (Age: 3; AttendedSchool: No; EnumerationDistrict: 26-11; GradeCompleted: None; MaritalStatus: Single; RelationToHead: Daughter). She lived in Provo, Utah, Utah, USA in 1956 (BYU Yearbook; Age: 20). She lived in Idaho Falls, Bonneville, Idaho, USA in 1957 (StreetAddress: 1525 12th St). She lived in Bountiful, Davis, Utah, USA in 1984. She lived in Bountiful, Davis, Utah, USA in 1993; StreetAddress: 958 Chelsea Dr; age 56). She lived in Las Vegas, Clark, Nevada, USA in 2004 (StreetAddress: 10636 Mission Lakes Ave; Age 67; StreetAddress: 958 Chelsea Dr. Race: (White).

Lela Waddoups grew up in a family of five children whose parents met each other when they were Idaho school teachers. Her mother Fern was also known for her many recipes for a variety of meals and desserts. Nevertheless, the family did make time to teach Lela and her siblings not only how to cook, but also how to ski, skate, swim, and fish.

Dennis Raymond Taylor and Lela Kaye Waddoups had the following children:

+4.   i.   TAMMI[3] TAYLOR was born on 01 Oct 1959. She married Bradley J Utter on 13 Jun 1992 in Idaho Falls, Bonneville, Idaho, USA (Idaho Falls LDS Temple). He was born on 10 Dec 1957.

+5.   ii. KURT RAYMOND TAYLOR was born on 01 Apr 1964 in Idaho Falls, Bonneville, Idaho, USA. He married Renee Christine Pecora on 19 Dec 1987 in Salt Lake City, Salt Lake, Utah, USA (Salt Lake City LDS Temple).

Left: Four generations of Taylor mothers meet in 1983, from left: Tammi Taylor, Hazel McClure, baby Ann Taylor, and Fern Whiting. From Dennis R. Taylor Collection.

3.   ARLENE HAZEL[2] TAYLOR (Artice Raymond[1], Richard Thomas[A], Richard Lemuel[B], John Dennis[C], Dempsey[D], William Abraham Lawrence[E], William Nathaniel[F], James Henry "The Elder"[G] I, John William "The Immigrant"[H], Capt. Thomas John[I] II, Thomas John[J] I, Rev. Dr. Rowland[K], John Thomas[L], John William[M] I, William[N] II, Sir John[O], William[P] I, Sir John[Q] Taylifer, Harger[R] Taylefer) was born on 27 Jun 1942 in Idaho Falls, Bonneville, Idaho, USA. She died on 23 Nov 2019 in Boise, Ada, Idaho, USA. . She married (1) **DONALD DELL EVANS** on 22 Aug 1964 in Idaho Falls, Bonneville, Idaho, USA. He was born in 1940 in Lewistown, Fergus, Montana, USA. She married (2) **NEIL JEROME PARISOT**, son of Albert Holland Parisot Sr and Elizabeth Patricia Mooney, on 15 Jul 1966 in Coeur d'Alene, Kootenai County, Idaho, USA. He was born on 24 Apr 1940 in Butte, Silver Bow, Montana, USA. He died on 22 Mar 2018 in Helena, Lewis and Clark, Montana, USA (St. Peter's Hospital).

Arlene Hazel Taylor lived in Ogden, Weber, Utah, USA in 1950 (StreetAddress: Washington; 7 Age: 7; ApartmentNumber: Office; AttendedSchool: Yes; EnumerationDistrict: 29-86; GradeCompleted: No; LiveOnFarm: No; SchoolYearsCompleted: S2; ThreeOrMoreAcres: No; SameHouse: Yes; Daughter RelationToHead: Daughter; Never Married MaritalStatus: Single). She graduated in 1960 in Idaho Falls, Bonneville, Idaho, USA (Idaho Falls High School). She received a BA (Education) degree in 1966 at Idaho State University. She lived in Pocatello, Bannock, Idaho, USA in 1966 (514 South Tenth). She lived in Great Falls, Cascade, Montana, USA in 1983. She received an MA degree in 1993 at Montana State University-Northern (MSU-Northern). She lived in Great Falls, Cascade, Montana, USA in 1993. She received a PhD degree in 1995 at MSU-Northern. She was employed as a Montana

Commission of Higher Education director of workforce planning between 1999–2008 in Helena, Lewis and Clark, Montana, USA. She lived in Helena, Lewis and Clark, Montana, USA in 2001 (Street Address: 748 S California Street). She tested her DNA in 2018 (Mary Guerra Shared DNA: 964 cM across 47 segments). DNA Match: 2018 (1st cousin to Mary Guerra). She was cremated on 24 Nov 2019 in Boise, Ada, Idaho, USA. She was buried on 17 Sep 2021 with her husband in Helena, Lewis and Clark, Montana, USA at the Montana State Veterans Cemetery (Sec C, Row 15, Plot 85); Find A Grave #215744422. Her cause of death was a stroke. Race: (White).

Born in 1942, four years after her older brother Dennis, Arlene grew up in Idaho and in Jackson Hole, Wyoming and loved to tell stories about skiing in Jackson Hole during the winter and horseback riding during the summer. A favorite memory was when she and some friends modeled ski gear for the November 15, 1965 issue of *Sports Illustrated* magazine (Sports Illustrated, 1965, pp. 74-76). Her brother Dennis admired her accomplishments as a horse rider, "We had horses when we were teenagers after we moved back from Ogden to Idaho Falls. That was in about 1951. Arlene rode in rodeos and did a lot of things with the horses." (Taylor D. , Dennis Taylor Family History Video Interview, 2016, p. 01:58).

Left: Arlene Taylor (on right) and friends model ski clothing near Jackson Hole, Wyoming. Courtesy Sports Illustrated magazine.

Arlene met her husband Neil when they both attended Idaho State University in the 1960s. They were married in 1966 in Coeur d'Alene, Idaho. Arlene and Neil started a family and began a series of moves that would span over thirty years and take them around the world. With their two sons, they lived and worked in numerous cities in the United States, Japan, Germany and Turkey, gathering experiences that would be retold during family gatherings and celebrations over the 51 years they were married.

Education was a driving force in Arlene's life. She first attended Utah State University, then completed a bachelor's degree in education at Idaho State University in 1966. Arlene received a Master of Arts degree from Montana State University-Northern in 1993, and a Doctorate in Education from Montana State University in 1995. She taught school in most places she lived. Overseas, she worked for the American School in Japan, the U.S. Department of Defense Dependent Schools at Hahn Air Base, West Germany as well as adjunct faculty for the Universities of Oklahoma and Maryland in their programs on military installations in Europe. Arlene taught extensively in Great Falls and held many positions with the MSU College of Technology-Great Falls. An article she coauthored about teaching classes with new television technology was published in a national magazine. In 1999 Arlene joined the staff of the Montana Commissioner of Higher Education as the director of workforce planning where she developed higher education programs until her retirement in 2008.

Right: Portrait of Arlene Taylor and Neil Parisot about the time they were married in 1966. From Art Taylor Collection.

Next to education, Arlene contributed her time and talent to the Democratic Party. In 1997, she was elected chairwoman of the Cascade County Democratic Central Committee and eastern district co-chairperson of the Montana State Democratic Party executive board. She volunteered, supported, wrote letters, and knocked on doors for many Democrats throughout her lifetime.

As many others in the Taylor family, Arlene was also a talented artist, focusing primarily in watercolors and abstract paintings. She exhibited in many art shows, at one point showing a watercolor technique using synthetic paper that evaporates water from the paint rather than absorbing it, leaving a vivid image. In 2008 she was appointed to the Montana Arts Council by then-Governor Brian Schweitzer, and was reappointed twice by Governor Steve Bullock. Besides creating artwork, she was active in her community promoting the visibility of art, including working with the Art Center of Helena among others.

Arlene was extremely active, enjoying particularly skiing, running, and hiking the public access trails around Helena. She loved dogs and kids. She was extremely proud of her two sons and grandchildren and they were her pride and joy. She was an excellent cook who loved to have dinner parties and try new recipes. Her friends said she was one of the most creative and nicest people you would ever meet. She developed a dynamic network of close friends she loved to socialize with, especially when it included live music and dancing. It was always fun with Arlene.

Neil Jerome Parisot was born on 24 Apr 1940 in Butte, Silver Bow, Montana, USA the youngest of five children of Albert Holland Parisot Sr. and Elizabeth Patricia Mooney. He died on 22 Mar 2018 in Helena, Lewis and Clark, Montana, USA (St. Peter's Hospital). When he was 26, he married Arlene Hazel Taylor, daughter of Artice Raymond Taylor and Hazel Florence McClure, on 15 Jul 1966 in Coeur d'Alene, Kootenai County, Idaho, USA.

Neil Jerome Parisot lived in Pocatello, Bannock, Idaho, USA in 1950 (Street Address: N 7th; Age: 9; Apartment Number: Nov; Enumeration District: 3-22; Live On Farm: No; Three Or More Acres: No; Son Relation To Head: Son; Marital Status: Single). He lived in Pocatello, Bannock, Idaho, USA in 1956 (Age: 16). He graduated in 1959 in Pocatello, Bannock, Idaho, USA (Pocatello High School). He served in the military between 1959 and 1962 at Fort

Devens, Massachusetts (SPC 4, US Army Security Agency). He received a BA degree in 1966 at Idaho State University. He lived in Pocatello, Bannock, Idaho, USA in 1966 (514 S 10th; Employer: Simplot; Occupation: Student). He received an MA degree in 1968 at the University of Nebraska. He lived in Helena, Lewis and Clark, Montana, USA in 1983 (StreetAddress: 748 S California St; age 43; StreetAddress: 3130 7th St; StreetAddress: 98 Sun River Rd Apt 1061; StreetAddress: 426 Fee St). He lived in Great Falls, Cascade, Montana, USA in 1992. He lived in Helena, Lewis and Clark, Montana, USA in 1996 (StreetAddress: 1931 9th Ave; StreetAddress: RR 1061; StreetAddress: 98 Sun River Rd # 1061). He lived in Helena, Lewis and Clark, Montana, USA in 2001 (StreetAddress: 748 S California St; PhoneNumber: 406-495-0831). He was buried on 11 May 2018 in Helena, Lewis and Clark, Montana, USA (MT State Veterans Cemetery (Sec C, Row 15, Plot 85); Find A Grave #189467470). His cause of death was congestive heart failure (family history). Race: (White).

Neil's father Albert was born and raised in Walkerville, Montana and Neil was born in nearby Butte, the fifth child born to a family of three brothers and one sister. Soon after his birth, the family moved to Pocatello, Idaho, where Neil graduated from Pocatello High School in 1959. After high school, he joined the US Army and was stationed at Fort Devens, Massachusetts.

Neil also served a tour of duty in the Army Security Agency in Southeast Asia including Vietnam. His total active service was 3 years after which he was honorably discharged.

Left: Arlene and Neil with their grandchildren, Christmas, 2012. From left: Arlene, Reilly, Neil, Maia, and Taylor. From Art Taylor Collection.

Higher education was always a major priority for Neil. However while going to college at Idaho State University in Pocatello, he noticed a young girl in one of his classes and wanted to meet her. That girl was Arlene Taylor who eventually became his wife, but only after a long period of time getting to know each other. Quick decisions were not part of their courtship. He had to travel to her hometown of Jackson Hole, Wyoming to offer his proposal for marriage. They both received bachelor's degrees in 1966 and they married that same year. By 1970 Neil and Arlene had become the proud parents of two boys. After they finished their bachelor's degrees, Neil obtained a full scholarship to the University of Nebraska and completed his master's degree there in about 1970.

Soon after, Neil began his federal career for the US Air Force as a Chief Education Officer at several Air Force Bases including: Mountain Home (Idaho); Luke (Arizona); Malmstrom (Montana); Yokota (Japan); and Hahn (West Germany). His family moved along with Neil and enjoyed many wonderful world travel experiences during this time. His last assignment was Education Officer at Izmir Air Base (Turkey). Upon returning from Turkey in about 1999, Neil retired after thirty years of service as a Federal employee.

Favorite activities for Neil, Arlene, and their two sons included traveling within foreign countries and the United States. Neil also was an avid reader, he could easily read several books in a week's time and move on to others, both fiction and non-fiction. He also enjoyed engaging in discussions related to various issues verging on the edge of debate. He usually won.

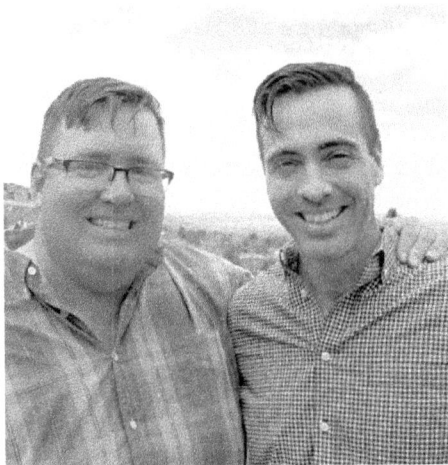

Left: Brothers George (left) and Peter Parisot in Helena, Montana. Author photo 12 May 2018.

Donald Dell Evans and Arlene Hazel Taylor had no children.

Neil Jerome Parisot and Arlene Hazel Taylor had the following children:

+6.	i.	GEORGE EDMOND[3] PARISOT was born on 24 Apr 1968 in Pocatello, Bannock, Idaho, USA. He married (1) JULIE WALKER on 20 Jun 2020 in Helena, Lewis and Clark, Montana, USA (at home). She was born on 27 Apr 1968 in Great Falls, Cascade, Montana, USA (Deaconess Hospital). He married (2) TAWNA LYNN MELDRUM on 18 Feb 1995 in Great Falls, Cascade, Montana, USA. She was born on 14 Nov 1971 in Havre, Hill, Montana, USA.

7.	ii.	PETER PARISOT was born on 30 Dec 1970 in Lincoln, Antelope, Nebraska, USA. He married Benjamin Richard Nystrom on 04 Oct 2015 in Canby, Clackamas, Oregon, USA. He was born on 03 Mar 1983 in Medford, Jackson, Oregon, USA.

Generation 3

4. TAMMI[3] TAYLOR (Dennis Raymond[2], Artice Raymond[1], Richard Thomas[4], Richard Lemuel[B], John Dennis[C], Dempsey[D], William Abraham Lawrence[E], William Nathaniel[F], James Henry "The Elder"[G] I, John William "The Immigrant"[H], Capt. Thomas John[I] II, Thomas John[J] I, Rev. Dr. Rowland[K], John Thomas[L], John William[M] I, William[N] II, Sir John[O], William[P] I, Sir John[Q] Taylifer, Harger[R] Taylefer) was born on 01 Oct 1959. She married Bradley Jay Utter on 13 Jun 1992 in Idaho Falls, Bonneville, Idaho, USA (Idaho Falls LDS Temple). He was born on 10 Dec 1957. She tested her DNA in 2018 (Mary Guerra Shared DNA: 500 cM across 21 segments). DNA Match: 2018 (Mary Guerra 1st cousin 1x removed). She was also known as Tammi Utter, Tammi Radford.

Bradley J. Utter and Tammi Taylor had the following child:

+8. i. ANN TAYLOR[4] RADFORD was born on 26 Dec 1982 in Idaho Falls, Bonneville, Idaho, USA. She married James Orrin Rockwell Porter on 10 Mar 2007 in Idaho Falls, Bonneville, Idaho, USA (Idaho Falls LDS Temple). He was born in May 1984.

5. KURT RAYMOND[3] TAYLOR (Dennis Raymond[2], Artice Raymond[1], Richard Thomas[A], Richard Lemuel[B], John Dennis[C], Dempsey[D], William Abraham Lawrence[E], William Nathaniel[F], James Henry "The Elder"[G] I, John William "The Immigrant"[H], Capt. Thomas John[I] II, Thomas John[J] I, Rev. Dr. Rowland[K], John Thomas[L], John William[M] I, William[N] II, Sir John[O], William[P] I, Sir John[Q] Taylifer, Harger[R] Taylefer) was born on 01 Apr 1964 in Idaho Falls, Bonneville, Idaho, USA. He married Renee Christine Pecora on 19 Dec 1987 in Salt Lake City, Salt Lake, Utah, USA (LDS Temple).

Kurt Raymond Taylor and Renee Christine Pecora had the following children:

9.   i.   ZACKARY DENNIS[4] TAYLOR was born on 28 Aug 1990 in Provo, Utah, Utah, USA.
10. ii. BRITTANY ANNE TAYLOR was born on 10 Apr 1993 in Salt Lake City, Salt Lake, Utah, USA.
11. iii. ZANE TAYLOR was born on 15 Dec 1997 in Idaho Falls, Bonneville, Idaho, USA.
12. iv. BRYSON KURT TAYLOR was born on 07 Jun 2002 in American Fork, Utah, Utah, USA.

6. GEORGE EDMOND[3] PARISOT (Arlene Hazel[2] Taylor, Artice Raymond[1] Taylor, Neil Jerome, Albert Holland Sr) was born on 24 Apr 1968 in Pocatello, Bannock, Idaho, USA. He married (1) **TAWNA LYNN MELDRUM** on 18 Feb 1995 in Great Falls, Cascade, Montana, USA. She was born on 14 Nov 1971 in Havre, Hill, Montana, USA. He married (2) **JULIE WALKER** on 20 Jun 2020 in Helena, Lewis and Clark, Montana, USA. She was born on 27 Apr 1968 in Great Falls, Cascade, Montana, USA (Deaconess Hospital). He tested his DNA (Mary Guerra Shared DNA: 535 cM across 24 segments). DNA Match: (1st cousin 1x removed to Mary Guerra).

George Edmond Parisot and Tawna Meldrum had the following children:

13. i.   REILLY STUART[4] PARISOT was born on 01 Sep 1995 in Great Falls, Cascade, Montana, USA.
14. ii. MAIA ELIZABETH PARISOT was born on 09 Jul 1998 in Helena, Lewis and Clark, Montana, USA (St Peters Hospital).
15. iii. TAYLOR LON PARISOT was born on 13 Oct 2004 in Helena, Lewis and Clark, Montana, USA (St Peters Hospital).

George and Peter Parisot with family and friends in Helena, Montana 25 Sep 2021.
Front, from left: Maia Parisot, Reilly Parisot, Taylor Parisot. Back, from left:
Tawna Meldrum, unknown, unknown, Peter Parisot, unknown, George Parisot, Julie Walker.
From Art Taylor Collection.

Generation 4

8. ANN TAYLOR⁴ RADFORD (Tammi³ Taylor, Dennis Raymond² Taylor, Artice Raymond¹ Taylor, Bradley Jay Utter) was born on 26 Dec 1982 in Idaho Falls, Bonneville, Idaho, USA. She married James Orrin Rockwell Porter on 10 Mar 2007 in Idaho Falls, Bonneville, Idaho, USA (Idaho Falls LDS Temple). He was born in May 1984. Although Ann was raised by her stepfather Bradley Utter, she uses her biological father's last name of Radford. She tested her DNA in 2018 (Mary Guerra Shared DNA: 3% 218 cM across 10 segments). DNA Match: 2018 (1st cousin 2x removed to Mary Guerra).

James Orrin Rockwell Porter and Ann Taylor Radford had the following children:
16.   i.   MARCUS S⁵ PORTER was born on 07 Apr 2010 in Logan, Cache, Utah, USA.
17.   ii.   OWEN RODNEY PORTER was born on 21 Nov 2013 in Logan, Cache, Utah, USA.

Left: Ann Taylor Radford and James Orrin Rockwell Porter celebrate their marriage in this 2007 photo. From Marjorie Taylor Collection.

Chapter 8. Nettie LaVonne Taylor and Guadalupe Guerra

Nettie Taylor

Generation 1

1. NETTIE LAVONNE*I* TAYLOR (Richard Thomas[A], Richard Lemuel[B], John Dennis[C], Dempsey[D], William Abraham Lawrence[E], William Nathaniel[F], James Henry "The Elder"[G] I, John William "The Immigrant"[H], Capt. Thomas John[I] II, Thomas John[J] I, Rev. Dr. Rowland[K], John Thomas[L], John William[M] I, William[N] II, Sir John[O], William[P] I, Sir John[Q] Taylifer, Harger[R] Taylefer) was born on 03 Feb 1915 in Okemah, Okfuskee, Oklahoma, USA. She died on 28 Apr 2002 in Boise, Ada, Idaho, USA (Age 87). She married Guadalupe Filiberto Guerra, son of Jose Antonio Guerra and Tecla Guerra de Guerra, on 18 Apr 1945 in Boise, Ada, Idaho, USA (First Christian Church). He was born on 16 Mar 1900 in Roma, Starr, Texas, USA (Rancho El Colorado). He died on 27 Dec 1982 in Boise, Ada, Idaho, USA (Age 82).

Right: Nettie Taylor became a Registered Nurse in 1939. From Nettie Taylor Guerra Collection.

Nettie LaVonne Taylor lived in White Cross, Ada, Idaho, USA in 1930 (Age 15; Marital Status: Single; Relation to Head of House: Daughter). She graduated on 19 May 1933 in Boise, Ada, Idaho, USA (Franklin High School with older brother Art). She graduated on 29 May 1939 in Enid, Garfield, Oklahoma, USA (University Hospital School for Nurses). She was employed as a Garfield County Hospital Director of Nurses in Jan 1940 in Enid, Garfield, Oklahoma, USA. She was employed as a Crippled Children's Hospital Head Nurse in Mar 1941 in Oklahoma City, Oklahoma, USA. She was employed as a US Veterans Hospital Registered Nurse in Sep 1942 in Boise, Ada, Idaho, USA. She lived in Boise, Ada, Idaho, USA in 1950 (308 Clithero Dr). She lived in Soldiers Home precinct, Ada, Idaho, USA in 1950 (Clithero Drive; Age 35; Enumeration District: 1-61; Is Employed: No; Live On Farm: No; Occupation Category: Keeping House; Seeking Work: No; Three Or More Acres: No; Worked Last Week: No; Wife Relation To Head: Wife; Marital Status: Married). She was employed as a St Luke's Hospital Pediatric Nurse in 1951 in Boise, Ada, Idaho, USA. She was employed as a Boise Independent School District Nurse between 1959 and 1976 in Boise, Ada, Idaho, USA. She lived in Boise, Ada, Idaho, USA in 1960 (308 Clithero Dr). She lived in Boise, Ada, Idaho, USA in 1993 (Street Address: 1000 N (was 308) Clithero Dr; Age 78). She was cremated on 30 Apr 2002 in Boise, Ada, Idaho, USA (Cloverdale Memorial Park (Sec 4VV-220-5); Find A Grave #193540239). Her cause of death was metastatic breast cancer to brain. Race: (White).

Nettie was the sixth of Richard Thomas Taylor and Roxie Ann Gibbs seven children. She had six siblings, namely: Elsie Blanche, Nommie Lee, Bessie Amanda, Richard Lamuel, Artice Raymond, and Marjorie Ellen. She was born less than three years after her brother Art and also grew up in Oklahoma on her father's farm, raised mostly by her older sisters. But in 1925 when she was ten years old, the family moved west with their four youngest children, first to New Mexico, then to Boise, Idaho, where her father began farming again in 1928.

Left: Nettie and her dog little Jacki at Eagle Ranch, Idaho in about 1936. From Nettie Taylor Guerra Collection.

In Boise, Nettie attended Meridian High School and graduated from Franklin High School in 1933. She always loved people and decided to become a nurse. So, she returned to Oklahoma to attend the University Hospital School of Nursing in Enid. To keep expenses down Nettie was able to live with her older sister Nommie and her family there. After graduation in 1939 Nettie worked as a Registered Nurse in Oklahoma City before moving back to Boise in 1942 during World War II to work at the Veterans Administration (VA) Hospital. Her daughters related a story about one of Nettie's patients at that time:

> She used to tell us about an old man that she 'specialed.'. . They stayed at home and the nurse would come to them. . . He was an old miner. . . When he died, he said he was going to give her an amethyst stone . . . and she just kind of forgot about it. His family contacted her and they had this stone that he faceted for her, and she had it made into a ring (Guerra T. , 2018, p. 45:19).

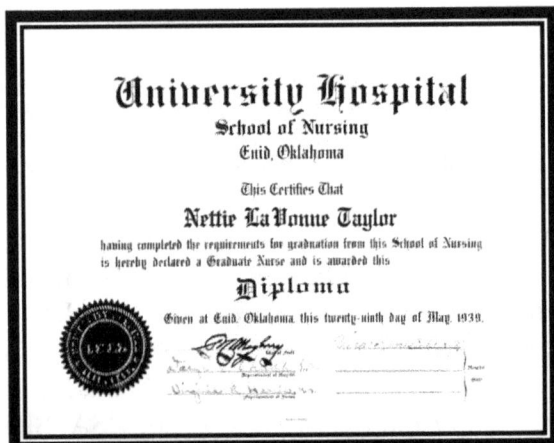

Nettie Taylor Nursing School Diploma.

Amethyst jewel stone given to Nettie by a patient.

Before Nettie died she gave instructions to give this ring to her granddaughter Dacia, who has it now, as amethyst is their birthstone since they were both born in February. While at the VA Hospital Nettie also met her future husband, Guadalupe "Lupe" Guerra, a tall handsome Texan who was stationed at Gowen Field during the war. Daughter Tecla says:

> Daddy [Lupe] was introduced by his friend to mama [Nettie]. . . She was trying to sneak out of the nurse's home, where the nurses lived, and she was hiding a shotgun . . . they were going to go hunting, my mother and her dad, [RT Taylor] . . . and she had a big coat on and had this under her coat. And here this friend showed up with a stranger and they got to talking, and mama always said she was so nervous that something would drop out of that coat and she would be kicked out of the nurse's home and lose her job over it. (Guerra T. , 2018, p. 38:55).

Tecla says she doesn't know how long they dated. They married in 1945 when the war ended and Tecla was born in 1946. Since Lupe had now received his discharge from the U.S. Army Air Corps, Nettie expected him to move their family back to Texas where his siblings lived. But after they drove their car back to meet his siblings, it became clear that his siblings would not recognize Lupe's marriage unless Nettie converted to Catholicism. She told Lupe that she would if he wanted her to, but Lupe did not want her to have to do that. Also Lupe grew up hunting and fishing on the ranchos of southern Texas, and living in Idaho was like living in a hunting and fishing paradise. According to Lupe's daughter Tecla, "He thought you could worship God in a boat on the edge of Lucky Peak Reservoir fishing." (Guerra T. , 2018, p. 34:46).

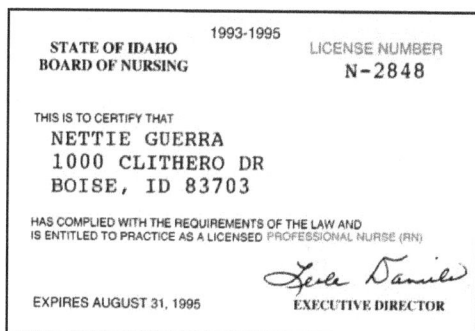

<table>
<tr><td></td><td>1993-1995</td><td></td></tr>
<tr><td>STATE OF IDAHO
BOARD OF NURSING</td><td></td><td>LICENSE NUMBER
N-2848</td></tr>
</table>

THIS IS TO CERTIFY THAT
NETTIE GUERRA
1000 CLITHERO DR
BOISE, ID 83703

HAS COMPLIED WITH THE REQUIREMENTS OF THE LAW AND
IS ENTITLED TO PRACTICE AS A LICENSED PROFESSIONAL NURSE (RN)

EXPIRES AUGUST 31, 1995   EXECUTIVE DIRECTOR

After Nettie and Lupe were married, they lived in an apartment about two blocks from St Alphonsis Hospital. The owners did not allow children, so when Tecla was born they went looking for a house to buy. After six months of searching, they bought one on Clithero Drive from a couple getting a divorce. The Guerra's paid $10,000 for the furnished house including furniture, dishes, towels, everything. Nettie was the last of the Guerra's to live in the house until she moved to an assisted living facility in 2000.

Soon after their marriage, Lupe found a job at the VA Hospital and their second child Mary was born in 1949. Then in 1951 Nettie began working as a St. Luke's Hospital Pediatric Nurse. A son Antonio Richard Guerra was born in 1954 but died from birth defects as an infant. But Nettie did not give up on her nursing career and in 1959 became a school nurse for the Boise Independent School district for the next seventeen years, retiring in 1976.

Not only was Nettie a nurse, a mother, and a wife, but she was also a great cook, saying "My mother couldn't boil water when she was married. . . So, she saw that all her girls learned cooking early" (Idaho Statesman, 1959). Like her sisters, Nettie was also an accomplished artist and painted landscapes and flower scenes throughout her retirement which she gave to family members who have her oil paintings prominently displayed in their homes.

Grandad RT Taylor also taught the kids how to hunt and fish, and Nettie and Lupe loved to take them for drives in the country, which often ended up at a favorite fishing hole for a picnic lunch. As Nettie's daughter Mary recalled, "We would go on picnics and we did everything together as a family." (Guerra M. , 2015, p. 15:44). Tecla said that one summer, "Daddy decided that if we were going to live in Idaho, we needed to learn something about it. . . We stopped at all the historical signs and went swimming in various places." (Guerra T. , 2018, p. 49:55). Tecla says they also visited Nettie's nursing colleagues and ended up making a two-week trip to see Northern Idaho, followed by another to see Southern Idaho.

But most of all Nettie was a people person, always joining and helping others. She was an active member of the University Christian Church, sang in the choir, and held leadership positions with the Daughters of American Veterans auxiliary and with the Idaho Nurses Association. For most of her life she lobbied for the betterment of nurses, nurse certification, and the welfare of children.

Nettie Taylor became an accomplished painter after she retired and loved to do oil paintings of landscapes and flowers such as this one she painted in 1986. From Nettie Taylor Guerra Collection.

Guadalupe Filiberto Guerra was born on 16 Mar 1900 in Roma, Starr, Texas, USA (Rancho El Colorado as the fourth child of Jose Antonio Guerra and Tecla Guerra de Guerra. He had eight siblings, namely: Teresa, Abel Eulalio, Victoria, Margarita, Maria Florinda, Herlinda, Fidencio Miguel, and Evangelina. He died on 27 Dec 1982 in Boise, Ada, Idaho, USA (Age 82). When he was 45 he married Nettie LaVonne Taylor, daughter of Richard Thomas Taylor and Roxie Ann Gibbs, on 18 Apr 1945 in Boise, Ada, Idaho, USA (First Christian Church).

Left: In 1945 Sergeant Guadalupe Guerra was serving in the U.S. Army Air Corps 141st Bomb Wing at Gowen Airfield, near Boise, Idaho. From Guadalupe Guerra Collection.

Guadalupe Filiberto Guerra lived in Justice Precinct 4, El Salineno, Starr, Texas, USA on 15 Jun 1900 (Marital Status: Single; Relation to Head of House: Son). He lived in Justice Precinct 4, Starr, Texas, USA in 1910 (Relation to Head of House: Son). Draft Registration: Bet. 1917–1918 in Hidalgo County, Texas, USA He lived in McAllen, Hidalgo, Texas, USA in 1920 (Marital Status: Single; Relationship: Head). He lived in McAllen, Hidalgo, Texas, USA in 1930 (Marital Status: Single; Relation to Head of House: Head). He lived in McAllen, Hidalgo, Texas, USA in 1935 (1716 Beaumont Ave; Agent, Magnolia Coffee Company). He lived in McAllen, Hidalgo, Texas, USA on 01 Apr 1940 (Age 40; Marital Status: Single; Relation to Head of House: Head). He was employed as a Salesman for Lee Auto Company. Age 41 on 15 Feb 1942 in McAllen, Hidalgo, Texas, USA. He was described as Complexion: Light; Eye Color: Brown; Hair Color: Brown; Height: 71"; Weight: 192 lbs; mole on right temple on 15 Feb 1942 in McAllen, Hidalgo, Texas, USA. He served in the military between 30 Jun 1942– 11 Sep 1945 in Fort Sam Houston, TX; Gowan Army Airfield, ID (Sgt, 141st Bomb Wing). He was employed as a VA Hospital Statistician Clerk in 1950 in Boise, Ada, Idaho, USA. He lived in Soldiers Home precinct, Ada, Idaho, USA in 1950 (Street Address: Clithero Drive; 50 Age: 50; Clerical Worker Occupation: Clerical Worker; Class of Worker: Government; Enumeration District: 1-61; Hours Worked: 40; Industry: Veterans Admin; Live On Farm: No; Occupation Category: Working; Three Or More Acres: No; Head Relation To Head: Head; Marital Status: Married). He lived in Boise, Ada, Idaho, USA in 1960 (308 Clithero Dr). He lived in Boise, Ada, Idaho, USA in 1982 (308 Clithero Dr). He was buried on 30 Dec 1982 in Boise, Ada, Idaho, USA (Cloverdale Memorial Park (Sec 4VV-220-5); Find A Grave #193540388). He was also known as Lupe. His cause of death was a heart aneurism (after several heart attacks). Race: (White.

For more information on Guadalupe Filiberto Guerra see Chapter 6 in *"The Descendants of Jose Antonio Guerra"* (Conklin D. G., 2020).

Guadalupe Filiberto Guerra and Nettie LaVonne Taylor had the following children:

+2. i. TECLA ANN*12* GUERRA was born on 14 Oct 1946 in Boise, Ada, Idaho, USA (St Alphonsis Hospital). She married Daniel Oakley Blood, son of Harold Clifton Blood and Marjorie Alene Jones, on 14 Jul 1973 in Boise, Ada, Idaho, USA (St Stephens Church). He was born on 27 Apr 1937 in Moscow, Latah, Idaho, USA. He died on 04 May 1977 in Potlatch, Latah, Idaho, USA.

+3. ii. MARY LAVONNE GUERRA was born on 15 Jun 1949 in Boise, Ada, Idaho, USA. She married David Gene Conklin, son of Charles Franklin Conklin and Betty Marinkovic, on 22 Nov 1969 in Moscow, Latah, Idaho, USA (Trinity Baptist Church). He was born on 03 Nov 1948 in Lynwood, Los Angeles, California, USA (St Francis Hospital).

4. iii. ANTONIO RICHARD GUERRA was born on 20 Mar 1954 in Boise, Ada, Idaho, USA as the third child of Guadalupe Filiberto Guerra and Nettie LaVonne Taylor. He had two siblings, namely: Tecla Ann, and Mary LaVonne. He died on 17 Apr 1954 in Boise, Ada, Idaho, USA (age: 28 days). He was described as red hair, bluish-green eyes, in Apr 1954 in Boise, Ada, Idaho, USA. He was buried on 19 Apr 1954 in Boise, Ada, Idaho, USA (Cloverdale Memorial Park (Sec 1LV-11-5; Find A Grave #132078861). His cause of death was congenital heart disease, harelip, cleft palate.

Generation 2

2. **TECLA ANN*2* GUERRA** (Nettie LaVonne*1* Taylor, Guadalupe Filiberto, Jose Antonio, Jesus Maria, Jose Lino de Jesus, Jose Manuel, Jose Antonio Albino Hinojosa, Joseph Ramon, Capitan Cristobal -Cañamar, Ignacio Guerra-Cañamar, Antonio Guerra-Cañamal II, Antonio Guerra-Cañamal) was born on 14 Oct 1946 in Boise, Ada, Idaho, USA (St Alphonsis Hospital). She married **Daniel Oakley Blood**, son of Harold Clifton Blood and Marjorie Alene Jones, on 14 Jul 1973 in Boise, Ada, Idaho, USA (St Stephens Church). He was born on 27 Apr 1937 in Moscow, Latah, Idaho, USA. He died on 04 May 1977 in Potlatch, Latah, Idaho, USA.

Right: Tecla Guerra on her wedding day 14 Jul 1973. From Guadalupe Guerra Collection.

Tecla Ann Guerra lived in Soldiers Home precinct, Ada, Idaho, USA in 1950 (308 Clithero Drive; 3 Age: 3; Enumeration District: 1-61; Live On Farm: No; School Years Completed: O; Three Or More Acres: No; Same House: Yes; Relation To Head: Daughter; Never Married Marital Status: Single). She lived in Boise, Idaho, USA in 1962 (Age: 16). She lived in Boise, Idaho, USA in 1963 (Age: 17). She graduated in June 1964 in Boise, Ada, Idaho, USA (Boise High School). She was employed as a McCall Elementary School music teacher from 1968 to 1971 in McCall, Valley, Idaho, USA. She received a University of Idaho, BS (Music

Education) degree in May 1969 in Moscow, Latah, Idaho, USA. She was employed as an Elementary music and orchestra teacher between 1971 and 1973 in Boise, Ada, Idaho, USA. She lived in Potlatch, Latah, Idaho, USA in 1973 (Duffield Flat Rd). She lived in Potlatch, Latah, Idaho, USA in 1993 (Duffield Flat Rd). She was described as brown hair, brown eyes, ruddy complexion, height 5'6" weight 225 lbs. (ID driver license) in 2014 in Moscow, Latah, Idaho, USA. Race: (White).

Tecla Ann was named after her grandmother on each side of the family. She remembers her childhood fondly as the older of two sisters:

> One of the fun things we used to do with Grandad Taylor: they would go to Lake Lowell and rent a rowboat, and Grandad would take a whole stack of gunny sacks and we would fish until those gunny sacks were full of catfish, hundreds of them. Then we would take them back to Grandad's place and dump them into galvanized tubs. The catfish would stay alive until we would have a little butchering party which took about a week. We liked catfish! (Guerra T. , 2018, p. 13:36).

Left: Grandad Richard T. Taylor and Tecla Guerra pose with the day's catch, Boise 1949. From Marjorie Taylor Collection.

Why Tecla became a music teacher is no mystery. She says, "I'm musical. I like to sing, to play the piano. I used to play the violin and the guitar. I started playing violin in the 4th grade. Grandad Taylor bought a violin from the Sears & Roebuck catalog in 1906, and I still have it" (Guerra, T, 2018). Tecla learned the piano in high school from a friend during lunchtime and school breaks.

Not only does Tecla like to sing, some say she is a very good singer. In 1969, she sent a tape recording of her songs to her Aunt Evangelina Guerra, a school teacher in Texas, who wrote back, "I took it to school and when my principal heard the songs from his office, he came and asked, 'Mrs. Guerra, I am so happy to hear you can sing so well. It sounds beautiful. May I listen to the rest?' I said, 'Yes of course, Mr. West,' and never told him it was my niece until the songs had finished" (Guerra E. , 1969). Tecla studied Music Education in college and after graduation taught music in McCall and Boise, Idaho, then moving to Palouse, WA, and Potlatch, ID, where she married Dan Blood in 1973. They had two children before his untimely death from heart failure in 1977.

Right: 1985 photo of Tecla Guerra. She raised her two boys while managing her husband's farm near Potlatch, Idaho. From Guadalupe Guerra Collection.

Tecla was left with two babies at Dan's death. Casey was three years old and Ellery was seven months old. Her parents wanted her and the boys to move back to Boise with them, but Tecla did not want to leave her widowed mother-in-law Marjorie Blood alone on the farm. Also, Tecla's home was debt free. So she and "Marge" created an informal partnership. Marge took care of her own land and all the milk cows while Tecla leased her own land to a neighbor and took care of all the cattle, sheep, horses, chickens, and later goats, while Marge helped her with the boys. They had a very good working relationship and did many things together over the years until Marge passed away in 2006. When her youngest son Ellery started first grade, Tecla began working for the Palouse school district, where she worked for 20 years.

Tecla has remained very active in the nearby communities of Palouse and Potlatch. She sang for 10 years with their large Community Chorus. In 1994, Tecla and her mother Nettie Guerra went with the chorus to sing in Austria and Hungary. They rehearsed in the same palace Haydn, Beethoven, Mozart, and other famous musicians worked, studied, and performed. Her mother was thrilled to make such a trip with Tecla and they brought back many happy memories. A year later, in 1995, Tecla was badly injured in a traffic accident near her home and as a result had to sell her livestock and curtail many of her farm activities. Then in 2017, she was injured in a second traffic accident and since then has had to really slow down. So in 2021, Tecla moved into a retirement complex in nearby Moscow, Idaho. The family farm is now owned by her oldest son Casey and his family, who remodeled and moved into his Grandma Marge's house next door.

Daniel Oakley Blood was born on 27 Apr 1937 in Moscow, Latah, Idaho, USA as the first child of Harold Clifton Blood and Marjorie Alene Jones. He died on 04 May 1977 in Potlatch, Latah, Idaho, USA. When he was 36, he married Tecla Ann Guerra, daughter of Guadalupe Filiberto Guerra and Nettie LaVonne Taylor, on 14 Jul 1973 in Boise, Ada, Idaho, USA (St Stephens Church).

Right: Daniel Blood on his wedding day 14 Jul 1973. From Guadalupe Guerra Collection.

Daniel Oakley Blood lived in Palouse, Latah, Idaho, USA in 1940 (Marital Status: Single; Relation to Head: Son). He graduated in Jun 1955 in Potlatch, Latah, Idaho, USA (Potlatch High School). He was employed as a grain and legume (peas and lentils) farmer and electrician in 1973 in Potlatch, Latah, Idaho, USA. He lived in Rt. 1, Potlatch in 1977. He was buried on 07 May 1977 in Potlatch, Latah, Idaho, USA (Freeze Cemetery; Find a Grave #24849229). His cause of death was a streptococcus infection leading to heart failure from a previously unknown defective heart valve.

Daniel Oakley Blood and Tecla Ann Guerra had the following children:

+5. i. CASEY GUERRA[3] BLOOD was born on 29 Apr 1974 in Moscow, Latah, Idaho, USA (Gritman Memorial Hospital). He married Cathy Hui-Ju Woo, daughter of George Tai Mei Woo and Nancy Fong Ju Chen, on 01 Jun 1996 in Palouse, Whitman, Washington, USA (Palouse Federated Church). She was born on 14 May 1976 in Taipei, Taiwan.

+6. ii. ELLERY ABNER BLOOD was born on 26 Sep 1976 in Moscow, Latah, Idaho, USA (Gritman Memorial Hospital). He married Alexandra Dickinson Broughton, daughter of William Cranston Broughton and Zena Marie Dickinson, on 25 Sep 2005 in Shawnee-on-Delaware, Monroe, Pennsylvania, USA. She was born on 19 Jul 1984 in Dayton, Columbia, Washington, USA.

3. MARY LAVONNE[2] GUERRA (Nettie LaVonne[1] Taylor, Guadalupe Filiberto, Jose Antonio, Jesus Maria, Jose Lino de Jesus, Jose Manuel, Jose Antonio Albino Hinojosa, Joseph Ramon, Capitan Cristobal-Cañamar, Ignacio Guerra-Cañamar, Antonio Guerra-Cañamal II, Antonio Guerra-Cañamal) was born on 15 Jun 1949 in Boise, Ada, Idaho, USA. She married **David Gene Conklin**, son of Charles Franklin Conklin and Betty Marinkovic, on 22 Nov 1969 in Moscow, Latah, Idaho, USA (Trinity Baptist Church). He was born on 03 Nov 1948 in Lynwood, Los Angeles, California, USA (St Francis Hospital).

Left: Mary Guerra poses with her daughter Dacia (center) and granddaughter Isabelle (right) in Helena, Montana. Author photo 2018.

Mary LaVonne Guerra graduated in Jun 1967 in Boise, Ada, Idaho, USA (Capital High School). She was employed at the Helena Public Library in 1974 in Helena, Lewis and Clark County, Montana. She was employed as a Veterinarian Assistant in 1977 in Helena, Lewis and Clark, Montana, USA. She was employed as a Montana Legislative Council Librarian in 1983 in Helena, Lewis and Clark, Montana, USA. She received an AS (Business Mgt) degree in May 1997 in Flathead Valley Community College. She was employed as a Flathead Valley Community College Instructor in 2001 in Kalispell, Flathead, Montana, USA. She was described as: fair complexion, brown hair, blue eyes, height 5'3" weight 190 lbs. (Montana driver license) on 13 Jun 2014 in Kalispell, Flathead, Montana, USA. She tested her DNA on 07 Jan 2017 in Ancestry Kit #A022185. DNA Match: 22 Nov 2018 (1st cousins: Leonard Guerra, Daniel Guerra, Gloria Garza, Arlene Taylor, Dennis R. Taylor) She has a medical condition of osteo-arthritis.

Mary was born and raised in Boise, Idaho. The Idaho summers were some of her fondest memories of childhood:

> I remember just summer times running through the neighborhood. We would do our chores first thing in the morning and then we were outside. . . We kids rode our bikes, we played in the dirt, and we went to the [Boise] River . . . and we would eat baloney sandwiches on white bread and drink Kool-Aid . . . and we had no helmets or seat belts or any kind of security, and we all lived through it somehow. (Guerra M. , 2015, p. 11:14).

Upon graduation from Capital High School in 1967, Mary attended the University of Idaho, where her sister Tecla was a senior at the time. Mary sang in the University's Vandaleer Chorale and played string bass in the orchestra.

She met and married her lifelong partner Dave Conklin in 1969 while in college. Their daughter Dacia was born the next year and in 1972, they moved to Helena, Montana, where Dave worked for State Parks, while Mary worked for the Lewis & Clark County Library and later the Montana Legislative Council Library. In 1980, they moved to Miles City, where their son Christopher was born in 1982. They returned to Helena in 1983, and in 1990, they moved to Kalispell, where Mary received her Associates Degree in 1997 and later joined the faculty of Flathead Valley Community College.

Right: This Conklin family portrait was made in Miles City, Montana shortly after their son Chris was born in 1982. From Mary Guerra Collection.

Mary explained, "I had numerous professions because Dave kept moving. I started out as an artist, then librarian, which I enjoyed the most because I loved books and research, especially trivia questions. I worked at a veterinary clinic. I taught computer classes both overseas and in Montana" (Guerra M. , 2015, p. 12:17).

Mary also took on the burden of managing the home, children, pets, and finances during the many times Dave was training or deployed overseas as an Army Reserve officer. In 1998, she and son Chris were able to join him for a year, where she taught computer classes at the Anglo-American School in Sofia, Bulgaria. During that time they were able to travel throughout Europe together. After Dave returned from two years in the Iraq War in 2006, she retired from teaching and moved with him to Hawaii for 7 years, where he worked as an IT technician and where Mary made many friends, became a Sea Turtle Guardian, and rescued and trained her service and therapy dog MaiTai. During that time, she also loved to travel throughout the Islands and to Australia with friends and family. Always ready for a new adventure, Mary again moved with Dave when his job was relocated to Camp Pendleton, California in 2012. When Dave retired, they bought a winter home and moved to Sun City, AZ where she was active in Crafts and other clubs.

Although she was raised in the city of Boise, Mary was always around horses, dogs, and cats and became an avid horsewoman, gardener, and dog trainer. The family home in Boise always included pet dogs, cats, and a garden full of flowers and vegetables. She was also an excellent cook, seamstress, and nurse which she learned from her mother and spent many loving hours passing her talents and skills on to her children Dacia and Chris, as well as grandchildren Justin Kunz and Isabelle Conklin. As for hobbies Mary says, "I like to read, I like to sew, crochet and knit, and cook, and go for walks" (Guerra M. , 2015, p. 13:22).

David Gene Conklin was born on 03 Nov 1948 in Lynwood, California (St Francis Hospital) as the first child of Charles Franklin Conklin and Betty Marinkovic. He had three siblings, namely: Rita Marie, Joan Louise, and Lorie Ann. When he was 21, he married Mary LaVonne Guerra on 22 Nov 1969 in Moscow, Latah, Idaho, USA (Trinity Baptist Church).

Right: Mary Guerra and Major Dave Conklin, U.S. Army Reserve, attend the Montana Centennial Ball in Helena, Montana, 11 Nov 1989. From Mary Guerra Collection.

David Gene Conklin graduated in May 1966 in South Gate, Los Angeles, California (South Gate High School). He served in the military between Jun 1969 and Oct 2008 in the US Army Reserve/National Guard (Combat Engineer / Broadcast Journalist). He received a BS (Forestry) degree in Jun 1970 at the University of Idaho. He received a MS degree (Natural Resources) in Dec 1972 at the University of Montana. Public Service: Between 1973 and 1999 in Montana (State Park Ranger). He received an MBA degree in Jun 1998 at the University of Montana. He was described as Gray hair, blue eyes, left-handed, 5ft 8in, 145 lbs, O+ blood type (Hawaii driver license) in 2006 in Honolulu, Hawaii. He had a medical condition of Parkinson's disease; on 03 Nov 2014 in Kalispell, Flathead, Montana. He tested his DNA on 07 Jan 2017 in Ancestry Kit #A858700 (Haplogroup Y= R1a (most common group in Tatars). DNA Match: 07 Jan 2017 (1st/2nd cousins: Diane Berg, Charlene Elfers, Savo Marinkovic, Ginger Walston, Alice Kirkman, James Mauzey) He had a medical condition of a Heart Attack while hiking on 08 Jun 2017 in Kalispell, Flathead, Montana. He tested his DNA on 08 Jun 2018 in Family Tree Y-DNA37 Kit #MK36621 (haplogroup Y= R-M269). He tested his DNA on 23 Nov 2018 in 23andMe Kit #72-9118-1743-3929 (haplogroup Y= R-L1066), X= H1c). He was also known as Dave and by the title of Lieutenant Colonel. He was affiliated with the Serbian Orthodox religion. For more information about David Gene Conklin see *"Conklin-Marinkovic Family History"* (Conklin D. G., 2018, p. 64).

David Gene Conklin and Mary LaVonne Guerra had the following children:

+7. i. DACIA MARIE[3] CONKLIN was born on 06 Feb 1970 in Moscow, Latah, Idaho, USA (Gritman Memorial Hospital). She had a child with (1) MYRON TROY KUNZ, son of Myron Logan Kunz and Sandra Lucille Nelson, on 21 Jul 1994 in Mesa, Maricopa, Arizona, USA (Partner split-up in 1998). He was born on 12 May 1968 in Sandy, Utah, USA. She married (2) RANDAL WILLIAM ENGLISH on 16 Mar 2000 in Bullhead City, Mohave, Arizona, USA. He was born on 26 Jan 1970 in Helena, Lewis and Clark, Montana, USA.

+8. ii. CHRISTOPHER ANDREW CONKLIN was born on 29 Apr 1982 in Miles City, Custer, Montana, USA (Holy Rosary Hospital). He had a child with (1) BRITTANY ELIZABETH SMITH on 29 Apr 2004 in Kalispell, Flathead, Montana, USA (Partner split-up in 2006). She was born on 1 Sep 1982 in Miles City, Custer, Montana,

USA (adopted daughter). He met his current partner (2) JESSICA SWANSON about 2007 in Kalispell, Flathead, Montana. She was born on 13 Apr 1984 in St Paul, Hennepin, Minnesota.

Generation 3

5. CASEY GUERRA[3] BLOOD (Tecla Ann[2] Guerra, Guadalupe Filiberto[1] Guerra, Daniel Oakley, Harold Clifton) was born on 29 Apr 1974 in Moscow, Latah, Idaho, USA (Gritman Memorial Hospital). He married **Cathy Hui-Ju Woo**, daughter of George Tai Mei Woo and Nancy Fong Ju Chen, on 01 Jun 1996 in Palouse, Whitman, Washington, USA (Palouse Federated Church). She was born on 14 May 1976 in Taipei, Taiwan.

Casey Guerra Blood graduated in Jun 1992 in Potlatch, Latah County, Idaho, USA (Potlatch High School). He lived in Potlatch, Latah, Idaho, USA in 1995. He received a BS (Agricultural Systems Management) degree in May 1997 in Univ of Idaho. He lived in Moscow, Idaho, USA between 1998 and 2000. He has lived in Potlatch, Latah, Idaho, USA since 2001. Casey has worked for fifteen years for the Wilbur Ellis Agribusiness Company providing seed and fertilizer for local pea, lentil, and wheat farmers and enjoys being a Boy Scout Troop and Venture Crew leader. **Cathy Woo** joined Washington State University in 2006 as a conference coordinator until December 2007, and then she transferred over to Food Science Human Nutrition Department, now School of Food Science. She also volunteers with Habitat for Humanity and Boy Scouts.

Casey Guerra Blood and Cathy Hui-Ju Woo had the following children:

9. i. DARRICK[4] BLOOD was born on 07 Sep 1996 in Spokane, Spokane, Washington, USA (Sacred Heart Hospital). He married Megan Rich on 01 Aug 2020 in Potlatch, Latah, Idaho, USA (Blood farm).
10. ii. LYSSA WOO BLOOD was born on 13 Sep 1998 in Moscow, Latah, Idaho, USA (Gritman Memorial Hospital).

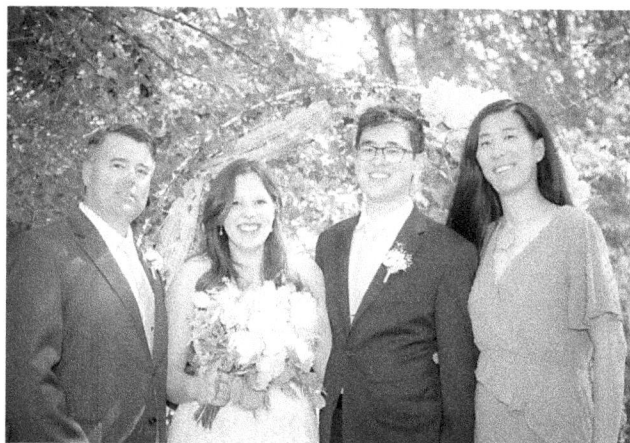

Darrick Blood with his bride and his parents on his wedding day 1 Aug 2020. From left: Casey Blood, Megan Rich, Darrick Blood and Cathy Blood. From Guadalupe Guerra Collection.

6. **ELLERY ABNER**[3] **BLOOD** (Tecla Ann[2] Guerra, Nettie LaVonne[1] Taylor, Daniel Oakley, Harold Clifton) was born on 26 Sep 1976 in Moscow, Latah, Idaho, USA (Gritman Memorial Hospital). He married **Alexandra Dickinson Broughton**, daughter of William Cranston Broughton and Zena Marie Dickinson, on 25 Sep 2005 in Shawnee-on-Delaware, Monroe, Pennsylvania, USA. She was born on 19 Jul 1984 in Dayton, Columbia, Washington, USA.

Ellery Abner Blood lived in Potlatch, Latah, Idaho, USA in 1993. He graduated in Jun 1994 in Potlatch, Latah, Idaho, USA (Potlatch High School). He lived in Rennselaer Polytechnic Institute, Troy, NY in 1996 (Street Address: 101 Warren Hall RPI Dorms; Street Address: 203 Cary Hall RPI). He lived in Potlatch, Latah, Idaho, USA in 1996. He served in the military between 1996–2022 (Commander, US Navy Reserve). He received a BS (Computer and Systems Engineering) degree in May 1999 in Rennselaer Polytechnic Institute, Troy, NY. He received a MS (Mechanical Engineering) degree about 2004 in US Naval Academy. He was employed as an Assistant Professor, Engineering Instructor and academic advisor in 2009 in US Naval Academy. He lived in Moscow, Latah, Idaho, USA in 2010. He lived in Annapolis, Anne Arundel, Maryland, USA in 2010. He received a PhD degree in 2012 in US Naval Academy. He lived in Potlatch, Latah, Idaho, USA in 2012. He has lived in Moscow, Idaho, USA since 2016. He was employed as a Principal Research Engineer at Schweitzer Engineering Laboratories on 20 Jul 2016 in Pullman, Whitman, Washington, USA.

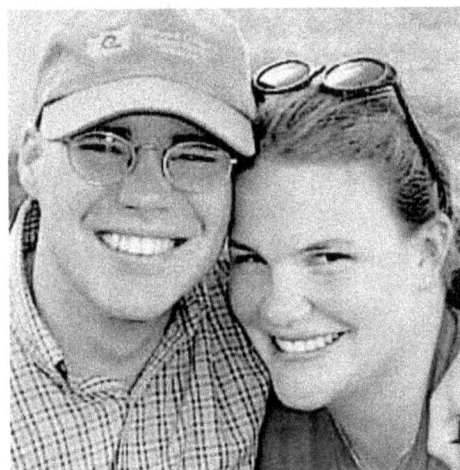

Left: Ellery Blood and fiancé Alexa Broughton in 2005. From Marjorie Taylor Collection.

Ellery Abner Blood and Alexandra Dickinson Broughton had the following children:

11. i. OLIVER ANDREW BROUGHTON[4] BLOOD was born on 02 Nov 2009 in Annapolis, Anne Arundel, Maryland, USA.
12. ii. IAN DANIEL BROUGHTON BLOOD was born on 12 Sep 2012 in Moscow, Latah, Idaho, USA.
13. iii. ANNEMARIE PEARL BROUGHTON BLOOD was born on 07 Dec 2014 in Moscow, Latah, Idaho, USA.

7. **DACIA MARIE**[3] **CONKLIN** (Mary LaVonne[2] Guerra, Nettie LaVonne[1] Taylor, David Gene, Charles Franklin) was born on 06 Feb 1970 in Moscow, Latah, Idaho, USA (Gritman Memorial Hospital). She had a child with (1) **MYRON TROY KUNZ**, son of Myron Logan Kunz and Sandra Lucille Nelson, on 21 Jul 1994 in Mesa, Maricopa, Arizona, USA (Partner split-up in 1998). He was born on 12 May 1968 in Sandy, Utah, USA. He died on 09 Dec 2020 in Mesa, Maricopa, Arizona, USA. She married (2) **RANDAL WILLIAM ENGLISH**, son of William Milton English and Diane Helen Launer, on 16 Mar 2000 in Bullhead City, Mohave, Arizona, USA. He was born on 26 Jan 1970 in Helena, Lewis and Clark, Montana, USA.

Left: Dacia Conklin and Husband Randy English both received Associate degrees from Flathead Community College in May 2002. From Mary Guerra Collection.

Dacia Marie Conklin was baptized in 1970 in Spokane, Spokane, Washington, USA (Holy Trinity Greek Orthodox Church). She lived in Helena, Montana, USA in 1985. She graduated in Jun 1988 in Helena, Lewis and Clark, Montana, USA (Helena High School). She lived in Mesa, Maricopa, Arizona, USA in Aug 1988 (Street Address: 930 S Dobson Road Rd). She lived in Helena, MT in 1990; Street Address: 1919 Grizzly Gulch; Street Address: 2107 W Broadway Rd Apt 159 (1996); Street Address: 930 S Dobson Rd. (1993); Street Address: 2060 North Cn 412; age 20). She lived in Kalispell, Flathead, Montana, USA in 1998. She received AAS, AAA (Business) degrees in May 2002 at Flathead Valley Community College. She lived in Bozeman, Gallatin, Montana, USA in Aug 2002. She received a BS (Business) degree in Dec 2003 at Montana State University. She was employed as an EMC2 Environmental Engineering Project Assistant in 2004 in Bozeman, Gallatin, Montana, USA. She was employed as a Blue Cross-Blue Shield Health Insurance Claims Adjuster in 2008 in Helena, Lewis and Clark, Montana, USA. She lived in Helena, Lewis and Clark, Montana, USA in 2008. She was employed as a Montana Department of Revenue Liquor Control Division compliance supervisor in Aug 2014 in Helena, Lewis and Clark, Montana, USA. She was described as blonde hair, blue eyes, right-handed, 5ft 2in, 167lbs (MT driver lic) in 2016 in Helena, Lewis and Clark, Montana, USA.

Randal William English was born on 26 Jan 1970 in Montana, USA. When he was 30, he married Dacia Marie Conklin, daughter of David Gene Conklin and Mary LaVonne Guerra, on 16 Mar 2000 in Bullhead City, Mohave, Arizona, USA.

Randal William English graduated in 1988 in Helena, Lewis and Clark, Montana, USA (Helena High School). He was employed as a Tower Meats meat cutter in 1988 in Helena, Lewis and Clark, Montana, USA. He was employed as an American Chemet maintenance man in 1992 in East Helena, Lewis and Clark, Montana, USA. He received an AA (Surveying) degree in May 2002 at Flathead Valley Community College. He lived in Bozeman, Gallatin, Montana, USA in Aug 2002. He received a BS (Civil Engineering) degree in Dec 2006 at Montana State University. He was employed as a Tetra Tech Environmental Engineering (Civil Engineer) in Apr 2007 in Helena, Lewis and Clark, Montana, USA. He lived in Helena, Lewis and Clark, Montana, USA in 2008. He was also known as Randy.

Randal William English and Dacia Marie Conklin had no children.
Myron Troy Kunz and Dacia Marie Conklin had the following child:

14. i. JUSTIN TROY[4] KUNZ was born on 21 Jul 1994 in Mesa, Maricopa, Arizona, USA (Mesa Lutheran Hospital).

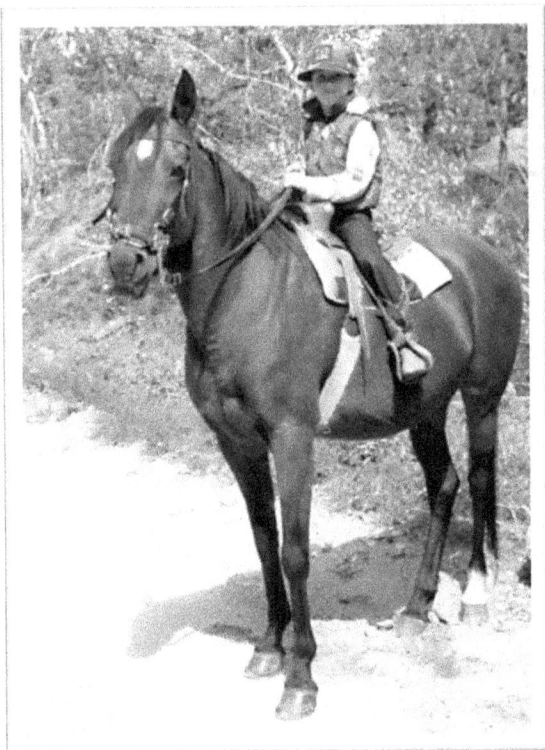

Left: Seven-year-old Christopher riding his mom's horse Rajah in Grizzly Gulch near Helena, Montana. Author photo 1989.

8. **CHRISTOPHER ANDREW³ CONKLIN** (Mary LaVonne² Guerra, Nettie LaVonne¹ Taylor, David Gene, Charles Franklin) was born on 29 Apr 1982 in Miles City, Custer, Montana, USA (Holy Rosary Hospital). He had a child with (1) **BRITTANY SMITH** on 29 Apr 2004 in Kalispell, Flathead, Montana, USA (Partner split-up in 2006). She was born in Kalispell, Flathead, Montana, USA (adopted daughter). He partnered with (2) **JESSICA SWANSON** about 2007 in Kalispell, Flathead, Montana, USA. She was born on 13 Apr 1984 in St Paul, Hennepin, Minnesota, USA.

Christopher Andrew Conklin and Jessica Swanson have no children.

Christopher Andrew Conklin and Brittany Smith had the following children:

15. i. ISABELLE IONA⁴ CONKLIN was born on 29 Apr 2004 in Kalispell, Flathead, Montana, USA.

Chapter 9. Marjorie Ellen Taylor and Allen Rayburne Lievsay

Marjorie Lievsay

Generation 1

1. MARJORIE ELLEN^I TAYLOR (Richard Thomas^A, Richard Lemuel^B, John Dennis^C, Dempsey^D, William Abraham Lawrence^E, William Nathaniel^F, James Henry "The Elder"^{G} I, John William "The Immigrant"^{H}, Capt. Thomas John^I II, Thomas John^J I, Rev. Dr. Rowland^K, John Thomas^L, John William^M I, William^N II, Sir John^O, William^P I, Sir John^Q Taylifer, Harger^R Taylefer) was born on 27 Dec 1916 in Okemah, Okfuskee, Oklahoma, USA. She died on 03 Mar 2016 in Boise, Ada, Idaho, USA (age 99). She married **Allen Rayburne Lievsay** on 31 May 1941 in Ada, Pontotoc, Oklahoma, USA. He was born on 02 Sep 1914 in Caddo, Bryan, Oklahoma, USA. He died on 22 Nov 2005 in Boise, Ada, Idaho, USA (age 91).

Right: Portrait of Marjorie Ellen Taylor and husband Allen Rayburne Lievsay, about 1979. From Marjorie Taylor Collection.

Marjorie Ellen Taylor lived in White Cross, Ada, Idaho, USA in 1930 (Age: 13; Marital Status: Single; Relation to Head of House: Daughter). She lived in Boise, Idaho, USA in 1948 (Street Address: 2607 N 36th). She lived in Boise, Idaho, USA in 1950 (Street Address: N 36th RD 9). She lived in Boise, Idaho, USA in 1953 (Street Address: 619 N 29th; Occupation: Office Secretary). She lived in Pendleton, Umatilla County, Oregon, USA in 1958. She lived in Boise, Idaho, USA in 1958. She lived in Boise, ID in 1993 (Street Address: 12134 West Keates Dr; Stree Address: 2822 N 32nd St; Age 77). She was buried on 05 Mar 2016 in Boise, Ada, Idaho, USA (Cloverdale Memorial Park (10VV-57-1); Find A Grave #159067839). She was also known as Marge. Her cause of death was mini-strokes exacerbated by shingles. Race: (White)

Marjorie or "Marge" as she was called, was born in Okemah, Oklahoma. Her middle name was from her Aunt Sarah Ellen Gibbs. She was the last of Richard Thomas Taylor and Roxie Ann Gibbs' seven children, born 19 years after her oldest sister Elsie. Marge said, "Elsie was my mother. . . I didn't like my mother [Roxie]. She slapped me on the head when I was little and my ear hurt for hours, and then later on she mistreated me." (Taylor M. , 2015, p. 07:10).

Marge was about nine years old in 1925 when her family left Oklahoma and moved west to New Mexico and then Boise, Idaho. This was a trying time for Marge as her oldest sister, Elsie, who was like a mother to her, elected to stay in Oklahoma with her new husband and family. Marge went to school in Pryor, Oklahoma and later Meridian, Idaho. In Idaho she attended high school in Meridian and graduated from Boise's Franklin High School in 1934.

Right: Marjorie Taylor's high school graduation photo, May 1934. From Marjorie Taylor Collection.

Marge went on to study at Boise Business University, then like her older sister Nettie moved back to Oklahoma to attend college. She hoped to keep expenses down by living with her older sister Elsie and her family while attending East Central State College in Ada. It was also helpful that her big sister Elsie was a home economics teacher at the college. Marge became a secretary for the president of the college. But soon her life and her job would change in a big way. In Ada she met and married native Oklahoman Allen Rayburne Lievsay in 1941. Ray worked for Denco Bus Lines in Ada but was soon transferred to Oklahoma City, where their son Larry was born in 1943. While in Oklahoma City, Marge worked for the Federal Wage and Hour Division.

Then a year later, in 1944, they moved to Tacoma, Washington, where Ray worked at the Pacific Naval Air Base during World War II. Two years later, the family moved to Boise, where Ray was station manager for the Pacific Trailways Bus Line for 11 years. In 1946, their second son, Jerry was born but died in less than a month from pulmonary disease. Marge went back to work and got a job as an accountant at St. Alphonsus Hospital for 6 years. In 1957, they moved to Pendleton, Oregon, where she assisted Ray in managing the Greyhound Bus Depot. Here, their son Larry graduated from Pendleton High School and was a standout pitcher on the high school baseball team. The family moved back to Boise in 1961, where Marge worked for the First National Bank and later as an executive secretary for the Small Business Administration until retiring in 1975. Meanwhile, Ray was employed by the State of Idaho Law Enforcement Department as a fuel and mileage auditor until retiring in December 1979 at age 65.

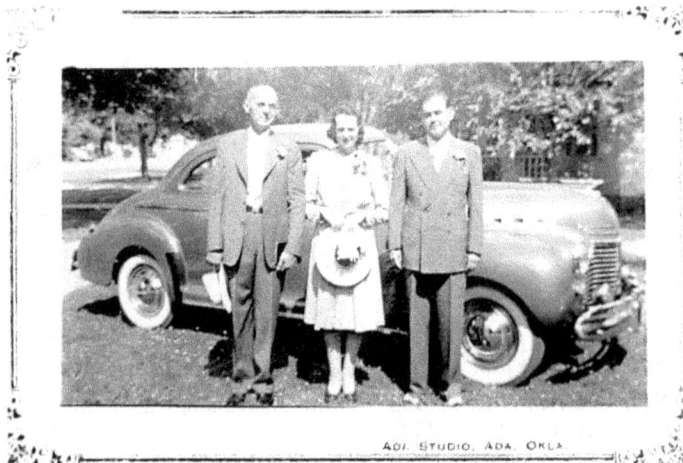

Left: Marge and Ray pose with their minister (left) on the way to their wedding in Ada, OK, 31 May 1941. From Marjorie Taylor Collection.

Besides work and raising their son, Marge enjoyed several hobbies. She was an excellent seamstress, made many of her own clothing items, and taught her niece Mary Guerra how to sew lingerie, skirts, blouses and jackets. Marge was raised on a farm and like all her siblings, always kept a vegetable garden in her back yard. Also, like all her sisters, Marge was an accomplished artist, with oil paints in particular. After she retired she took classes and it

Although Marge was the youngest of her siblings, she was also a talented artist.
From Marjorie Taylor Collection.

became her favorite hobby. When she was 99 years old she reflected, "I really enjoyed painting more than anything. Every once in a while I think 'gee I wish I had my paints.' It was fun." (Taylor M. , 2015, p. 36:36). Marge painted primarily flower and bird scenes and landscapes. Her paintings were proudly displayed in her home and also given to family members.

She was also an excellent cook and taught her niece Mary Guerra to make pies of all kinds. Her pecan pies were legendary. Marge remembered gathering pecans as a child:

> The pecans in Oklahoma when I was little they grew wild; and my dad made a long pole with a crosspiece and he called it a bumper and he'd bump that tree and it would just rain pecans. Us kids would have to pick them up. (Taylor M. , 2015, p. 25:45).

After husband Ray passed away in 2005, Marge lived alone until 2011 when she moved to the Valley View Retirement Center, where she met many wonderful residents and members of the staff. She enjoyed her life there very much, and she would say, "Never a dull day." Marge died there of natural causes at the well-advanced age of 99.

Allen Rayburne Lievsay was born on 02 Sep 1914 in Caddo, Bryan, Oklahoma, USA as the first of Rayford Lievsay and Lottie Ann Beckham's two children. He had one sister, namely: Frances Marie. He died on 22 Nov 2005 in Boise, Ada, Idaho, USA (age 91). When he was 26, he married Marjorie Ellen Taylor, daughter of Richard Thomas Taylor and Roxie Ann Gibbs, on 31 May 1941 in Ada, Pontotoc, Oklahoma, USA.

Right: Ray Lievsay and Marge Taylor in Ada, Oklahoma, 1941. From Marjorie Taylor Collection.

Allen Rayburne Lievsay lived in Chickasha, Chickasha, Grady, Oklahoma, USA in 1930 (Street Address: Fifteenth; Age: 15; Able To Speak English: Yes; Attended School: Yes; Can Read Write: Yes; Enumeration District: 0007; Registration District: 0007; Marital Status: Single; Relation To Head: Son). He lived in Chickasha, Grady, Oklahoma, United States in 1930. He graduated in 1933 in Chickasha, Grady, Oklahoma, USA (Chickasha High School). He lived in Chickasha, Grady, Oklahoma, USA in 1935. He lived in Ada, Pontotoc, Oklahoma, USA in 1940 (Street Address: West 14th; Age: 25; Occupation: Ticket Agent; Attended School: No; Class of Worker: Wage or salary worker in private work; Employment Code: 1; Employment Details: No; Employment History: No; Enumeration District: 62-7; Grade Completed: High School, 4th year; Hours Worked: 48; Income: 1320; Income Other Sources: No; Is Employed: Yes; Public Emergency Work: No; Residence Farm Nineteen Thirty Five: No; Seeking Work: No; Weeks Worked: 52; Marital Status: Married; Relation To Head: Lodger). He was described as Occupation: Denco Bus Line; Complexion: Dark; Eye Color: Brown; Hair Color: Brown; Height: 5'11"; Weight: 180 lbs. on 16 Oct 1940. He lived in Boise, Idaho, USA in 1948 (Street Address: 2607 N 36th; Occupation: Manager). He lived in West Boise, Ada, Idaho, USA in 1950 (Street Address: Wo-36; 35 Age: 35; Manager Occupation: Manager; Apartment Number: RV9; Class of Worker: Private; Enumeration District: 1-71; Hours Worked: 72; Industry: Bus Depot; Live On Farm: No; Occupation Category: Working; Three Or More Acres: No; Head Relation To Head: Head; Marital Status: Married). He lived in Boise, Idaho, USA in 1950 (Street Address: N 36th RD 9; Occupation: Manager). He lived in Boise, Idaho, USA in 1953. He lived in Boise, Idaho, USA in 1958. He lived in Pendleton, Umatilla County, Oregon, USA in June 1958 (Occupation: Manager Greyhound Bus Depot). He was employed as a bus station manager (Trailways and Greyhound) in 1960. He lived in Boise, Ada, Idaho, USA in 1968 (fuel and mileage auditor for the state of Idaho). He lived in Boise, Ada, Idaho, USA in 1994 (Street Address: 12134 W Keates Dr). He was buried on 25 Nov 2005 in Boise, Ada, Idaho, USA (Cloverdale Memorial Park (10VV-57-1); Find A Grave #214875763). He was also known as Ray. His cause of death was cancer. FamilySearch ID: (L2JL-JJ1) Race: (White).

Rayburne, or Ray as he was known, went to school in Alex and Chickasha, Oklahoma, graduating from Chickasha High School in 1933. He got his first job at the Oklahoma Transportation Company working for Denco Bus Lines for 11 years in Ada and Oklahoma City. While living in Ada, he met and married Marjorie Taylor in 1941. They soon moved to Oklahoma City, where their son Larry was born in 1943.

Left: Ray Lievsay WW II draft card, 16 Oct 1940. From Ancestry.com.

During World War II they moved to Tacoma, Washington in 1944 and Ray worked at the Pacific Naval Air Base there. His wife Marge said, "Ray was a 4F -- flat feet. He tried to get in the Navy and nobody would take him" (Taylor M. , 2015, p. 20:00). The family moved to Boise in 1946, where Ray became station manager for the Pacific Trailways Bus Line for 11 years. Also in 1946, their second son, Jerry was born but died in less than a month from pulmonary disease. In 1957, they moved to Pendleton, Oregon where he was the manager for the Greyhound Bus Depot. Their son Larry graduated from Pendleton High School and was a standout pitcher on the high school baseball team.

In 1961 they returned to Boise where Ray was employed by the State of Idaho Law Enforcement Department as a fuel and mileage auditor until retiring in December 1979 at age 65.

Ray and his family enjoyed many outdoor activities such as golf, fishing, camping, bird hunting, and gardening. Ray was always talking about his last fishing trip or planning the next one with his son Larry. It was a common sight to see him working with his Labrador retriever bird dog before duck hunting season.

Allen Rayburne Lievsay and Marjorie Ellen Taylor had the following children:

2.   i.   LARRY RAY[2] LIEVSAY was born on 07 Apr 1943 in Oklahoma City, Oklahoma, Oklahoma, USA. He married (1) JANET FREELAND on 20 Apr 1973 in Boise, Ada, Idaho, USA (University Christian Church). She was born on 23 Feb 1947. He married (2) PATRICIA A MARTIN on 03 Jul 1985 in Winnemucca, Humboldt,

Nevada, USA. He married (3) RHONDA REED on 30 May 1992 in Boise, Ada, Idaho, USA. She was born on 31 Jan 1952.

3.   ii.   JERRY THOMAS LIEVSAY was born on 12 Aug 1946 in Boise, Ada, Idaho, USA as the second child of Allen Rayburne Lievsay and Marjorie Ellen Taylor. He died on 07 Sep 1946 in Boise, Ada, Idaho, USA. Jerry Thomas Lievsay was buried on 09 Sep 1946 in Boise, Ada, Idaho, USA (Cloverdale Memorial Park (Sec 1LV-28-5); Find A Grave #210612190). His cause of death was pulmonary disease.

Generation 2

2. LARRY RAY² LIEVSAY was born on 07 Apr 1943 in Oklahoma City, Oklahoma, Oklahoma, USA as the first child of Allen Rayburne Lievsay and Marjorie Ellen Taylor. He had one sibling, namely: Jerry Thomas. When he was 30, he married Janet Freeland on 20 Apr 1973 in Boise, Ada, Idaho, USA (University Christian Church). When he was 42, he married Patricia A Martin on 03 Jul 1985 in Winnemucca, Humboldt, Nevada, USA. When he was 49, he married Rhonda Reed on 30 May 1992 in Boise, Ada, Idaho, USA.

Far left: Larry Lievsay (Pendleton High School) photo, 1962. From Marjorie Taylor Collection.

Left: Larry Lievsay photo, 2016. From Marjorie Taylor Collection.

Larry Ray Lievsay lived in West Boise, Ada, Idaho, USA in 1950 (Street Address: Wo -36; 7 Age: 7; Apartment Number: RV9; Enumeration District: 1-71; Live On Farm: No; Three Or More Acres: No; Son Relation To Head: Son; Marital Status: Single). He lived in Pendleton, Umatilla, Oregon, USA in 1958. He lived in Pendleton, Umatilla, Oregon, USA in 1961 (Age: 16). He lived in Pendleton, Oregon, USA in 1961. He graduated in May 1962 in Pendleton, Umatilla, Oregon, USA (Pendleton High School). He received a BS Forestry (Range Mgmt) degree in 1966 from the Univ of Idaho. He served in the military between 1966–1972 in Boise, Ada, Idaho, USA (Idaho National Guard, Maint. Battalion). He was employed by the US Bureau of Land Management between 1966 and 1996 in Boise, Ada, Idaho, USA. He lived in Denver, Colorado in 1976 (Occupation: BLM Real Estate specialist). He lived in Boise, Ada, Idaho, USA in 1988 (Street Address: 8885 W Canterbury St; Postal Code: 83709-6059 (1993); Street Address: 7216 Snohomish St; Postal Code: 83642-6658 (1993); Street Address: 950 E Kingsford Dr; Age: 45). He lived in Meridian, Ada, Idaho, USA in 1992. He lived in Boise, Ada, Idaho, USA in 1993 (Street Address: 7216 Snohomish St; Phone Number: 208-362-4584). He lived in Meridian, Ada, Idaho, USA in 1995. He lived in Meridian, Ada, Idaho, USA in 2006 (Street Address: 1971 S Weimaraner Way; 63 Age: 63; Street Address: 1971 E Weimaraner Dr; Street

Address: 2660 S Spring Bar Way; Street Address: 950 E Kingsford Dr). He had a medical condition of multiple myeloma bone marrow cancer in 2012 in Boise, Ada, Idaho, USA. Race: (White).

Larry Ray Lievsay and Janet Freeland had no children.
Larry Ray Lievsay and Patricia A Martin had no children.
Larry Ray Lievsay and Rhonda Reed had no children.

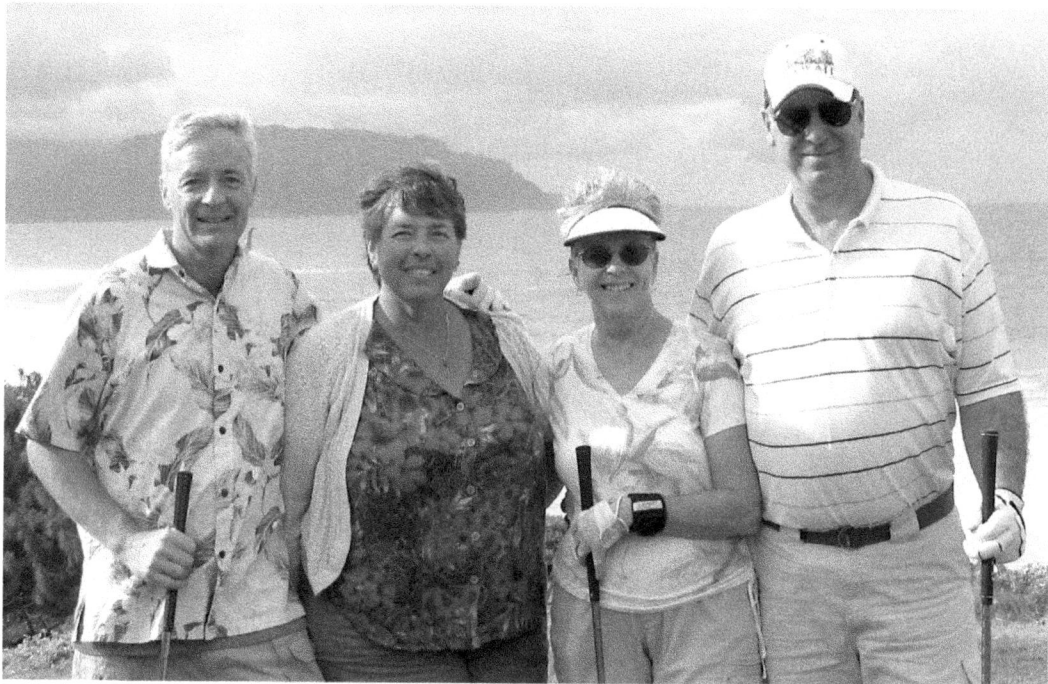

Mary Guerra caddies for her husband Dave and Cousin Larry Lievsay on Kaneohe Golf Course in Hawaii. From left: Dave Conklin, Mary Guerra, Shirley Cain, and Larry Lievsay. Author photo 25 Jan 2008.

Appendix 1: Nettie Taylor Ancestors Pedigree Chart

Note: (1-48) = direct decendant's chapter number & NGSQ reference number beginning in Chap. 1 (i.e. Dempsey Taylor = chapter 1 person 48 [p. 33]; Nettie Taylor = chapter 8, person 1 [p. 125]).

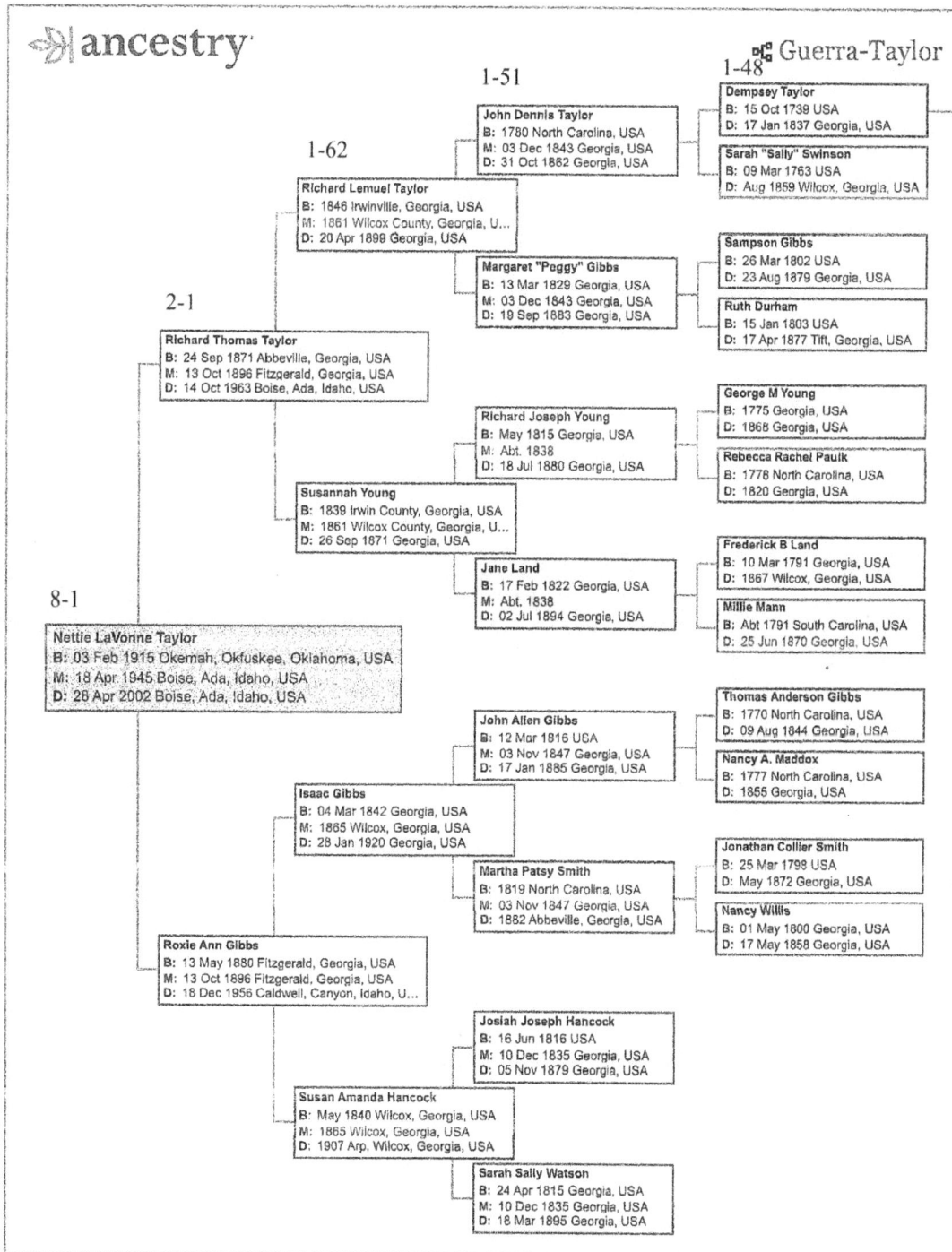

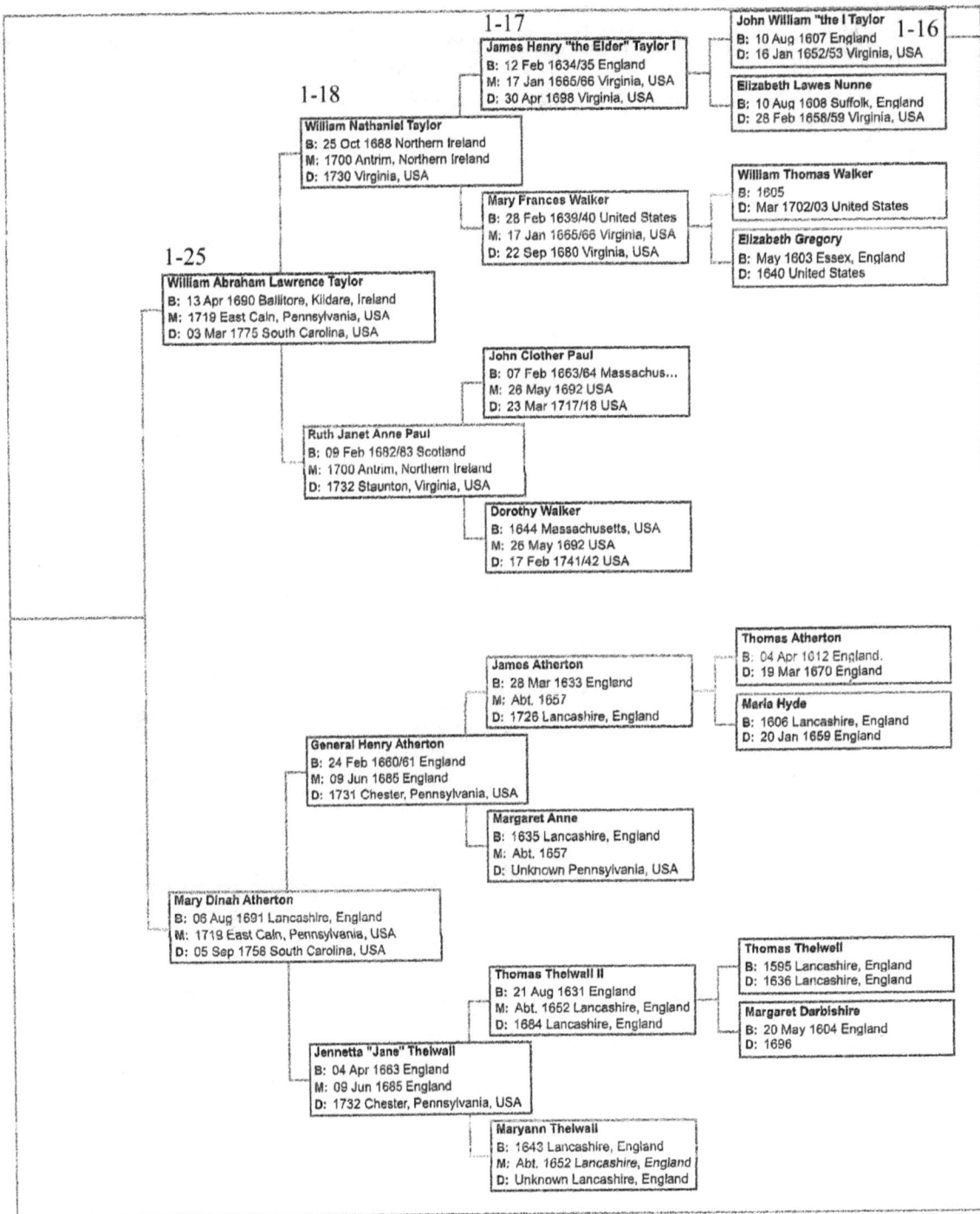

James Henry "the Elder" Taylor I
B: 12 Feb 1634/35 England
M: 17 Jan 1665/66 Virginia, USA
D: 30 Apr 1698 Virginia, USA

John William "the I Taylor
B: 10 Aug 1607 England
D: 16 Jan 1652/53 Virginia, USA

Elizabeth Lawes Nunne
B: 10 Aug 1608 Suffolk, England
D: 28 Feb 1658/59 Virginia, USA

William Nathaniel Taylor
B: 25 Oct 1688 Northern Ireland
M: 1700 Antrim, Northern Ireland
D: 1730 Virginia, USA

Mary Frances Walker
B: 28 Feb 1639/40 United States
M: 17 Jan 1665/66 Virginia, USA
D: 22 Sep 1680 Virginia, USA

William Thomas Walker
B: 1605
D: Mar 1702/03 United States

Elizabeth Gregory
B: May 1603 Essex, England
D: 1640 United States

William Abraham Lawrence Taylor
B: 13 Apr 1690 Ballitore, Kildare, Ireland
M: 1719 East Cain, Pennsylvania, USA
D: 03 Mar 1775 South Carolina, USA

John Clother Paul
B: 07 Feb 1663/64 Massachus...
M: 26 May 1692 USA
D: 23 Mar 1717/18 USA

Ruth Janet Anne Paul
B: 09 Feb 1682/83 Scotland
M: 1700 Antrim, Northern Ireland
D: 1732 Staunton, Virginia, USA

Dorothy Walker
B: 1644 Massachusetts, USA
M: 26 May 1692 USA
D: 17 Feb 1741/42 USA

Thomas Atherton
B: 04 Apr 1612 England.
D: 19 Mar 1670 England

James Atherton
B: 28 Mar 1633 England
M: Abt. 1657
D: 1726 Lancashire, England

Maria Hyde
B: 1606 Lancashire, England
D: 20 Jan 1659 England

General Henry Atherton
B: 24 Feb 1660/61 England
M: 09 Jun 1685 England
D: 1731 Chester, Pennsylvania, USA

Margaret Anne
B: 1635 Lancashire, England
M: Abt. 1657
D: Unknown Pennsylvania, USA

Mary Dinah Atherton
B: 06 Aug 1691 Lancashire, England
M: 1719 East Cain, Pennsylvania, USA
D: 05 Sep 1758 South Carolina, USA

Thomas Thelwall
B: 1595 Lancashire, England
D: 1636 Lancashire, England

Thomas Thelwall II
B: 21 Aug 1631 England
M: Abt. 1652 Lancashire, England
D: 1684 Lancashire, England

Margaret Darbishire
B: 20 May 1604 England
D: 1696

Jennetta "Jane" Thelwall
B: 04 Apr 1663 England
M: 09 Jun 1685 England
D: 1732 Chester, Pennsylvania, USA

Maryann Thelwall
B: 1643 Lancashire, England
M: Abt. 1652 Lancashire, England
D: Unknown Lancashire, England

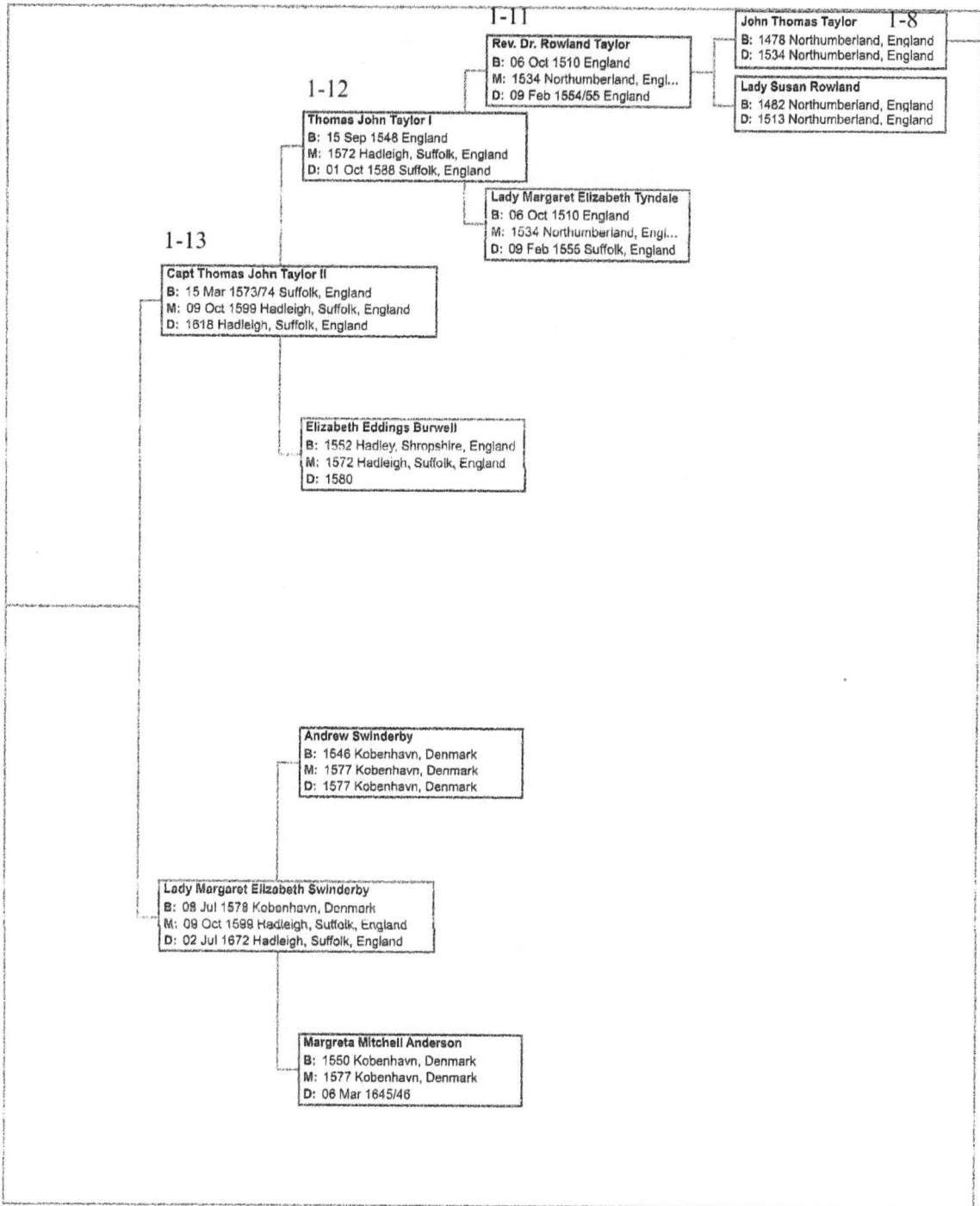

1-11

Rev. Dr. Rowland Taylor
B: 06 Oct 1510 England
M: 1534 Northumberland, Engl...
D: 09 Feb 1554/55 England

John Thomas Taylor   **1-8**
B: 1478 Northumberland, England
D: 1534 Northumberland, England

Lady Susan Rowland
B: 1482 Northumberland, England
D: 1513 Northumberland, England

1-12

Thomas John Taylor I
B: 15 Sep 1548 England
M: 1572 Hadleigh, Suffolk, England
D: 01 Oct 1588 Suffolk, England

Lady Margaret Elizabeth Tyndale
B: 06 Oct 1510 England
M: 1534 Northumberland, Engl...
D: 09 Feb 1555 Suffolk, England

1-13

Capt Thomas John Taylor II
B: 15 Mar 1573/74 Suffolk, England
M: 09 Oct 1599 Hadleigh, Suffolk, England
D: 1618 Hadleigh, Suffolk, England

Elizabeth Eddings Burwell
B: 1552 Hadley, Shropshire, England
M: 1572 Hadleigh, Suffolk, England
D: 1580

Andrew Swinderby
B: 1546 Kobenhavn, Denmark
M: 1577 Kobenhavn, Denmark
D: 1577 Kobenhavn, Denmark

Lady Margaret Elizabeth Swinderby
B: 08 Jul 1578 Kobenhavn, Denmark
M: 09 Oct 1599 Hadleigh, Suffolk, England
D: 02 Jul 1672 Hadleigh, Suffolk, England

Margreta Mitchell Anderson
B: 1550 Kobenhavn, Denmark
M: 1577 Kobenhavn, Denmark
D: 06 Mar 1645/46

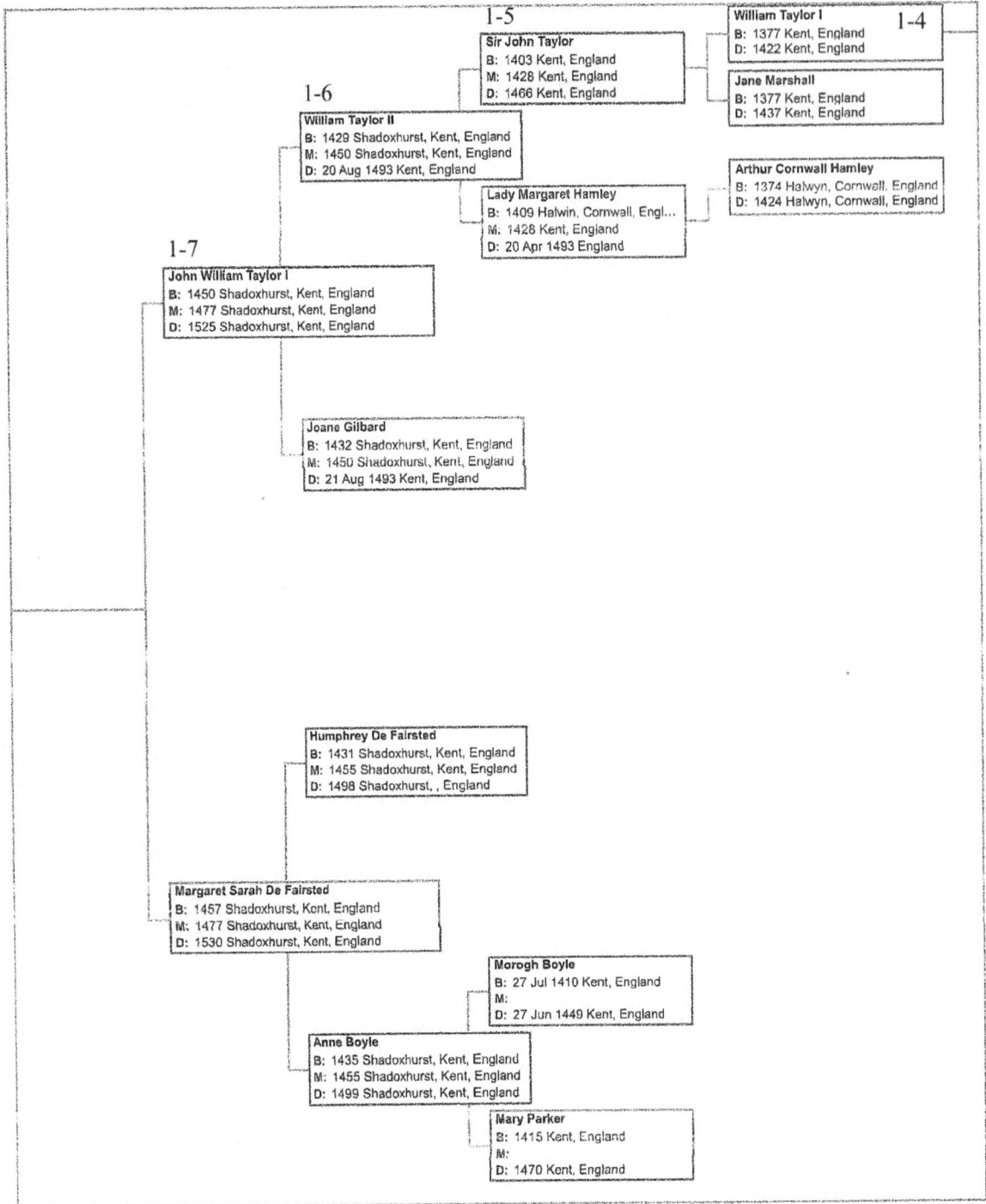

1-5

Sir John Taylor
B: 1403 Kent, England
M: 1428 Kent, England
D: 1466 Kent, England

William Taylor I **1-4**
B: 1377 Kent, England
D: 1422 Kent, England

Jane Marshall
B: 1377 Kent, England
D: 1437 Kent, England

1-6

William Taylor II
B: 1429 Shadoxhurst, Kent, England
M: 1450 Shadoxhurst, Kent, England
D: 20 Aug 1493 Kent, England

Lady Margaret Hamley
B: 1409 Halwin, Cornwall, Engl...
M: 1428 Kent, England
D: 20 Apr 1493 England

Arthur Cornwall Hamley
B: 1374 Halwyn, Cornwall, England
D: 1424 Halwyn, Cornwall, England

1-7

John William Taylor I
B: 1450 Shadoxhurst, Kent, England
M: 1477 Shadoxhurst, Kent, England
D: 1525 Shadoxhurst, Kent, England

Joane Gilbard
B: 1432 Shadoxhurst, Kent, England
M: 1450 Shadoxhurst, Kent, England
D: 21 Aug 1493 Kent, England

Humphrey De Fairsted
B: 1431 Shadoxhurst, Kent, England
M: 1455 Shadoxhurst, Kent, England
D: 1498 Shadoxhurst, , England

Margaret Sarah De Fairsted
B: 1457 Shadoxhurst, Kent, England
M: 1477 Shadoxhurst, Kent, England
D: 1530 Shadoxhurst, Kent, England

Morogh Boyle
B: 27 Jul 1410 Kent, England
M:
D: 27 Jun 1449 Kent, England

Anne Boyle
B: 1435 Shadoxhurst, Kent, England
M: 1455 Shadoxhurst, Kent, England
D: 1499 Shadoxhurst, Kent, England

Mary Parker
B: 1415 Kent, England
M:
D: 1470 Kent, England

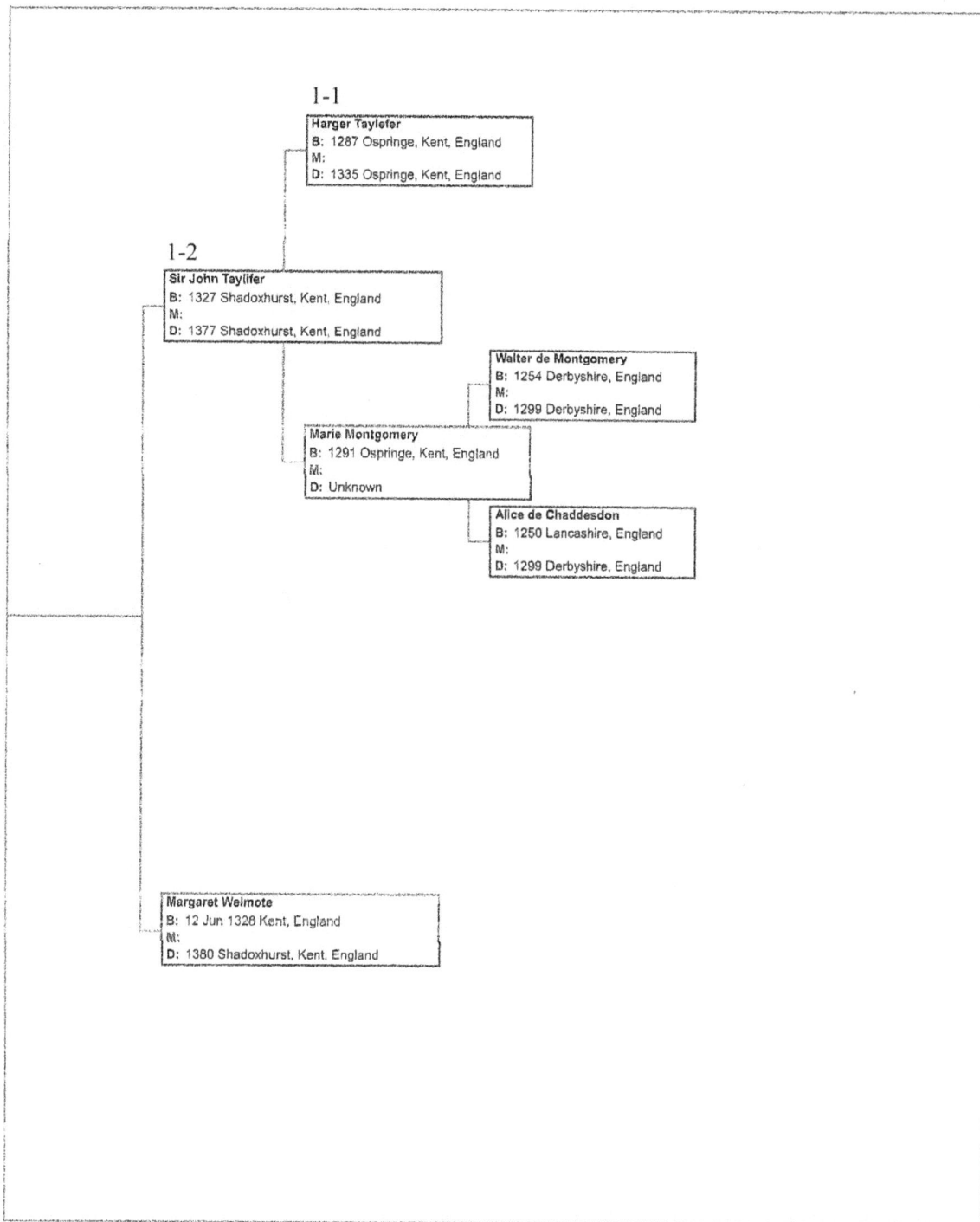

1-1

Harger Taylefer
B: 1287 Ospringe, Kent, England
M:
D: 1335 Ospringe, Kent, England

1-2

Sir John Taylifer
B: 1327 Shadoxhurst, Kent, England
M:
D: 1377 Shadoxhurst, Kent, England

Walter de Montgomery
B: 1254 Derbyshire, England
M:
D: 1299 Derbyshire, England

Marie Montgomery
B: 1291 Ospringe, Kent, England
M:
D: Unknown

Alice de Chaddesdon
B: 1250 Lancashire, England
M:
D: 1299 Derbyshire, England

Margaret Welmote
B: 12 Jun 1328 Kent, England
M:
D: 1380 Shadoxhurst, Kent, England

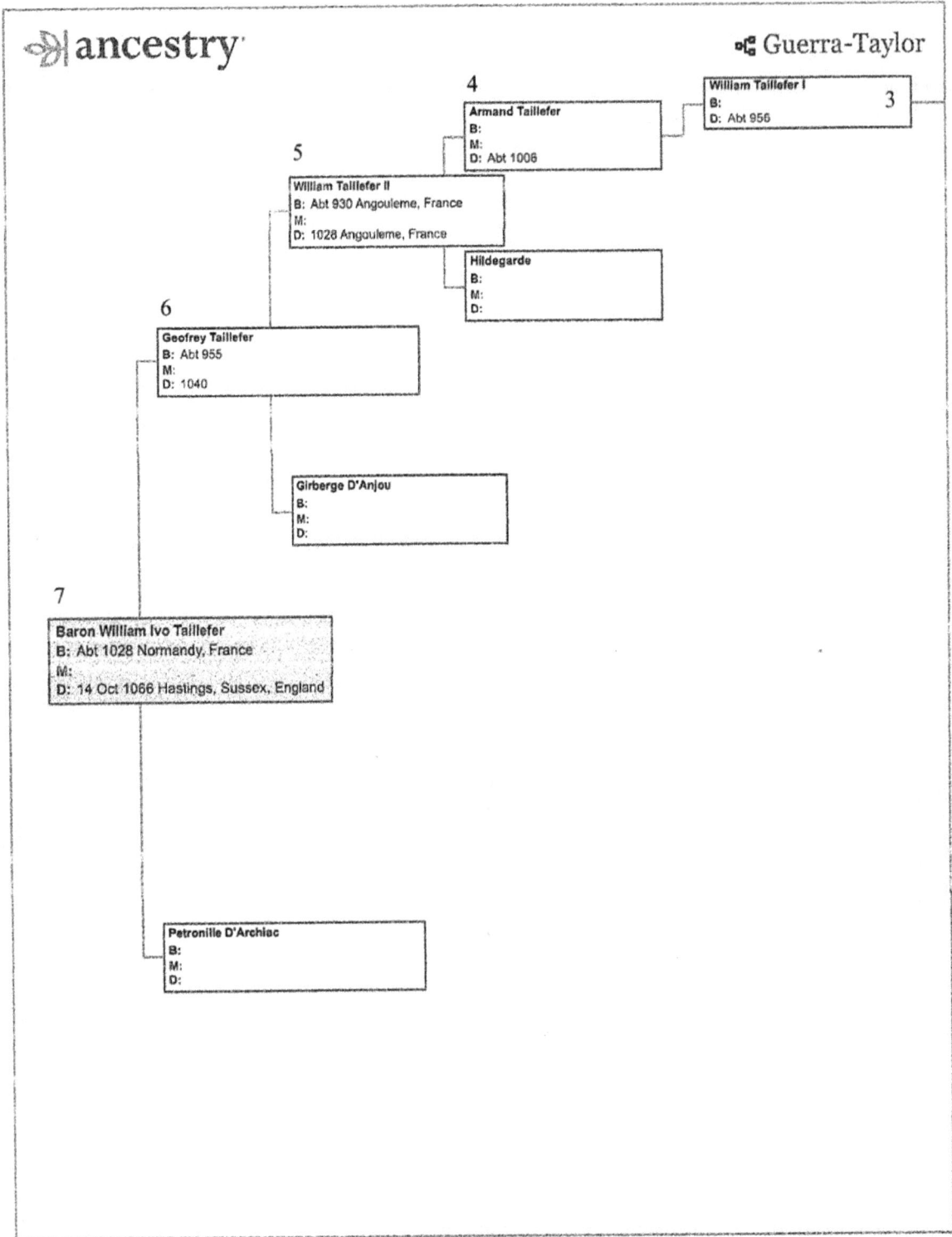

4

Armand Taillefer
B:
M:
D: Abt 1006

William Taillefer I
B:
D: Abt 956

3

5

William Taillefer II
B: Abt 930 Angouleme, France
M:
D: 1028 Angouleme, France

Hildegarde
B:
M:
D:

6

Geofrey Taillefer
B: Abt 955
M:
D: 1040

Girberge D'Anjou
B:
M:
D:

7

Baron William Ivo Taillefer
B: Abt 1028 Normandy, France
M:
D: 14 Oct 1066 Hastings, Sussex, England

Petronille D'Archiac
B:
M:
D:

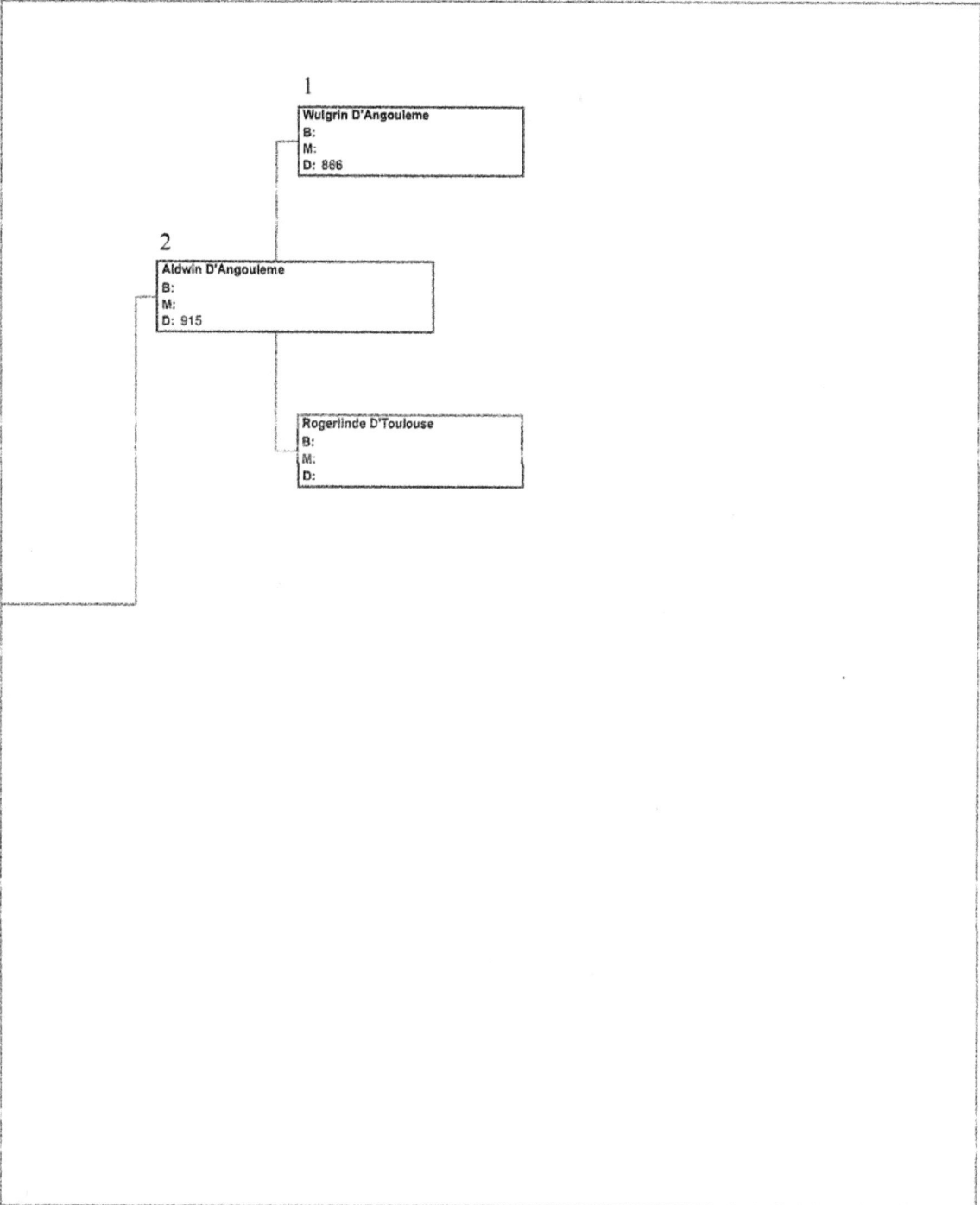

1
Wulgrin D'Angouleme
B:
M:
D: 886

2
Aldwin D'Angouleme
B:
M:
D: 915

Rogerlinde D'Toulouse
B:
M:
D:

Appendix 2: DNA Ethnicity Reports

Introduction to Taylor Family DNA Ethnicity Reports

Each of the following DNA ethnicity reports include information on: 1) an Actual *versus* Predicted Relationship to the home person, Mary Guerra (Ancestry Kit #A022185), based on documentation *versus* DNA analysis; 2) the approximate amount of shared DNA (in centimorgans (cM), a unit used to measure the length of DNA) in the relationship. and 3) a DNA Ethnicity Estimate that graphically shows which regions of the world the approximate percentage of DNA for that person is estimated to be from.

Although the AncestryDNA web page shows that Mary Guerra currently has more than 1000 4th cousins or closer, only 3 DNA reports are included at this time. These reports were selected for the following reasons: 1) they all used the same AncestryDNA test kit and results display; 2) they all have separate documentation as to their actual location in the Taylor family tree; and 3) they all have given permission to view their reports.

AncestryDNA Match Confidence Score:
When AncestryDNA compares your DNA to the DNA of one of your matches, they calculate a confidence score for you. This score lets you know how much DNA evidence there is for you and your match actually being related.

The confidence score is based on the amount and location of the DNA that you share with your match. AncestryDNA shows the shared amount using centimorgans (cM). The higher the number, the higher the confidence, and in general, the closer the relationship. Since you can share DNA with your match on one or more segments in different locations in the genome, AncestryDNA shows you how many. Note that the number of segments and number of centimorgans (cM) that they show reflects only those segments that they believe were inherited from a recent common ancestor. In other words, segments that are likely to be identical by descent).

Confidence Score	Approximate amount of shared centimorgans: cM	Likelihood of a single recent common ancestor	Description
Extremely High	More than 60	Virtually 100%	You and your match share enough DNA to prove that you're both descendants of a common ancestor (or couple), and the connection is recent enough to be conclusive.

Confidence Score	Approximate amount of shared centimorgans: cM	Likelihood of a single recent common ancestor	Description
Very High	45—60	About 99%	You and your match share enough DNA that we're almost certain you're both descendants of a recent common ancestor (or couple).
High	30—45	About 95%	You and your match share enough DNA that it is likely you're both descendants of a common ancestor (or couple), but there's a small chance the common ancestor(s) are quite distant and difficult to identify.
Good	16—30	Above 50%	You and your match share some DNA, probably from a recent common ancestor (or couple), but the DNA may be from distant ancestors that are difficult to identify.
Moderate	6—16	15—50%	You and your match might share DNA from a recent common ancestor (or couple), share DNA from very distant ancestors, or you may not be related.

The amount of centimorgans (cM) you share with a match can also help you understand your relationship to them. For example, you'll usually share about 120 cM with a 3rd cousin, but it's possible to share as few as 90 or as many as 200. Be aware that the precise amount of shared DNA can vary beyond the ranges shown in the table below (Ball, Catherine. et al., 2016).

Approximate amount of shared centimorgans (cM)	Possible Relationship
3,475	Parent, child, or identical twin
2,400—2,800	Full sibling (including fraternal twins)
1,450—2,050	Grandparent, aunt, uncle, half sibling
680—1,150	1st cousin, great grandparent
200—620	2nd cousin
90—180	3rd cousin
20—85	4th cousin
6—20	Distant cousin: 5th cousin — 8th cousins

AncestryDNA Ethnicity Estimate:

AncestryDNA uses two different processes to determine the regions provided in your DNA Story: a reference panel and Genetic Communities™.

Building a reference panel:
One way AncestryDNA create estimates of your genetic ethnicity is by comparing your DNA to the DNA of other people who are native to a region. The AncestryDNA reference panel contains 40,017 DNA samples from people from around the world.

AncestryDNA builds the reference panel from a larger reference collection of 97,000 DNA samples collected from people whose genealogy suggests they are native to one region. Many of these samples were originally collected by the Sorenson Molecular Genealogy Foundation. Each panel member's genealogy is documented so we can be confident that their family is representative of people with a long history (hundreds of years) in that region.

Each volunteer's DNA sample from a given region is then tested and compared to all the others to construct the AncestryDNA reference panel. In the end, 40,017 samples were carefully selected to represent 60 global regions for the reference panel (Ball, Catherine. et al., 2019, p. 10).

Comparing your DNA to the reference panel:
AncestryDNA then compares your DNA to the DNA in the reference panel to see which regions your DNA is most like. The ethnicity estimate you see on the web site is the result of this comparison.

Your AncestryDNA Results reveal your unique story —
who your ancestors were and where they came from.

Results as of:
21 Sep 2020

DNA Results Summary for Mary Guerra

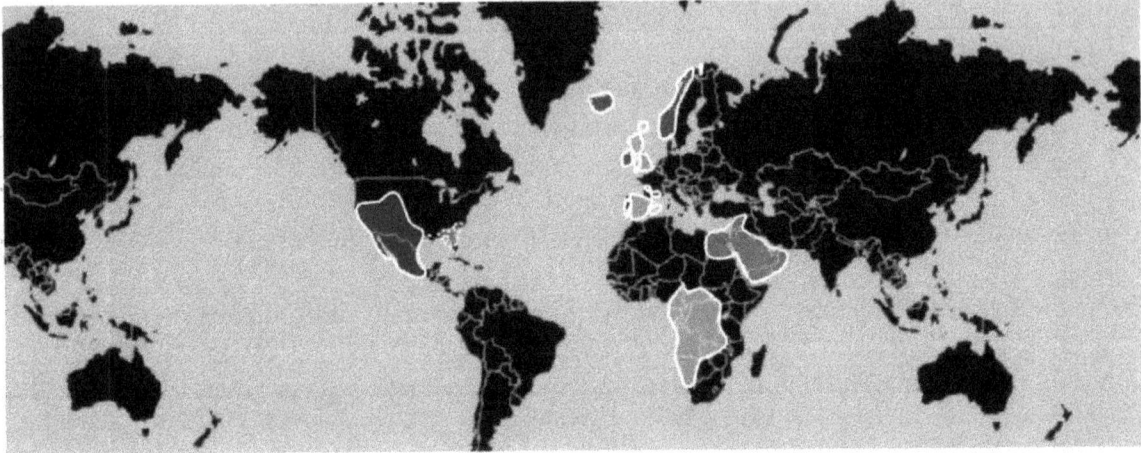

© Mapbox, © OpenStreetMap

Ethnicity Estimate

Spain	33%
England & Northwestern Europe	28%
Scotland	13%
Wales	6%
France	5%
Indigenous Americas—Mexico	5%

- Nuevo León, Tamaulipas & South Texas
  - Northeastern Nuevo Leon & South Texas
  - Rio Grande Valley

Portugal	4%
Norway	2%
Ireland	2%
Middle East	1%
Cameroon, Congo & Western Bantu Peoples	1%

Additional Communities

- Georgia & Florida Settlers
  - Southeast Georgia Settlers
  - Central Georgia Settlers
- South Carolina Settlers
  - Coastal Carolinas Settlers

Dennis R. Taylor—Maternal 1st Cousin (actual)

Amount of Shared DNA: 1,001 centimorgans shared across 38 DNA segments
Possible range: 1st - 2nd cousins; *1st Cousins*
Confidence: Extremely High
Ancestry Kit #

Relationship Info: 1st Cousin (Predicted)
Our analysis of your DNA predicts that this person you match with is your first cousin. The exact relationship however can vary. It could be a great nephew or great-great grandmother.

While there may be some statistical variation in our prediction, it's likely to be a four-degree separation. However, the relationship could range from three to five degrees of separation.

Here are some examples of possible relationships separated by 4 degrees:

1st Cousins
1st Cousins share your grandparents

Grandparent (Richard Thomas Taylor)
2 degrees

Parent (Nettie Taylor)
1 degree

Uncle (Artice Taylor)
3 degrees

You (Mary Guerra)
0 degrees

1st Cousin (Dennis R. Taylor)
4 degrees

Your AncestryDNA Results reveal your unique story —
who your ancestors were and where they came from.

Results as of:
21 Sep 2020

DNA Results Summary for Dennis Taylor

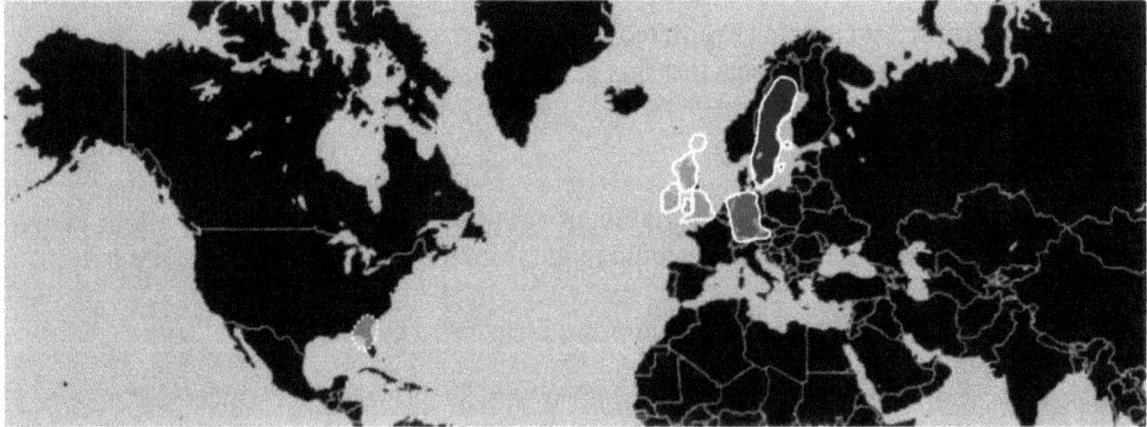

© Mapbox, © OpenStreetMap

Ethnicity Estimate

England & Northwestern Europe	51%
Scotland	18%
Ireland	13%
Wales	11%
Germanic Europe	4%
Sweden	3%

Additional Communities

Georgia & Florida Settlers
  Southeast Georgia Settlers
  Central Georgia Settlers

Arlene (Taylor) Parisot—Maternal 1st Cousin (actual)

Amount of Shared DNA: 1,001 centimorgans shared across 38 DNA segments
Possible range: 1st - 2nd cousins; *1st Cousins*
Confidence: Extremely High
Ancestry Kit #

Relationship Info: 1st Cousin (Predicted)
Our analysis of your DNA predicts that this person you match with is your first cousin. The exact relationship however can vary. It could be a great nephew or great-great grandmother.

While there may be some statistical variation in our prediction, it's likely to be a four-degree separation. However, the relationship could range from three to five degrees of separation.

Here are some examples of possible relationships separated by 4 degrees:

1st Cousins
1st Cousins share your grandparents

                         Grandparent (Richard Thomas Taylor)
                                 2 degrees
Parent (Nettie Taylor)
1 degree

                                                    Uncle (Artice Taylor)
                                                        3 degrees

You (Mary Guerra)
0 degrees

                                                    1st Cousin (Arlene Taylor)
                                                        4 degrees

Your AncestryDNA Results reveal your unique story —
who your ancestors were and where they came from.

Results as of:
21 Sep 2020

DNA Results Summary for Arlene Parisot

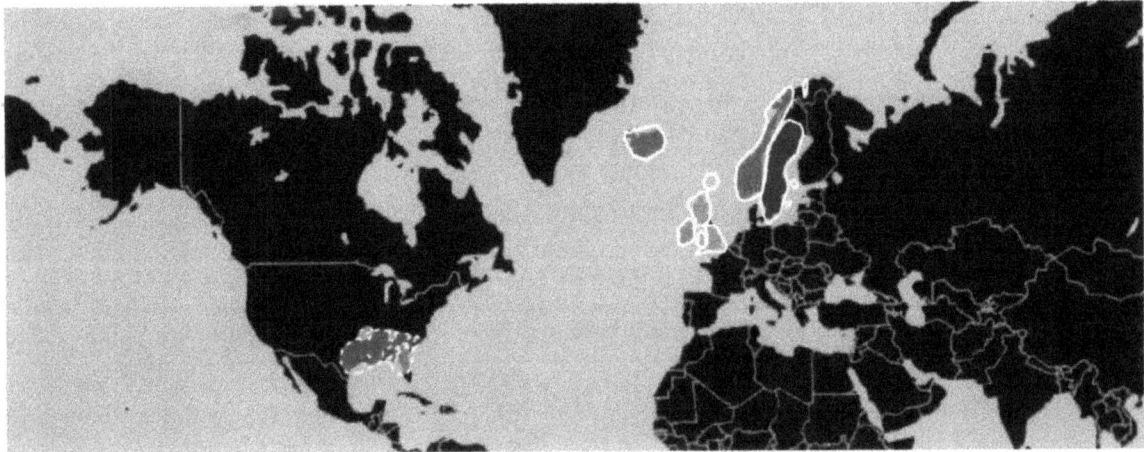

© Mapbox, © OpenStreetMap

Ethnicity Estimate

England & Northwestern Europe	49%
Scotland	40%
Wales	4%
Ireland	3%
Norway	2%
Sweden	2%

Additional Communities

Georgia & Florida Settlers
   Southeast Georgia Settlers
   Central Georgia Settlers
Northern Arkansas & Middle Tennessee
Settlers
   Middle Tennessee & Ozarks Settlers
South Carolina Settlers
Southern States Settlers

George Parisot—Maternal 1st Cousin 1x removed (actual)

Amount of Shared DNA: 535 centimorgans shared across 24 DNA segments
Possible range: 1st - 2nd cousins; *1st Cousins*
Confidence: Extremely High
Ancestry Kit #

Predicted Relationship Info: 2nd Cousins
Our analysis of your DNA predicts that this person you match with is probably your second cousin.
The exact relationship can vary. It could be a first cousin once removed, or a great-great aunt. While there may be some statistical variation in our prediction, it's likely to be a second cousin type relationship – which are separated by 6 degrees or six people. However, the relationship could range from four to seven degrees of separation.

Here are some examples of possible relationships separated by 6 degrees:

1st Cousins (1x removed)
1st Cousins (1x removed) share your great-great grandparents

Grandparent (Richard Thomas Taylor)
2 degrees

Parent (Nettie Taylor)
1 degree

Uncle (Artice Taylor)
3 degrees

You (Mary Guerra)
0 degrees

1st Cousin (Arlene Taylor)
4 degrees

1st Cousin 1x removed (George Parisot)
5 degrees

Your AncestryDNA Results reveal your unique story —
who your ancestors were and where they came from.

Results as of:
05 Apr 2020

DNA Results Summary for George Parisot

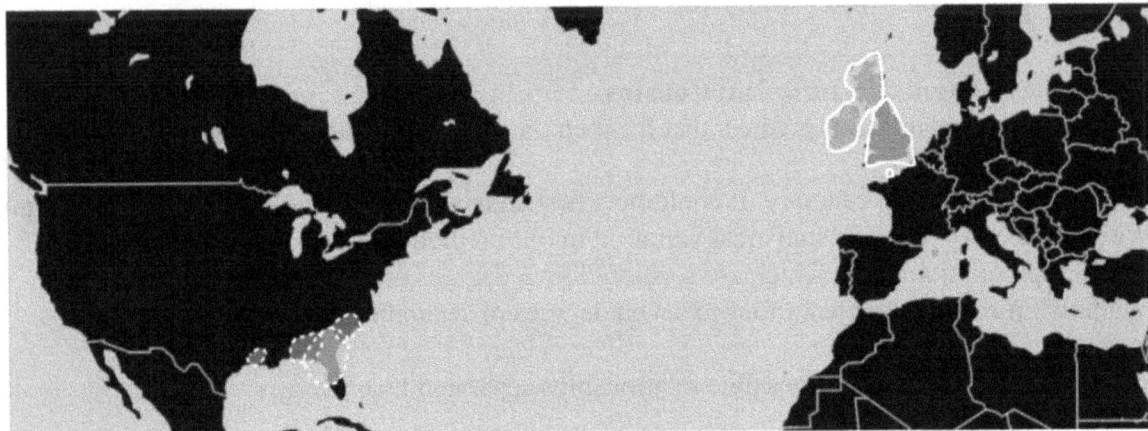

© Mapbox, © OpenStreetMap

Ethnicity Estimate

Ireland & Scotland   60%
* Munster, Ireland
  * South West Munster
  * Beara Peninsula
  * West Beara Peninsula

England, Wales & Northwestern Europe   40%

Additional Communities

* Georgia & Florida Settlers
  * Central Georgia Settlers
* South Carolina Settlers

Taylor Ancestors Grave Locations
Online Find A Grave Memorials (www.findagrave.com)
as of 29 Dec 2022

NAME: LAST	FIRST	MIDDLE	MAIDEN	MEMORIAL #	CEMETERY	CITY / STATE	ADDRESS
Abston	Martha	Sue	Lucas	82967806	Resthaven Gardens Cem	Oklahoma City, OK	500 SW 104th St
Abston	Oliver	Gene		225971521	Arlington National Cem	Arlington, VA	1 Memorial Ave
Blood	Daniel	Oakley		24849229	Freeze Cemetery	Potlatch, ID	917 W Freeze Rd
Cooper	Susie	Amanda	Tiegreen	103480075	Restland Mem Park	Dallas, TX	9220 Restland Rd
Davis	Sarah (Knoxie)	Knox	Taylor	20981	Locust Grove Cemetery	St Francisville, LA	Bains Rd
Davis	Jefferson	Finis (CSA Pres)		260	Hollywood Cemetery	Richmond, VA	412 S Cherry St
Gibbs	Isaac				Gibbs Cemetery?	Arp, Ben Hill Co, GA	1-1/2 Mi NW on Astor Rd
Gibbs	Susan	Amanda (Mandy)	Hancock		Gibbs Cemetery?	Arp, Ben Hill Co, GA	1-1/2 Mi NW on Astor Rd
Gibbs	Sampson			55267377	Turner Church Cemetery	Tift County, GA	Ferry Lk & Smith-Coker Rd
Gibbs	Ruth		Durham	55267378	Turner Church Cemetery	Tift County, GA	Ferry Lk & Smith-Coker Rd
Gibbs/Taylor	Ruth		Clements	126393649	Clements Cemetery	Irwin County, GA	Big Creek Rd
Gilstrap	Billy	Burt			Ashes at wife Sara's home	Colorado Spgs, CO	
Guerra	Nettie	LaVonne	Taylor	193540239	Cloverdale Mem Park	Boise, ID	11825 W Fairview Ave
Guerra	Guadalupe (Lupe)	Filiberto		193540388	Cloverdale Mem Park	Boise, ID	11825 W Fairview Ave
Guerra	Antonio	Richard		132078861	Cloverdale Mem Park	Boise, ID	11825 W Fairview Ave
Hancock	Josiah	Jackson		98440012	Paulk Cemetery	Rebecca, GA	Young Rd
Hancock	Sarah	Sally	Watson	98440065	Paulk Cemetery	Rebecca, GA	Young Rd
Lievsay	Marjorie	Ellen	Taylor	159067839	Cloverdale Mem Park	Boise, ID	11825 W Fairview Ave
Lievsay	Allen	Rayborne		214875763	Cloverdale Mem Park	Boise, ID	11825 W Fairview Ave
Lievsay	Jerry	Thomas		210612190	Cloverdale Mem Park	Boise, ID	11825 W Fairview Ave
Lucas	Nommie	Lee	Taylor	82967883	Resthaven Gardens Cem	Oklahoma City, OK	500 SW 104th St
Lucas	Elmer	Lawrence		82967918	Resthaven Gardens Cem	Oklahoma City, OK	500 SW 104th St
Madison	James (4th Pres)			661	Montpelier Plantation	Orange County, VA	Montpelier Station
Madison	Dorthea (Dolley)		Payne	660	Montpelier Plantation	Orange County, VA	Montpelier Station
Parisot	Arlene	Hazel	Taylor	215744422	MT State Veterans Cem	Helena, MT	1900 Williams St
Parisot	Neil	Jerome		189467470	MT State Veterans Cem	Helena, MT	1900 Williams St
Porter	Elsie	Blanche	Taylor	5679778	Kechi Township Cemetery	Park City, KS	N Hillside St
Porter	James	Glenn				Marathon, FL?	
Porter	Elsie	Christine		167584504	Fairview Cemetery	Pryor, OK	NE 1st St
Porter	James	Laddie		5679780	Kechi Township Cemetery	Park City, KS	N Hillside St
Porter	Virgina	Beth	Quillan	23119255	Kechi Township Cemetery	Park City, KS	N Hillside St
Porter	Quillin	F				Marathon, FL?	
Scott	Virgina (Josie) (Jo)	Josephine	Porter			Marathon, FL?	

Scott II	Ferdinand	Winfred				Chicago, Il?	
Stofer	Robert	Maxwell			Wright State Univ Cem?	Dayton, OH	
Stofer	Lawrence	Edward		200720745	Rockafield Cemetery	Fairborn, OH	Circle Dr
Stofer	Robert	Maxwell Jr				Jacksonville, FL?	
Taylor	Richard	Thomas		214874752	Cloverdale Mem Park	Boise, ID	11825 W Fairview Ave
Taylor	Roxie	Ann	Gibbs	214875255	Cloverdale Mem Park	Boise, ID	11825 W Fairview Ave
Taylor	Richard (Dick)	Lamuel		555993360	Morris Hill Cemetery	Boise, ID	317 N. Latah
Taylor	Mabel (Mabe)	Ruth	Crone	555993302	Morris Hill Cemetery	Boise, ID	317 N. Latah
Taylor	Artice (Art)	Raymond		67111788	Meridian Cemetery	Meridian, ID	895 E Franklin Rd
Taylor	Hazel	Florence	McClure	67111777	Meridian Cemetery	Meridian, ID	895 E Franklin Rd
Taylor	Richard	Lemuel			Morris Hill Ministry Cem?	Rutledge, GA	
Taylor	Suzannah		Young		Morris Hill Ministry Cem?	Rutledge, GA	
Taylor	John	Dennis		67475277	Salem Baptist Church Cem	Fitzgerald, GA	Salem Church Rd
Taylor	Margaret (Peggy)	Mackall	Smith	1023	Zachary Taylor Nat Cem	Windy Hills, KY	4701 Brownsboro Rd
Taylor	Zachary (12th Pres)			8626	Zachary Taylor Nat Cem	Windy Hills, KY	4701 Brownsboro Rd
Taylor	Margaret (Peggy)		Gibbs			Irwin County, GA	
Taylor	Dempsey					Wilcox County, GA	
Taylor	Sarah		Swinson	10224789	Old Waxhaw Church Cem	Lancaster County, SC	2814 Old Hickory Rd
Taylor	William	Abraham Lawrence		10224788	Old Waxhaw Church Cem	Lancaster County, SC	2814 Old Hickory Rd
Taylor	Mary	Dinah	Atherton	116206202	Taylor-Quarles Family Cem	Orange County, VA	Bloomsbury Rd
Taylor	Martha	Montague	Thompson	18531133	Hare Forest Plantation Cem	Greenfield, Locustville, VA	
Taylor	William	Nathaniel		18538707	unknown	Staunton, VA	
Taylor	Ruth	Janet	Paul			Hopewell, VA	10th Ave & Davis St
Taylor	Mary	Bishop	Gregory			Caroline County, VA	
Taylor	Frances		Walker	219294247	Wicomico Parish Church	Northumberland Co, VA	5191 Jessie Ball Dupont Hwy
Taylor	John	William "the Immigrant"	Nunne	219354565	Wicomico Parish Church	Northumberland Co, VA	5191 Jessie Ball Dupont Hwy
Taylor	Elizabeth		Swinderby	18652168	St. Mary's Churchyard	Hadleigh, Suffolk, England	Babergh Dist
Taylor	Lady Margaret			18685777	St. Mary's Churchyard	Hadleigh, Suffolk, England	Babergh Dist
Taylor	Elizabeth	Eddings	Burwell	23000159	St. Mary's Churchyard	Hadleigh, Suffolk, England	Babergh Dist
Taylor	Rev Dr Rowland			18671473	St. Mary's Churchyard	Hadleigh, Suffolk, England	Babergh Dist
Taylor	Lady Margaret		Tyndale	114966811	unknown	England	
Taylor	John	Thomas		114966875	unknown	Rothbury, Northumberland, Eng	
Taylor	Lady Susan		Rowland	18538665	Hare Forest Plantation Cem	Hopewell, VA	10th Ave & Davis St
Taylor	James I	Henry "the Elder"		18685743	St. Mary's Churchyard	Suffolk, England	Hadleigh, Babergh Dist
Taylor	Thomas	John I		116206295	Taylor-Quarles Family Cem	Orange, VA	Bloomsbury Rd
Taylor	James	Walker II		18652140	St. Mary's Churchyard	Hadleigh, England	Hadleigh, Babergh Dist
Taylor	Capt Thomas	John II					
Tiegreen	Bessie	Amanda	Taylor	114356095	Southern Memorial Park	Biloxi, MS	2076 Beach Blvd
Tiegreen	Carl	Mandeville		52616423	Southern Memorial Park	Biloxi, MS	2076 Beach Blvd
Tiegreen	Judith (Judy)		Tatum	186026917	Decatur Cemetery	Decatur, GA	299 Bell Street

References

Ball, Catherine. et al. (2016). *AncestryDNA Matching White Paper.* AncestryDNA. Retrieved Mar 6, 2020, from https://www.ancestry.com/corporate/sites/default/files/AncestryDNA-Matching-White-Paper.

Ball, Catherine. et al. (2019). *Ethnicity Estimate White Paper.* AncestryDNA. Retrieved Mar 3, 2020, from https://www.ancestrycdn.com/dna/static/pdf/whitepapers/EV2019_white_paper_1.

Brown, N. (1941, Sep 25). Richard Taylors meeting kin they never saw before. *The Leader-Enterprise & Press.*

Browning, Arnold J. & Justin W. Wilder. (2009). *The Descendants of Emory R. Wilder: 1889-1967.* Camas, WA: Arnold J. Browning.

Churchill, W. (1991). *Churchill's History of the English Speaking Peoples. NY.* (H. S. Commager, Ed.) NY: Greenwich House.

Clements, J. (1932). *History of Irwin County (Georgia).* Atlanta, GA: Foote & Davies Co.

Conklin, D. (1975). *Montana Historic Preservation Plan.* Helena, MT: Montana Dept of Fish, Wildlife & Parks.

Conklin, D. (2002). *Montana History Weekends: 52 Adventures in History.* Guilford, CT: Globe Pequot Press.

Conklin, D. G. (2018). *Conklin-Marinkovic Family History.* Kalispell, MT: Published privately by the author. Moore Graphics, Youngtown, Arizona. 177 pp.

Conklin, D. G. (2020). *The Descendants of Jose Antonio Guerra.* Kalispell, MT: David G. Conklin. Published privately by the author. Moore Graphics, Youngtown, Arizona. 166 pp.

Crawford, A. (2007). The Swamp Fox. *Smithsonian Magazine.* Retrieved Feb 20, 2022, from https://www.smithsonianmag.com/history/the-swamp-fox-157330429/

Crone, D. (2008). *Mabel Crone Eulogy.* Alden-Waggoner Funeral Chapel, Boise, ID. Retrieved Dec 12, 2008

Foxe, J. (2001). *The New Foxe's Book of Martyrs.* Gainesville, FL: Bridge-Logos.

Guerra, E. (1969). *Evangelina Guerra letter to Guadalupe and Nettie Guerra.* San Manuel: Evangelina Guerra Collection in author's Guerra Family History files. Retrieved Oct 18, 1969

Guerra, M. (2015, Nov 28). Mary Guerra Family History Video Interview. (D. G. Conklin, Interviewer)

Guerra, T. (2018, Aug 17). Tecla Guerra Family History Video Interview. (D. G. Conklin, Interviewer)

Halbert's Family Heritage. (1998). *The New World Book of Conklins.* New York: Halbert's Family Heritage.

Hanks, P. (2003). *Dictionary of American Family Names.* New York: Oxford University Press.

Harding, K. (1987, Mar 7). Elsie Porter, 89, of Biloxi does her aerobic workout. *The Sun Herald.*

House of Names. (2021, Mar 27). Taylor. *House of Names.* Retrieved from https://www.houseofnames.com/Taylor-family-crest#ContemporaryNotables

Idaho Statesman. (1959, Dec 3). Holiday Dishes Can Include Date Cake, Vegetable 'Toss'. *The Idaho Evening Statesman.*

Jones, D. B. (1994). *Children's Literature Awards & Winners: A Directory of Prizes, Authors, and Illustrators* (2nd ed.). Farmington Hills, MI: Thomson Gale.

Landers, A. (1996, Apr 13). Family letters become treasures forever. *Idaho Statesman.*

Logan, M. (1926). *Taylor Typescript. Louisville, KY.* Retrieved Dec 26, 2021, from Taylor Genealogy: www.nltaylor.net/taylor/MTLogan_1926.pdf

Lucas, S. (2019, May 9). Sara Lucas Family History Video Interview. (D. G. Conklin, Interviewer)

Lucas, W. (2017, Aug 23). Wanda Lucas Family History Video Interview. (D. G. Conklin, Interviewer)

Lytton, E. B. (1895). *Harold: The Last of the Saxon Kings: The Battle of Hastings* (Vol. 12). London: Routledge.

MacKiev. (2019). Family Tree Maker. Boston, MA. Retrieved from https://www.mackiev.com/ftm/index.html.

McDonald, M. L. (1987). *Passing of the Pines: History of Wilcox County Georgia.* Roswell, GA: WH Wolfe Association.

Pioneers of Wiregrass Georgia. (1951). *5.* Homerville, GA. Retrieved Apr 2020, from Huxford Genealogical Society: https://www.ancestry.com/mediaui-viewer/tree/%20%20%20%20%20%20%20%2045280133/person/6337891577/media/04429d2a-6ccc-49d9-8ec0-c8a97161817

Porter, J. P. (1997). *Eulogy for James Laddie Porter.*

Porter, V. Q. (1995). *Eulogy for Elsie T. Porter.*

Rigdon, J. C. (2002). *Historical Sketch and Roster of The Georgia 49th Infantry Regiment.* Cartersville, GA: Eastern Digital Resources. Retrieved from www.researchonline.net

Rixford, E. M. (1993). *Families Directly Descended from all the Royal Families in Europe (495 to 1932).* Baltimore, MD: Genealogical Publishing.

Sports Illustrated. (1965, Nov 15). Skiing (1965-66). *Sports Illustrated, 23*(20), pp. 74-76.

Taylor Ancestors. (2020, Jun 21). Retrieved from Our Famous Taylor Ancestors, in: Born of Greatness: https://bornofgreatness.weebly.com/our-famous-taylor-ancestors.html

Taylor, D. (2014, Aug 6). *Taylor Clan Family History.* Retrieved from McClure Family: https://sites.google.com/site/taylorclanhistory/home

Taylor, D. (2016, Jan 28). Dennis Taylor Family History Video Interview. (D. G. Conklin, Interviewer)

Taylor, D. (2021). *Taylor Clan Family History.* Retrieved Feb 24, 2021, from Richard Lemuel Taylor: https://sites.google.com/site/taylorclanhistory/home

Taylor, D. (2022, Dec 19). Dennis Taylor email to David G. Conklin. *From Dennis Taylor Collection in author's Taylor Family History files.* Kalispell, MT.

Taylor, E. (1903). *History of John Taylor of Hadley.* Boston, MA: Taylor Reunion Association.

Taylor, I. T. (1945). *History of the Taylor Family p. 287.* Retrieved Jun 21, 2020, from History of the Shrode Family: www. Ancestry.com

Taylor, M. (2015, Oct 15). Marjorie Taylor Family History Video Interview. (M. L. Conklin, Interviewer)

Tiegreen, A. F. (2021, Apr 18). Alan Tiegreen Family History Video Interview. (D. G. Conklin, Interviewer)

Tiegreen, C. H. (2012). *Ancestors of Alan F. Tiegreen.* Lilburn, GA: Privately held by Carl Tiegreen.

Trabue, A. E. (1925). Taylors in the Making of a Nation. *The Taylor Family Association, Second Annual Meeting.* Frankfort, KY. Retrieved Jul 2020, from www. Ancestry.com

Walker, O. T. (1964). The Taylor Family in Virginia. In *Historical Southern Families* (Vol. 8). Redwood City, CA: Genealogical Publishing Co.

Wikipedia. (2020). Taillefer. Retrieved Dec 9, 2020, from https://en.wikipedia.org/wiki/Taillefer

Index of Individuals

Females are indexed under both maiden and married names. Dates of birth/baptism and death (where available) are provided for many of the numerous same names to help the reader find a specific individual.

A

Abston, Oliver Gene, 74, 78, 79, 80
Abston, Sue. *See* Lucas, Martha Sue
Allen, Elizabeth, 32, 33
Anderson, Margreta Mitchell, 23
Atherton, Gen Henry, 28, 31
Atherton, Mary Dinah, 28, 31, 32, 34

B

Beadles, William David, 83
Bennett, Laura, 98
Blood, Casey Guerra, 137
Blood, Cathy. *See* Woo, Cathy Hui-Ju
Blood, Daniel Oakley, 130, 132, 133
Blood, Darrick, 137
Blood, Ellery Abner, 138
Blood, Harold Clifton, 130, 132
Blood, Lyssa Woo, 137
Blood, Tecla. *See* Guerra, Tecla Ann
Boyle, Anne, 8, 19
Broughton, Alexandra Dickinson, 133, 138
Broughton, William Cranston, 133, 138
Broughton-Blood, Alexa. *See* Broughton, Alexandra Dickinson
Burwell, Elizabeth Eddings, 22, 23

C

Clark, Mayme Lee, 74, 80, 82
Clements, Eliseh, 38, 40, 42
Clements, Mary Ann, 38
Clements, Ruth, 40, 42
Conklin, Christopher Andrew, 140
Conklin, Dacia Marie, 139
Conklin, David Gene, i, ii, iv, 130, 133, 135, 136, 139
Conklin, Isabelle Iona, 135, 140
Conklin, Mary. *See* Guerra, Mary LaVonne
Conway, Eleanor Rose, 32, 35
Crone, Mabel Ruth, 56, 101, 103, 105
Crone, Thomas Otha, 101, 103
Crone, William Delbert "Del", 105

D

D'Angouleme, Aldwin, 14
D'Angouleme, Wulgrin, 13, 14
D'Anjou, Girberge, 14
D'Archiac, Petronille, 15
Davis, Jefferson (CSA Pres.), 10, 39
De Fairsted, Humphrey, 8, 19
De Fairsted, Margaret Sarah, 8, 19, 20
Dickinson, Zena Marie, 133, 138
Doby, Nancy Hopper, 97
D'Toulouse, Rogerlinde, 14
Dyess, Stella Wolverton, 92, 94

E

English, Dacia. *See* Conklin, Dacia Marie
English, Randal William, 139
Evans, Donald Dell, 120

F

Fletcher, Mary Van, 38, 43, 44
Fox, Nancy J., 93

G

Gibbes, Robert John, 1
Gibbs, Allen (d.1861), 37
Gibbs, Isaac, 41, 45, 53, 54, 55, 62
Gibbs, John Allen (1838-1862), 39, 41, 42
Gibbs, Margaret "Peggy", 34, 37, 39, 41, 42, 46, 54
Gibbs, Roxie Ann, ii, 1, 2, 41, 45, 53, 54, 55, 56, 57, 61, 63, 69, 71, 89, 103, 110, 126, 129, 141, 144
Gibbs, Sarah Ellen, *46, 141*
Gibbs, Temperance Zemfa, 39, 42
Gibbs, William, 38, 39, 42
Gilbard, Joane, 18, 19
Gilstrap, Bertrum Bernard, 74, 80, 82
Gilstrap, Billy Bert, 74, 80, 82, 83
Gilstrap, Christine Suzanne, 83
Gilstrap, James Paul, 83
Gilstrap, Sara. *See* Lucas, Sara Ann
Gilstrap, Stephen Lawrence, 85

Gregory, Mary Bishop, 25, 27
Guerra de Guerra, Tecla, 56, 125, 129
Guerra, Antonio Richard, 127
Guerra, Evangelina, 131
Guerra, Guadalupe, 1, 8, 125, 129, 130, 132, 133, 137
Guerra, Jose Antonio, iv, 56, 125, 129
Guerra, Mary LaVonne, iii, 1, 8, 46, 53, 55, 70, 76, 79, 80, 113, 117, 120, 121, 122, 134, 135, 136, 139, 143, 147, 157, 161, 163, 165
Guerra, Nettie. *See* Taylor, Nettie LaVonne
Guerra, Tecla Ann, iii, 47, 55, 56, 79, 125, 130, 131, 132, 133

H

Hamley, Arthur Cornwall, 18
Hamley, Lady Margaret, 18
Hancock, Catherine Sarah Jane, 41
Hancock, Susan Amanda, 41, 45, 53, 54, 88
Hansen, Lady Agnes, 20
Hanson, Sir John of Woodhouse, 8
Hencmann, Gunnar, 97, 99
Henry, Thursa, 56, 107, 110, 111
Hildegarde, 14
Hinely, Hannah, 98
Hogan, Mary Sandra, 93
Horton, Elizabeth Taylor, 24
Hurt, Helen, 96
Hurt, Isabella, 27, 30
Hurt, Walter Harvey Jr., 92, 94

J

Johansdotter, Elisabeth Engmark, 56, 87, 89
Jones, Marjorie Alene, 130, 132

K

King, James W., 54
Knowles, Martha Wilmina, 69, 71
Kunz, Justin Troy, 135, 139
Kunz, Myron Logan, 136, 138
Kunz, Myron Troy, 139

L

Land, Jane Jincy, 38
Lee, Elizabeth (1709-1743), 29, 32
Lievsay, Allen Rayburne, 56, 141, 144, 145, 146
Lievsay, Larry Ray, 146, 147
Lievsay, Marjorie, iii, *See* Taylor, Marjorie Ellen
Lievsay, Ray. *See* Lievsay, Allen Rayburne
Lucas, Elmer Lawrence, 56, 69, 71, 74, 76, 78, 79, 80, 82

Lucas, Jessie E., 69, 71
Lucas, Martha Sue, 78, 79, 80
Lucas, Sara Ann, 46, 52, 68, 69, 70, 71, 72, 73, 78, 79, 80, 82, 83, 85, 92, 102
Lucas, Tomi. *See* Taylor, Nommie Lee
Lucas, Wanda Lee, 73, 74, 76, 77, 81
Luke, Jesse Jackson, 41
Luke, Margaret Abigail. *See* Taylor, Margaret Abigail
Luke, Mary. *See* Taylor, Mary Elizabeth
Luke, William Robert, 41

M

MacNalley, Abigail, 34, 36
Madison, Ambrose, 29, 32
Madison, Frances. *See* Taylor, Frances
Madison, James (Pres.), 6, 9, 23, 26, 28, 30, 35
Marion, Francis "Swamp Fox", 33
Marshall, Jane, 17, 18
Martin, Carrie May, 101, 103
McAnally, Rebecca Abigail, 37, 39
McClure, Hazel Florence, 8, 9, 56, 107, 109, 110, 111, 112, 115, 116, 118
McClure, Joseph Taylor, 56, 107, 110
McNatt, Leona Neomi, 63
Meldrum, Tawna, 121, 122
Mixon, John, 46
Montgomery, Marie, 16
Mooney, Elizabeth Patricia, 112, 116, 118

N

Nelson, Sandra Lucille, 136, 138
Nunne, Elizabeth Lawes, ii, 23, 24, 25
Nystrom, Benjamin Richard, 120

P

Parisot, Albert Holland Sr., 118
Parisot, Arlene. *See* Taylor, Arlene Hazel
Parisot, George Edmond, 121
Parisot, Maia, 122
Parisot, Neil Jerome, 118, 120
Parisot, Peter, 120, 122
Parisot, Reilly, 122
Parisot, Taylor, 122
Pate, Elizabeth Cornelia (1856-1951), 39
Paul, Ruth Janet, 27, 28
Pecora, Renee Christine, 116, 121
Pendleton, Catherine (1699-1774), 27, 30
Pendleton, Henry, 27
Pendleton, Philip, 27, 30
Porter, Elsie. *See* Taylor, Elsie Blanche

www.ingramcontent.com/pod-product-compliance
Lightning Source LLC
Chambersburg PA
CBHW080518030426
42337CB00023B/4562